COLORADO

Rio Grande

NEW MEXICO

SANTA FE

ALBUQUERQUE

Pecos

EL PASO

C. JUAREZ

CHIHUAHUA

CHIHUAHUA

Conchos

Rio

Sinaloa

DURANGO

CULIACAN

DURANGO

SINALOA

ZACATECAS

OKLAHOMA

OKLAHOMA CITY

DALLAS

River

TEXAS

AUSTIN

Rio Grande

COAHUILA

SALTILLO

NUEVO

MONTERREY

LEON

C. VICTORIA

TAMAULIPAS

GULF OF MEXICO

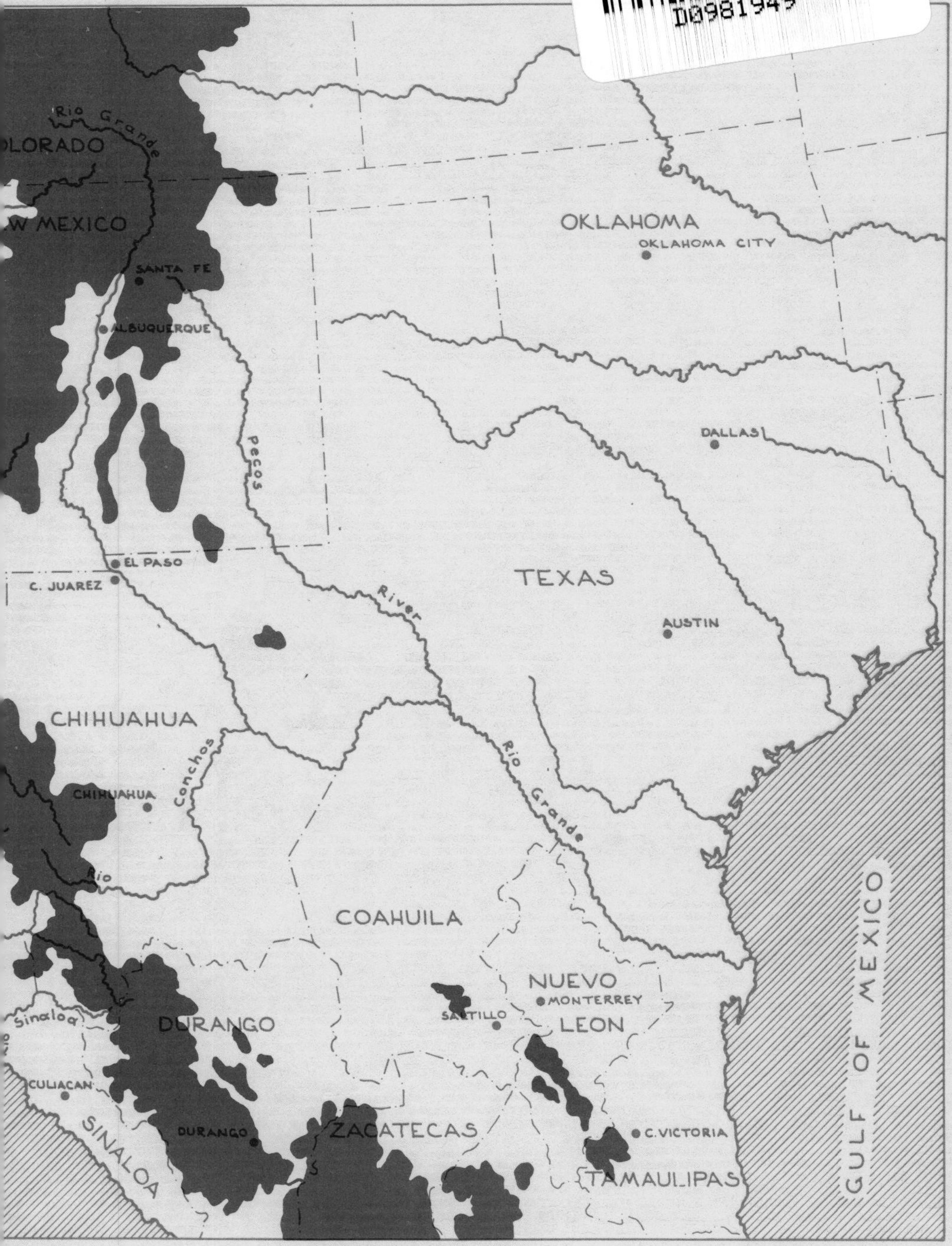

PLURAL SOCIETY IN THE SOUTHWEST

PLURAL
SOCIETY
IN THE
SOUTHWEST

Editors: Edward H. Spicer
Raymond H. Thompson

A Publication of the Weatherhead Foundation

Interbook, Incorporated
New York

Interbook, Incorporated
Box 872
New York 10022

Foreword

The Founder of the Weatherhead Foundation, Albert J. Weatherhead, Jr., like his father before him, was fascinated by the Southwest. In the 1880's, the elder Weatherhead went from Cleveland, Ohio, where he lived, to New Mexico and southern Arizona in search of gold and other rich ores and was lucky enough to find mines that brought him modest rewards. Although he maintained his principal business and family activities in Ohio, for a time he owned mining property in Socorro, New Mexico ("Deadwood Mine") which still produces ore and dividends. His son, although an inventor and manufacturer of automotive parts in midwest America, felt the same, and probably a stronger, lure of the Southwest and its people. In the late 1930's, he and his family made frequent visits to a dude ranch not far from Nogales, Arizona/Sonora, and in the early 1940's he purchased property in the same area and began building his own ranch. A good part of his life was shaped by his image of the cowboy and the rancher and his familiarity with the changing yet enduring landscape of the country.

When its founder died in 1966, it seemed appropriate for the Foundation to convert his personal liking for the Southwest into one of its main fields of endeavor. Not only would his particular interest be continued and expanded, but also the Foundation would be doing work in an important section of America. In the Southwest—defined for the Foundation's purposes as a core area of New Mexico, Arizona, Sonora and Chihuahua, and parts of Texas and California where there are significant populations of Mexican-Americans—the Foundation could develop and carry out socially useful projects in an instructive cultural and demographic laboratory of the United States.

In the Southwest there are three basic cultural identities: the Indian, the Mexican, and the Anglo-American (and varieties of blendings and unblendables as they are discussed in this volume).

I

Over the past one hundred years or so, these groups have learned to adjust to one another in the rugged rural setting and more recently in the compact communities of the cities. The Southwest is a vast, imposing land where man is never entirely in control of the fell forces of nature—the desert, the mountains, the sudden heavy rains, the big scale of the land and its incredible beauty; all somehow work to return man to his elemental concerns of spirit and survival, even in this latter part of the twentieth century. In this region one can study the ways that cultural groups living side by side have developed for tolerating each other or one can study the improbable rise of such cities as Los Alamos and Phoenix. The Southwest, then, is an ethnic and ecological region unique in the United States, but sharing common characteristics with other parts of the world, as, for example, in the Middle East.

These were some of the reasons which led the Weatherhead Foundation to develop its program, *The Culture and Society of the Southwest*. The activities in this program include the encouragement of new knowledge about the region, support of the traditional and contemporary arts, efforts to help relieve groups suffering from ill health or in need of greater educational opportunities, and a concern with the historic ecological balance in an era of "progress" and technology.

The essays in this volume are the result of a conference held by the Foundation in August, 1970. At an earlier conference in the summer of 1969, some ten experts on the Southwest were brought together for the purpose of outlining broad areas of activity for the Foundation and, within these areas, typical projects which might be endorsed and funded. One such project was the conference on "Plural Societies in the Southwest," an effort to study the unique features of the region and the mechanisms on which plural societies run. The papers which were discussed at this meeting are presented in somewhat revised form in the pages of this book.

Richard W. Weatherhead
President

August 9, 1971

Preface

This volume is the result of a conference on "Plural Societies in the Southwest" held at Patagonia, Arizona, August 24-28, 1970. The conference was the first of a series of meetings on Southwestern topics that the Weatherhead Foundation plans to hold. The Plural Societies conference had its beginning in mid-1968 when Richard W. Weatherhead and Richard Eells visited the University of Arizona to discuss possibilities for conferences with Edward H. Spicer and Raymond H. Thompson. In September, 1969 this group was joined by Fernando Cámara, Joseph Maier, James Officer, John Parry, and Charles Wagley for an informal meeting to lay more specific plans for the projected conference series and especially to organize the Plural Societies conference, the basic conception for which had been presented by Edward Spicer. At that time the details of the Plural Societies conference were worked out. Participants in the Plural Societies conference were Richard Eells, Ernesto Galarza, Miguel León-Portilla, Thomas O'Dea, John H. Parry, Ithiel de Sola Pool, Emory Seka-quaptewa, Edward Spicer, Raymond Thompson, Richard W. Weatherhead, and Robert Young. The papers from the conference were revised and submitted to the editors by mid-November, 1970. Carroll Barber, University of Arizona doctoral candidate, handled editorial details with great skill and patience. Clarice Mathis produced the final typed manuscript.

Tucson, 1971   R.H.T.

Contents

MAPS

Introduction

This book presents some ideas which it is hoped can be built upon for a clearer understanding of the implications of the human cultural variety which is so striking a characteristic of the "Southwest"—a term used here to include the Mexican Northwest as well. Its contrasting ways of life have been a major source of interest shown in the region, not only by tourists and casual visitors, but also by artists, educators, administrators, and most of the ordinary residents.

The Literary Description of the Southwest

Interest in the region's diversity is documented from as early as a work written in 1763, by an "unknown Jesuit" missionary and commentator ([Nentuig] 1951), to as late as a symposium held in 1970, with the title *Thoughts on Community and Diversity in the Southwest*, by Indian, Mexican-American, Black, and Anglo-American spokesmen (Brown and others 1970). Moreover, judging from the oral traditions of some Indian groups, it appears that differences in race and custom were a theme for religious speculation centuries before the written word was used, for example, among the Pima (Russell 1908: 206-230) and among the Hopi (Nequatewa 1936).

It was the Jesuit commentator who produced one of the first, and certainly the best, early surveys of the ethnic groups of the region. He was interested in more than mere description and, as a result, dared to put himself on record with the judgment that certain Indians, among them the Pimas, were not civilizable. He recommended that they be deported somewhere else, so that the Spanish colonial program could proceed peacefully for the

1

benefit of the other Indians ([Nentuig] 1951: 149). A little over 100 years later Anglo-Americans, making the trek westward for gold and finding that they could rely on the Pimas of the Gila Valley for food supplies, wrote that the most civilized of all the natives of the region were the Pimas (Hackenberg 1955: 30-31). Thus judgments have been passed by one group on others through the centuries, and predictions have continually been made about capacity for peaceful coexistence or for constructive leadership.

The persisting diversities of human ways have stimulated far more description than serious analysis and interpretation. The level of interest has continued high and has resulted in descriptions of most of the region's Indian languages and cultures, in a steady flow of novels and paintings directly portraying its contrasting customs, in many volumes by historians presenting the conflicts among Spaniards, Indians, and Anglos, and even in some comparisons by philosophers of the ways of thought of Indians and Europeans. There is an abundance of such portrayal, a rich and growing store contributed to by a host of observers, commentators, and scholars from the earliest periods of contact to the present. But there have been few attempts at overall surveys; most are incomplete in some sense, such as that of Fergusson (1940), which covers only the United States Southwest. Moreover, only occasionally, and usually in piecemeal fashion, has description led to interpretation of the nature and significance of the varied cultural scene (for example, Austin 1924).

Questions and Assumptions

One suspects that the right questions which could lead to broad and general understanding have not been asked. Yet, as any museum director, national monument ranger, or similar public servant in the region knows, tens of thousands of questions are asked every year about the different peoples—about their origins, about their history, and about their future. Somehow significant inquiry ought to be based on and grow out of this persistent and vigorous popular curiosity.

Visitors often ask, "Are the Indian cultures disappearing?" Repeatedly one hears the answer, by old Southwestern hands, "Of course." But the visitors' attention ought to be called to the fact that prophecies of such doom have been made by white men—and by some Indians—at least annually now for more than 100 years. Perhaps a more revealing question which could lead to an understanding of the nature of the relations between Indians and others would be "Why do travellers, legislators, educators, and many others make these prophecies?" An Indian might well ask, "Will the present kinds of Anglo-American or Mexican city culture disappear, as the frontier varieties of those cultures did before our eyes?"

There was a time barely 100 years ago when Spanish-Mexican culture in the hands of the cattlemen was dominant in the whole region; with the shift in technology from windmills to monster dams, it appears that Anglo-American culture is enjoying a period of prestige and dominating influence. What factors bring about the dominance of one culture over another—and shifts in dominance? What will the next phase bring in the relative influence of these two great Western cultures—the Anglo-American and the Mexican?

The region nurtured contrasting cultures, such as the Anasazi and the Hohokam, and varieties of each, 1000 years ago. There has been no reduction in the number of distinct cultural traditions since. Do conditions in the region continue to nurture cultural diversity, or is this, like miracles, a thing of the past?

Until the 1930's, in both the United States and Mexico the federal governments sought to eliminate the various distinctive Indian ways of life. At present in 1970 in both countries there are thousands more people who speak Indian languages and identify themselves as Indians than there were before the government efforts were instituted. Is it possible that the government programs had reverse effects? What can be learned, if anything, from the failure of these assimilation efforts?

If one looks to past events for practical guidance in making public policy about Indian affairs, or the relations between Mexicans and Anglos, one ought to be clear about the values one is espousing. Has the variety which has existed in the Southwest been a creative circumstance? Under what conditions and to

3

what extent does cultural variety contribute to human growth and development?

Questions of these kinds should be pursued further, if we are to give answers to the questions which everybody asks—answers which are not snap judgments but based on real knowledge. The abundant information relevant to them has barely been tapped. Yet from the time of the Jesuit writer answers based on the short view and the narrow range have been offered. The answers have rested ordinarily on one of two common assumptions. On the one hand, most missionaries, Spanish colonial administrators, employees of government departments of Indian affairs in both Mexico and the United States, professional educators (until recently), and the man in the street of both dominant societies have generally assumed that other people either are becoming, or ought to become, like themselves in all important respects. This is of course the usual ethnocentric assumption that people who are in control of the institutions of a region make. In the Southwest it is very difficult, unless one ignores most of the well-established facts, to make a plausible case in support of the assumption. Nevertheless the beliefs based on it continue to be held on a wide scale and form the basis, often quite unconsciously, for all sorts of development and improvement programs. This is true on both sides of the international border. The fact that so many action programs affecting so many different people proceed from such ideas makes it very important that they be examined in the long-term perspective of human experience in the Southwest.

When serious discussion of the issues has not rested on the belief in the necessity for assimilation, it has usually been guided by an opposing assumption. This view holds that assimilation to a dominant society's customs and values is not inevitable. In contrast with its opposite, this has never been a widespread view. Even the nondominant peoples who might be expected to espouse such a position have not been noted, until very recently, for adherence to this view. The data from the Southwest, at least on cursory inspection, nevertheless indicate that this assumption is more consistent with the facts that we know. This view is frequently held by persons who also believe that a condition of cultural diversity is desirable, because cultural differences lead to

4

mutual enrichment of cultural traditions. They frequently maintain that diversity makes for creative and dynamic development. However, there are very few data from the Southwest which clearly support such a view; there are more perhaps which indicate that diversity leads to conflict of a not always constructive kind.

These opposing positions are usually held with a good deal of passion and obviously do not stem from a reasonable assessment of facts, but rather from emotionally colored convictions about human values. The Southwest, as a region where one cannot ignore the cultural diversity, becomes a battleground for the opposing values.

The Need for New Concepts

What is needed, if the vigorous interest in Southwestern diversity is to bring wisdom, is not simply more facts. The facts are abundant. We require new ideas, new concepts, which can be used for systematic and consistent interpretation of these facts.

A beginning in the formulation of usable concepts was made in the 1940's by a team of investigators headed by Clyde Kluckhohn of Harvard University (Vogt and Albert 1966). This group of scientists from many different fields focused intensive research efforts on a small area of the Southwest in western New Mexico, where peoples of five different cultural traditions live in constant association: Zunis, Navajos, Hispanos, Mormons, and Texans (to list them in the order of their appearance in the area). The investigators were interested primarily in defining clearly the nature of the five different cultures in which these people participated. They decided that this would best be done, if significant comparisons were eventually to be made, by isolating and describing the basic value orientations by which the people guided their lives. The studies laid foundations for general understanding of what really constitutes cultural diversity, but fell short of delineating the processes by which coexistence goes on under those conditions. The conceptual tools developed by Kluckhohn and his co-workers, for description and analysis of the phenomena of cultural difference, need to be sharpened by further use if their value is to be realized.

5

We hope that the present volume builds on this foundation, as well as on some other useful ones. We have not followed the microcosmic approach of what Kluckhohn called the Rimrock Project, but have broadened it to include the whole Southwest. This involves not merely the placement of the societies in fuller geographical context; it seeks also to point up the need for a theoretical framework inclusive of the whole range of cultural types and processes. The Spanish-speaking people of the Rimrock area, for example, are one instance of a range of varieties of people of Spanish-Mexican background; their values and their relations with other groups in the Rimrock area are best understood in the context of the cultural development of other Spanish-speaking people. Similarly the representatives of Indian and Anglo-American groups chosen for study have their being in wider contexts as varieties of their general types. Awareness of these ranges is important for adequate understanding of the internal and external factors which make them what they are in the Rimrock area. It is when the Zuni value system is seen as a particular instance of the general Pueblo Indian system, forged during centuries in the conflicts and growths of the varied Southwestern society, that systematic understanding has begun. The papers in this volume seek to suggest the necessity for this more inclusive approach, which can serve as the theoretical frame for other intensive microcosmic and comparative studies such as the Rimrock Project.

While we hope that our effort may stimulate studies along the lines of those done at Rimrock, we hope also that it will lead to some which go beyond, in emphasizing the dynamic, or processual, aspects of ethnic relations. The internal structures of the various cultures of the Southwest are in part products of the kind of social relationships which the different groups have maintained with one another; these contacts and relations have changed decade by decade in response to requirements of new population distributions, changing technology, development of new economic systems, differing political environments, and shifting religious dominance and influences. A first step has been taken towards enabling us to grasp what in fact is involved in the basic nature of coexistent cultural systems. A second step can be taken in the direction of learning how the diversity is maintained and how stable it may be, by systematically organizing the information we have about the history of the relations of Southwestern peoples as they have developed through the centuries.

This kind of study, like that of the fundamental nature of the different cultural traditions, depends on the use of a framework which treats all the traditions on the same basis, regarding each—whether of the Indian, Mexican, or Anglo variety—as one among many similar phenomena. The tendency to regard most of the cultures of the region as essentially determined by two others—Mexican if one is a member of that dominant society, and Anglo-American if one participates in that—has led not only to uncritical acceptance of the basic assumption that assimilation to dominant ways is inevitable, but also to the corollary that only this one cultural process need be considered. Ignorance of all other processes and their effects on people has been encouraged, and fundamental understanding of cultural developments has thus been impeded. Probably the most important idea in the approach adopted here, as it was in the Rimrock studies, is simply that something more is happening in the region than one-way adjustment to the currently dominant societies of Mexico and the United States. Once this expectation is taken seriously, the way is cleared for examining the multiform cultural influences which transform cultures currently dominant as well as those which are not. This is the foundation both of a long-term and of an authentic comparative approach.

The Conference Approach

The topics chosen for treatment at the Weatherhead Conference on the Southwest are not regarded as constituting anything like a complete coverage of essential concepts. They were nevertheless selected with reference to an overall and, we hope, integrated viewpoint. Some elements of the approach have been outlined above. The others need to be explicitly stated as an aid to the reader in seeing the outlines of the whole.

First, exposition of our guiding conception of the nature of the region will illuminate some features of the approach. The boundaries might be specified in the usual way of doing so for a geographical study. Defined in the broadest terms conceivably by

7

current political divisions, for example, the region may be regarded as including primarily seven states in modern Mexico and six in the United States: (1) Chihuahua, Durango, Nayarit, Sinaloa, Sonora, and the two divisions of Baja California; (2) Arizona, California, Colorado, New Mexico, Texas, and Utah. To leave the delimitation in these terms, however, suggests a fixity which is not consistent with our interest in the changing relationships of the varied people of the region. It might help if we defined the region more simply as composed of former northwestern New Spain, a political entity which was never very sharply bounded.

But probably in order to avoid any linkage with a particular phase in the political development of the region, it would be more in the spirit of the inquiries to define it in terms of natural features: three major river systems of North America, namely, the Rio Grande, the Colorado, and the Sacramento-San Joaquín, and several minor river systems, namely, the Sonora, the Yaqui, the Mayo, the Fuerte, and the Sinaloa. The use of natural features, which are relatively unchanging, would be more consistent with our approach. Political divisions have changed extensively in the past and may be expected to do so in the future. However, it should not be assumed that definition in physical terms implies any view that they are the determining factors of the social and cultural relations upon which we wish to focus attention. It may be true that the great mountain ranges and the vast deserts of this region have had important influences at various times on the distribution of populations and their communications with one another, but we hold no brief for viewing such influences as a constant, under changing technological, political, and other conditions.

The fact remains that, while we have some conception of the Southwest as a whole, we are not at all happy with the names by which the region is usually designated. One ought to have a name, simple and suggestive of its distinctive qualities, because to lack a name is to invite fuzziness of treatment for any entity which one singles out for systematic study. Nevertheless, there is no presentation in this book of a term which the contributors found themselves completely agreed upon as appropriate. In his paper on northwest Mexico, Miguel León-Portilla proposes a name which has two great virtues; it emphasizes the borderlands concept discussed below, and it gets away from the employment of a label which merely indicates that the region is some direction from somewhere else, such as Northwest or Southwest. The sooner a name is found which can help direct attention to the distinctive features of the region, the better. A new and meaningful term is likely to emerge only after a good deal more study along lines such as those we have suggested. We are not convinced yet that we know what are the essential and basically significant characteristics which a useful name should in some measure connote.

Taken at any historical phase, at least in the last 2000 years, the region has contrasted with neighboring ones and has somehow maintained a character of its own. This distinctiveness is in respect to the extent of cultural diversity.

Four Aspects of Southwestern Diversity

In selecting topics for papers we were especially concerned with the importance of four aspects of this diversity, consideration of which seemed to provide a broad foundation for a long-term and comparative approach.

The Indian Presence

The first of these has to do with the number and nature of the Indian societies to be found in the region. In this respect it is unique as compared with any other regions of Mexico or the United States. The central part, including the four modern states of Sonora, Chihuahua, Arizona, and New Mexico, is and has been for centuries the scene of varied and thriving Indian communities, ranging from settled, compact, highly organized towns like those of the Pueblos to shifting, nomadic, loosely organized bands like those of the Seris of the Sonoran coast. The wide range of cultural types is not quite duplicated elsewhere, nor has it been in the past, in any region of the United States or Mexico. There are other regions of Mexico, such as the Chiapas highlands, where there is much contrast of language and custom, but the overwhelmingly greater number of all the communities in these regions conform to a single cultural type. In the United States there is no region of so many and such contrasting Indian societies. Migrations, conquests, and other factors elsewhere in the United States and Mexico have produced much greater homogeneity among surviving Indians, while in the Southwest, in the past as well as in the present, the Indian societies have been more numerous and more different from one another. Moreover, the Indian societies have developed for most of their history entirely outside the traditions of Western cultures, and in some respects continue that distinctive development, even though they have become linked to Western civilization. The region, then, is one which is characterized by a continuous, varied, and vigorous Indian presence developing along diverse lines.

Hispano-Anglo Contact

A second characteristic of the region which makes it of special interest in the study of cultural diversity is that it has been the scene of contact and mutual influence between two of the most vigorous representatives of the ancient Western European tradition. There is no region of the Americas where there has been such intimate contact across international boundaries between people of Spanish-American and Anglo-American backgrounds. For nearly 200 years this contact has been maintained, with shifting cultural dominance and mutual interpenetration of language, food habits, and other customs. In this respect historians have recognized the region as of special interest and have studied and analyzed it sometimes in the framework of the concept of a "borderland." They have labelled it the "Spanish Borderlands," because much of their work has been focused on the period when the Spanish empire was expanding into the region (Bannon 1964). In line with our approach, the concept can be modified and expanded in terms of a "Hispano-Anglo Borderlands." The idea might be made still more applicable by recognizing that for each Indian society living in the region, it is a multifaceted borderland area. In the historical studies of the Spanish Borderlands the triumphs and frustrations of an expanding frontier have inevitably been emphasized. Since the frontiers of two expanding Western nations have met in the region, a new phase of intercultural influence has begun. Thus, there is a diversity involving not only the cooperation and clash of European societies with the aboriginal societies, but also the interweaving of two Western societies with markedly contrasting traditions.

The Impact of Immigration

A third characteristic, closely related to the second, is that the region has been the goal of a northward migration which has had profound effects on both sides of the border. This movement began before the United States appeared in the region, when in 1598 the first Spanish colonists entered what had been named "New Mexico." The more recent phases of this northward movement have affected the population and culture of the United States in ways which are unique in its vast experience with immigration. Unlike the millions of willing and unwilling immigrants from Europe, Africa, and Asia, the millions of immigrants from Mexico have not been cut off from continuing person-to-person contact with their homeland. This continuing close contact has brought about different cultural effects on immigrant adaptation. The processes of change do not follow closely those of immigrants from other countries of the world, especially within the borderland region where most of the six million people of Mexican background remain. The Mexican immigrants, moreover, have exerted powerful influences of various kinds within Mexico, especially since the Mexican and U.S. governments have seen fit to encourage temporary migration in the form of the bracero programs. The international encouragements and restraints have also brought about a piling-up of population on the Mexican side of the border. This has been of such a magnitude as to result in a significant demographic shift in Mexico as a whole, and the effects of this shift are still unfolding in both countries. The Southwest is thus a region in which a long-existing cultural diversity has been augmented by the invasion of two contrasting European peoples, and where, further, after the relative stabilization of the boundaries of the invading nations, the situation has been complicated by an interchange of population under circumstances not duplicated elsewhere in the two countries.

11

Cultural Variation

There is a fourth characteristic of the region important for any effort to understand the most recent processes of social and cultural change. This involves developments which are by no means unique, but which have, outside of the Rimrock studies, usually been overlooked. This is the phenomenon of cultural variation. Many cultures become differentiated in the course of their history, sending off variant forms which achieve a greater or less degree of independence from the parent stock. This has happened in many parts of Mexico and the United States, where one readily recognizes such variants as the Yucatecan Mexican and the New England Yankee. The process has taken place also in the region that we are calling the Southwest; two of the papers are devoted to description and analysis of variant cultures on either side of the international boundary. Recognition of variation within the dominant societies makes clear the significant fact that they are not monolithic and unchanging entities, but that they vary greatly in response to circumstances—including cultural diversity itself.

Topics Not Covered and Why

Perhaps the four aspects of the region just discussed provide some understanding of why the papers which follow were devoted to the topics selected rather than to others. It may be helpful at this point to say something about those topics which were not dealt with. It became apparent, for example, as discussion proceeded that some felt that there was a persistent tendency to consider the different groups largely apart from the technological influences and the economic life of the nation—states of which they are parts. Only in the paper by Ernesto Galarza on Mexican-Americans, it was held, did aspects of the economy of the region receive adequate consideration. The other papers said little or nothing about the profound influence of changing technology on the life of the Indians or of the other peoples. It is unfortunate that an economist was not persuaded to write a paper or to join the conference for discussion. This would have added what undoubtedly all would have regarded as an important dimension.

However, the willingness of the participants to postpone consideration of economic influences indicated a kind of compen-
satory reaction against the superficial analyses so often made of
the phenomena of cultural diversity in the name of economic
science.

One of the most notable examples, pervasive among Anglos,
has been mentioned above—namely, the recurrent prediction that
Indians are on the point of disappearance as distinct groups. This
kind of prophecy turns out usually to be based on casual observations of the selection by Indians of some products or techniques of the U.S. or Mexican technology—such as window glass,
cowboy clothing, pick-up trucks, or tractors—or is merely an
application of the assumption that 20th-century technology
homogenizes, through the operation of some natural law, all
elements of cultures. This assumption seems not only to ignore,
rather than to explain, Southwestern facts, but also seems to
defy all that we do know about the processes of industrialization
in Japan, China, India, and many other countries. In view of
these tendencies it seemed worthwhile to devote our efforts to
defining as clearly as possible the phenomena with which we are
concerned, since clarity about the nature of the relationships
among elements of cultures is so often lacking in the approach of
economists. The very important questions of how technological
and economic factors do affect a people's sense of identity and
their customs and beliefs can then be tackled.

Another aspect of the life of Southwestern ethnic groups
may seem also to be somewhat slighted in the papers. This is the
political framework within which the various groups have their
being. Most of the papers have a little to say about the subject,
but it is true that nowhere is it the focus, unless it be in the
presentation by Robert Young on the Navajo. The interesting
point was made in our discussions that the reservation system,
which is certainly one foundation of the maintenance of distinctive Indian life on the U.S. side of the border, could be snuffed
out at one stroke by Congress. This is undoubtedly true in some
never-never land of politics, but not in the realities of U.S.
political life. The important fact is that Congress has *not* eliminated the Indians or the reservation system. Majority decisions
have several times during the past 100 years moved national

policy in that direction, in 1887 and again in 1954, for example, but these decisions led to national reactions against such policy with consequent reversals by Congress. This swinging of national Indian policy in the United States (and there are interesting parallels in Mexico) between opposing poles is a most significant phenomenon. We need a better understanding of all that is involved. The fruitful question to ask is not "When will Congress move to snuff out distinctive Indian existence?" Instead, one should ask, "What are the factors, symbolic and otherwise, which operated to make United States policy what it has been over the past 150 years" The role of the Southwestern Indians has been particularly important in shaping this national policy. We need a much more careful analysis of this role, and when we have proceeded with it we shall have a much better understanding, not merely of the Southwestern Indians, but also of the United States as a whole.

The fact that no paper isolated either the economic or the political factors for special consideration does not indicate that the conference was conceived in terms of an unrealistic abstraction of ethnic groups from their full contexts. It rather was a result of an effort to lay foundations for introducing much wider considerations into the study of ethnic phenomena in the Southwest. It is hoped that the approach suggested may lead to critical consideration of two widely accepted propositions: (1) that modern technology levels significant cultural differences such as those discussed in this book and brings about a common unitary identification among peoples of varying historical experience, and (2) that national policy decisions in modern states, made in isolation from solid knowledge of ethnic differences, can result in the reduction or elimination of those differences. It is precisely such propositions which the existence of a region like the Southwest challenges.

To sum up the general basis on which the conference was conceived, it was felt that the subject of cultural differences and their persistence in the Southwest was an important focus for understanding and appreciation of the distinctive quality of life in the region. For fruitful discussion the topic required greater precision in the definition of the essential features of the phenomena and the development of a general framework of concepts in terms of which all the varied groups could be viewed and compared. Greater clarity in the conception of what a distinct cultural, or ethnic, group is and what cultural processes have led to its formation and persistence would moreover be a necessary basis for understanding the role of the Southwestern groups in the national economy and political life. On this broad basis we proceeded to select a few features of the cultural groups and their interrelationships for special attention.

The Conference Papers

The first essay is devoted, in part, to getting at the nature of the contrasting cultural groups, from the viewpoints of the members of these groups. Adopting the term "ethnic" as the most useful label, a beginning is made by bringing together the well-known facts about differing customs and beliefs, and the less well-understood manifestations of the identifications which people make, or refuse to make, with others. The view is offered that common historical experience, rather than common customs, constitutes the essential element in the sense of identity, and hence lies at the root of the maintenance of differences. A beginning is also made at a comprehensive listing of the variety of ethnic groups in the Southwestern region, such a list being an indispensable tool for systematic analysis and comparison. The concept of ethnic policy is introduced in the sense of a universal dimension of ethnic relations, every ethnic group having and believing in an ideal set of relationships with others which embodies their conception of themselves. The difficulties of defining the changing boundaries of ethnic groups are discussed and illustrated, and finally a preliminary consideration is offered of the nature of intercultural borrowing and exchange among groups in the Southwest. This first essay is based on the view that ethnic groups give rise to a distinctive kind of phenomena, and that these can be studied in themselves, apart from other related phenomena such as class identification. The point is not discussed at length, but is implicit, that ethnic identification can be separated in analysis from class identification and that it is important to do so, despite the fact that both systems of identification are employed together in most individuals' ultimate placement of themselves in complex societies. The important relations between ethnic and class identification in the changing societies of the Southwest is a subject for further investigation.

The title of the essay requires some explanation, since the specific meaning attached to "plural society" is not explicit in the essay. It should be clear, nevertheless, as the essay is developed, that this term is given the meaning simply of "a political entity which contains two or more groups making separate identification from one another in ethnic terms." In short, a plural society is a political unit with several ethnic components. It would seem, however, that the term "polyethnic society," employed by Miguel León-Portilla in the second paper, is actually more suitable and far less ambiguous, once "ethnic" has been usefully defined.

The second and third essays share a common general theme, namely, the nature and development of variant groups within the dominant societies of the region. The Rimrock investigators identified two variants of Anglo culture, which they called "Mormon" and "Texan," and showed how with respect to basic value structures they differed profoundly, even though many of their culture traits, including language, were closely similar. We thought it important, in developing a concept of the Southwest as a whole, to apply the concept of ethnic variation to Mexican society and culture, and accordingly asked a Mexican scholar, Miguel León-Portilla, to consider the matter. He presents a description of the historical foundations of that variant of Mexican culture which developed in the Spanish Borderlands, and which has had an important influence in Mexican political leadership. His paper lays the basis for the necessary fuller definition of this variant in terms of ethnographic details, much of which might be gathered by employing an analytical approach to already existing literature by and about the Sonorans and other Mexicans of the North.

The other variant of a dominant society of the region, the Mormon, has been described before by Thomas O'Dea, who brought his studies up to date and amplified them for the purposes of the conference. He is careful about giving the label "ethnic group" to the Mormon society, or subsociety; instead he prefers the term "quasi-ethnic group." His reasons for doing so are well worth studying and pondering as a further development of the general approach adopted in this volume. The fact that two out of five papers are devoted to variants of the dominant societies is a reflection of the importance attached to considering them in the same general framework with the "minority," or nondominant, societies. As pointed out in the first essay, members of dominant societies are prone to be much less conscious—indeed if they are so at all—of their own ethnic traits. Therefore some special emphasis is required in our effort to develop a common analytical scheme.

The fourth essay is a conservative presentation of a particular instance of what might be called "cultural emergence." Robert Young was asked to write an account of the development of the Navajos as an illustration of this general process, because of his deep knowledge and years of intensive participation with the Navajos in the building of their emergent political institutions. His account shows that the political development of the Navajos is not an isolated growth, but that it has been accompanied by others—for instance, the continued use of the Navajo language. In political affairs, particularly, the Navajo language, which requires the employment of certain distinctive Navajo concepts of social and political organization, has played and continues to play an important role. The account demonstrates that the Navajos are engaged in a process of making their own selection from among their own traditional ways. This process of selection from various cultural traditions with a consequent integration into something new is what we mean by cultural emergence. The Navajo is just one among several emergent cultures among Indians in the Southwest. This kind of process is also notable among some of the tribes which made early intensive contact with Spaniards, such as the Yaquis of Sonora. Moreover, the process has also been going on among the Navajos for a long time, following their contacts in the 1600's with Pueblo Indians, and shortly thereafter with the Spaniards. In some measure, all the Indian societies which have survived their contacts with Europeans during the past 350 years are emergent societies.

Even when the process can be identified as "emergence," the creative growth may not affect all aspects of the culture equally. It is important that a better understanding of the process be gained through systematic comparison of the various instances in the Southwest. By way of contributing to this sort of comparison, Emory Sekaquaptewa offers here a summary of political developments among the Hopis, inspired by his hearing of the Navajo account. It is clear from his short paper that the political development of the Hopis contrasts strongly with that among the Navajos, since it cannot be said that they have developed an emergent new synthesis in political organization as a result of the modification of Anglo-American institutions. The causes for this lie both in the nature of the native Hopi institutions and the methods employed by Anglos in trying to introduce political innovations.

For good balance, the conference might have dealt more extensively with the very important processes of mutual influence between the two dominant societies as they have expressed themselves on both sides of the border. It might for example have followed the lead of Loomis and others (1966) and asked someone to present a paper on recent technological influences from the United States as they have affected not only agriculture, but also many other aspects of culture in northwestern Mexico. Or the conference might have considered a comparative study of the sometimes surprisingly different developments in twin border cities such as Nogales-Nogales, Juárez-El Paso, or Laredo-Nuevo Laredo (for example, Stone and others 1963). In the face of the many and significant possibilities, we chose to limit ourselves to one set of these contact processes—the question whether or not a kind of emergent culture is evolving among the descendants of Mexican immigrants in the United States. Ernesto Galarza was asked to describe what has happened over the last quarter-century in the life patterns of immigrants from Mexico. The story is not a happy one; after each successive adaptation of the immigrants was well under way and they seemed headed for a stable condition within which they could maintain some control of their lives, a new technological or new organizational change has upset the trend. Periodically, then, the immigrants have had to change their mode of adaptation. Galarza is pessimistic about the growth of a Mexican-American society, or subsociety, with any measure of control in the building of its own new institutions, though he freely admits that other Mexican-American scholars might see the facts of the immigrant adaptation in a quite different light. His interpretation should give impetus to the better understanding of this many-sided situation of culture contact.

The two papers which complete the volume arose in the course of the conference out of discussions of the original papers. John Parry, as a historian, places the consideration of Southwestern ethnic groups in a broad historical perspective. He makes a beginning at providing that comparative framework without which we are unlikely to develop fruitful analyses of the Southwestern instances. One of his most interesting points is his distinction between "plural" and "composite" societies. His suggestion that a plural condition, which he regards as being exemplified in the Indian societies in the Southwest, is more likely to produce conflict than creative growth should be examined further in the light of the history of ethnic groups in the Southwest.

Ithiel de Sola Pool, considering the materials presented from the viewpoint of a political scientist, was inspired to present an outline of an ideal set of relationships among ethnic groups. This set of relations is ideal in the sense that it could be expected to produce cooperative effort towards shared goals and thus to give scope for mutual enrichment of the different traditions. Since attempts have been made in the Southwest, as elsewhere, to institutionalize such relationships—in recent Office of Economic Opportunity programs, for example, this paper has great relevance to current development planning and offers possibilities for application.

A final comment on terminology may make this book more readable for those who have not lived in the Southwest—and also give them some small further introduction to the complexity of Southwestern society. The term "Anglo-American" has come into use in the Southwest north of the Mexican border to fill a need for recognizing a distinction between English-speaking and Spanish-speaking descendants of Europeans. It strikes Anglo-Americans from other parts of the United States as peculiar and unnecessary; they ordinarily think of themselves simply as "Americans." However, "American" is unacceptable to Mexicans, who customarily call Anglo-Americans *norteamericanos*

(North Americans). Therefore, despite the fact that "American" is actually used widely by members of all ethnic groups in ordinary conversation, in this introduction and in the essays which follow the authors have employed the more technical term "Anglo-American" or its short form "Anglo."

Edward H. Spicer

Plural Society in the Southwest

Edward H. Spicer

Like most other regions of comparable size, the greater Southwest is a region of many cultural traditions and ethnic groups. The cultural diversity has existed for 2000 or more years. Moreover, there has been no trend towards decreased diversity, despite the expansion into the region during the past 150 years of two modern nation-states which try to promote cultural homogeneity within their borders. The acquisition of territory in the region by Mexico and the United States has, in fact, led to an increase in cultural variety.

It is our purpose in this paper to describe the various ethnic groups which compose the population of the Southwest, or at least to describe features of these groups which are relevant to an understanding of the kinds and degrees of diversity that exist. It is our purpose further to characterize the interrelations of the ethnic groups and to delineate the trends of change in these relations. We shall adopt the view that society in the region is some sort of a whole—a sociocultural system which maintains characteristics differentiating it in some respects from other regions of the United States and Mexico. Our focus of concern will be with that part of the whole which can be discussed in terms of ethnic differences and similarities. We assume that there is a subsystem of the whole society which may be understood as a system of ethnic relations, maintained by definable social and cultural processes, and which changes in response to factors both within and outside of the system. We are thus embarked on an effort to characterize the structure and the dynamics of what we shall call the ethnic system of Southwestern regional society.

The Meanings of Ethnic Terminology

Our starting point is the fact that the various peoples of the Southwest recognize differences among themselves and that they have names for themselves in distinction from others, names the meanings of which have to do with these recognized differences. Individuals are by no means always able to be explicit about the differences, however strongly they feel them and however their contacts with other individuals are guided by them. In broad terms the differences have to do with ease of association and are most usually discussed in those terms (if discussed at all) rather than in terms of what anthropologists might identify as "cultural traits." Simple tests are promptly, and probably usually unconsciously, applied by anyone in first contacts with others. The cues may be given through language or dialect, but perhaps more decisively through silent language in demeanor, in overtones of etiquette, in manner of speaking, and sensed attitude. The basic point is that people do categorize themselves in relation to others and seek continuing or closer association, or limitation of association, on the basis of these cues in others' behavior. It is such considerations that give meaning to the names which people employ for identifying themselves as we-group members.

The fact of the existence of such names is the elementary phenomenon of the ethnic system and the usages associated with these names are basic for an understanding of the system. Yet it is true that there is very little systematic description of the native terminology, let alone the web of meanings associated with the terms. We do know enough, however, to make a beginning at delineating this feature of the Southwestern system of ethnic relations. While we shall not attempt here a full exposition of what is known, we shall attempt to indicate some of the major features of the ethnic terminology. There are as many sets of terms for the different ethnic groups as there are ethnic groups in the region. In other words, each group has its own distinctive view of ethnic relations, which does not wholly coincide with any other group's, and there is a vocabulary for expressing the viewpoint. This produces difficulties for any effort to describe the ethnic system in over-all terms aimed at establishing an as-objective-as-possible standpoint for understanding the inter-relations. The usual solution is to adopt the terms employed by the politically dominant ethnic group, Anglo or Mexican, occasionally calling attention to lack of coincidence between the dominant group's terminology and that of various of the others. That in fact will be the approach adopted in this paper, but it must be emphasized that this gives rise to bias and that a better set of terms should be devised. Another difficulty is that the terminology of any group is closely related to the nature of the interethnic relations at a given time. Thus the terminology may in the space of ten years change rather extensively as economic, educational, and other conditions change. The terminology is no more stable than the relations among groups and is an index to the changing conditions.

We may illustrate with the example of terms employed by the Spanish-speaking people of the United States. By the 1930's Spanish-speaking people used at least six different terms in referring to themselves. The descendants of Spanish colonists living almost exclusively in New Mexico frequently referred to themselves as *manitos* or *hispanos*, the former being used by the rural and less highly educated members of the group, the latter by those more highly educated. They made a sharp distinction between themselves and immigrants from Mexico, and the terms carried the connotation of this distinction. Among the immigrants several terms were in use. When speaking Spanish, they customarily used the term *mexicano*. In speaking English, perhaps the term most often used was "Mexican," but some of the more highly educated distinguished themselves from lower-income, and usually more recent, immigrants by employing the term "Spanish-American," which, they felt, had connotations of higher social class. Furthermore a term of uncertain origin had come into use in ordinary conversation among the lower-income Spanish-speaking people, namely, *chicano*. The only one of the five terms much known to English-speaking people was the term "Mexican," and this as used by them usually had connotations of inferiority. The English-speaking people generally tended to lump all Spanish-speakers together under this term, which was objected to by Spanish-speaking people, even those who customarily used it among themselves.

23

By the 1960's the terminology had altered, reflecting a considerable shift in the interethnic relations. The term *hispano* had come into general use among descendants of Spaniards in New Mexico and carried with it the meaning of the still important distinction between themselves and immigrants from Mexico. But among the latter there was a profound change. In general, during the 1950's, the term "Mexican-American" had come into use by persons of Mexican background when communicating with English-speaking people, although "Mexican" was still often used among themselves. "Spanish-American" was still occasionally used by persons who wanted to avoid any derogatory implication, but only a minute minority used the term and it was widely regarded by others of Mexican background as inaccurate, pretentious, and snobbish. It was definitely on the way out. Meanwhile, the term formerly regarded as vulgar by educated Mexican-Americans, "Chicano," had by the end of the 1960's come into wide use. It was used in every context, that of intimate association among themselves or that of communication with English-speaking and other peoples. It had risen to the status of a nationality term with connotations of pride in its use and was the major symbolic term of all militant leaders. It was rejected, usually in favor of "Mexican" or "Mexican-American," by those who shunned militant associations and who were inclined to use *la raza* as a collective term when they wished to express pride in their cultural background.

These shifting usages and terms illustrate a principle which is fundamental in the analysis and understanding of the ethnic system of the Southwest. Each group has a terminology which is an important feature of its identity system and symbolizes its conception of the group in relation to all other groups. If, for simplicity's sake, we fall into the use of the dominant group's terminology, it must be emphasized that we are aware of the biases so introduced and will try to correct these where it is most important to do so. The ethnic terminology may be regarded as an instrument employed by a group for the expression and reinforcement of its sense of distinctness and of common identification. The content, or meaning, of the set of terms is by no means uniform for those who use them, because their experience of ethnic relations is not identical, and the intensity of common identification and sense of distinctness varies. It seems possible however to indicate in a general way what is involved in the content of any set of ethnic terms.

Cultural Content

In the first place, there is always a cultural content, a feeling for, if not a conscious and articulated awareness of, behavioral differences. How many and which of the cultural differences that an outside observer can identify as important to individuals using the terms varies greatly. There is a selection. Usually there is an association of language difference with every set of ethnic terms, and yet it is clear as a result of some intensive studies of ethnic groups in the Southwest that language is not always decisive in the distinctions made. In the case of a number of Indian groups, such as Yaquis who have been separated from Yaqui-speaking communities for years, or Navajos educated far from Navajo communities, persons unable to use the native language may identify themselves with and be identified by other Yaquis or Navajos as of the we-group. Language is not a universal essential, but it is usually of great importance as an element in the identity system. Awareness of and willingness to give high priority to traditional forms of kinship obligation, in other words, to fulfill traditional kinship behaviors, are usually of great importance in the common identification. These may be rather narrow in scope, as among most Anglo groups as compared with many Indian and Spanish-speaking groups, but whatever the character, family roles have a considerable importance. Beyond language and kinship, a record of participation in wider organizations distinctive of the group, such as ritual kinship and ceremonial sodality networks, may be emphasized. The combination of cultural behaviors on the basis of which membership is recognized varies, and there seems to be no uniform set of minimum cultural traits which is required. The emphasis on what is important varies from group to group, and all groups recognize and define degrees of identification. It is important for understanding the ethnic system to realize that there is this leeway with respect to specific cultural behaviors. A given group, as among some of the Indians, may appear to an outsider to be lacking in distinctive culture from the dominant or other groups, but a sense of distinctive identity may nevertheless be very strong.

Historical Experience

The identity systems evidently, then, depend on other factors besides specific customs. One of the most important is a sense of distinctive historical experience. Perhaps the most common form of this is what is usually lumped under the term "discrimination." That is, there is an awareness of being identified as a member of an ethnic group and on this basis denied some privilege or right or given a derogatory classification. An actual or even vicarious experience may lead to a sense of being an outsider in some situation involving contacts with other ethnic groups. The experience is common enough among Indians and Mexican-Americans in the United States and among Indians in Mexico. This is what might be called the negative historical experience of being identified by others as of a certain ethnic group and suffering in some way as a result. There is also a positive aspect of historical experience. It is the nature of this which seems so seldom grasped by the dominant ethnic groups, and which has until recently not been recognized in the systems of formal education in the region.

The Indians, for example, have, in every case where they survive with an active sense of identity, undergone distinctive experiences as compared with non-Indians. They have seen portions of their land appropriated by others, land associated with a mythology of the past and regarded as sacred. They have experienced the invasion of their communities by traders, bureaucrats, and missionaries, who insist on maintaining their own ways of life and pushing these ways on the Indians. They have been made aware of the ethnic classifications used by the invaders and have watched the success or failure of various plans for changing the Indians' ways. They have been hard put to it to teach their children about these experiences and the actions of their leaders in response, because of the absence of information about these events in the school curriculum. But in some degree the nature of the events and of the relations established with the non-Indians have been apparent to each generation. They have reacted in different ways. The historical experience has bred militants, Uncle Toms, and moderates. It is in some form or other a part of Indian consciousness, but not until recently perceived by dominants.

Currently there is a movement on the part of Indians toward new positive evaluations of their history. If the emphasis is on the narrow, discrimination range of experience, this may stimulate merely a negative valuation of the dominant group along with negative valuation of one's own. If the emphasis is on the broader awareness of a respectable past with worthy leaders, then a strongly positive valuation of the nondominant group may develop, as has already among militant leaders. The sense of history, in whatever specific form, may be the most important part of an Indian's identification with others of his tribal group, while his cultural ways of doing and believing may contribute little to this identification.

It is not only among Indians, but also among all other groups that the sense of common historical experience must be regarded as an essential feature of the identity system. It is true of the dominant Anglos and Mexicans, as well as the nondominant groups. There is, however, an important difference. The nondominants are in an important way more conscious of their distinctive historical experience than are the dominants. They are aware of having to assert that they do have a history, because of the common failure of the dominants to recognize their history. This requires a process of constant comparison and contrast leading to a more acute awareness of all ethnic groups in the effort to focus attention on their own history. This process of comparison is intensifying under present conditions and actually makes the nondominants better historians of the multi-ethnic Southwest in the sense, not of objective knowledge of history, but certainly in the sense of more realistic and greater completeness of view.

Group Image

The third vital element in every group's identity system is separable only analytically from the cultural and the historical components. This is the "image" of the group vis-a-vis all the other groups, or at least vis-a-vis the dominant group. It involves

27

placing value on the cultural differences and the historical performance of the group. It is no fixed and static picture of themselves, although there may be well-defined and persistent features of the image over extended periods. Like the combination of selected culture traits and the conception of historical experience, the group image changes in content and in relative valuations in response to changing interethnic relations. However, at any given period it may be identified and described.

What we mean by an image may be illustrated by reference to a study of the Yaqui view of themselves in relation to other ethnic groups in the Southwest (Spicer 1953). What we present contains only the common features of the views of a selection of adult male Yaquis resident in Arizona in the 1940's. They believed that Yaquis had "in the beginning times" (a mythical past) a special relationship with God. They were commanded to mark the boundaries of their common land by marching and singing in the company of angels around their whole territory marking points so that the boundary would be known. Within the territory they were informed by prophets of the sacred locations of eight towns which were to be located in those places forever. Later the King of Spain confirmed these boundaries. This was therefore exclusively Yaqui land. The land myth sanctioned the defensive wars during the 19th century, when Yaquis who lived in the eight towns were ready to lay down their lives to maintain the sacred territory with its towns as their own. The Mexicans, who were a very different breed of men, always angry and pugnacious, were to be kept out of the territory. The Mexicans moreover were not very serious about religious devotions, while Yaquis were always ready to perform the hard labor necessary to maintain the trust of God and the saints. The Mexicans were cruel, undependable, and unable to understand the most simple requirements of good government. They were powerful, but not good and not to be trusted. Other Indians, like the Papagos for example, were uncivilized country people and inferior to Yaquis, as is evident in their inability to build towns or organize government and the right ceremonies, although they were capable of learning some of these things from Yaquis. The Americans were helpful and have allowed the Yaquis freedom, such as the religious freedom which the Mexicans did not.

The elements of the image are clearly a moral valuation of the group in relation to others, not in abstract terms but in terms of experiences in contact, and this valuation is maintained in terms of ratings regarding the cultural characteristics of the groups. The Yaqui self-image is itself a standard of moral values. These values may remain long after the specific circumstances giving rise to them have altered profoundly.

Ethnic Groups, Past and Present

A precise enumeration of all the ethnic groups in the Southwest is not yet possible for any historical phase. Our knowledge, for example, of the period following the Spanish entrada is very approximate. By 1700 the Spaniards had not yet identified all the Indian groups in the region, nor did they record the nature of the differences among themselves during the succeeding century. Coming to the 20th century, there is a total lack of information in printed sources for groups like the Czechs of the Arizona mining towns, and data is quite inadequate concerning such groups as the Greeks of Tucson, as to whether they should be regarded merely as a religious denomination or as a full-fledged ethnic group. As a matter of fact no close studies have as yet been made of any of the ethnic groups, except (1) the Indians, all of whom have been described with greater or less degree of adequacy; (2) unrepresentative portions of the Spanish-speaking people; and (3) two varieties of Anglo-Americans: Texans and Mormons.

Nevertheless it is essential that a listing be attempted, for the purpose of providing some sort of overall view with respect to the degree of complexity and general nature of the ethnic system. A fundamentally important quality of any social system is its degree of complexity, in the sense of the number of parts which are integrated into the whole. A two-part ethnic system is a very different kind of entity from a 20-part ethnic system, no matter how similar may be some of the basic institutions. Thus we find it essential to make the attempt, however difficult, under present conditions of ignorance of detail, to list all the ethnic groups as of the middle of the 20th century. In making the list we shall simplify the task by limiting our survey to only a por-

29

tion of the region, that which is perhaps best known, namely, the four states of Arizona, New Mexico, Sonora, and Chihuahua. Here, it appears, are exemplified most, if not all, the kinds of ethnic relations of the total region, and we may take this area therefore as a beginning point in what can be readily expanded into an understanding of the whole. What is presented is admittedly incomplete, but the very presentation should result in fruitful efforts to correct and expand the list, in the process of which we are sure to learn a great deal about the Southwestern ethnic system.

The list of ethnic groups below should be understood as applying to the decade of the 1960's. It uses for the most part the terms employed by the most highly educated Anglo middle class and should in no sense be taken as indicating in itself, without elaboration, the ethnic distinctions as seen from the standpoint of any other ethnic group. This list is tentative, subject to change in the light of research which it is hoped it may stimulate. It is based not on a single criterion of ethnic distinctness, such as language, but on several combined. Moreover it is felt that what are listed here as "varieties" of "types" are not all precisely the same sort of entities, a matter which will be discussed more on opposite page.

SOUTHWESTERN ETHNIC GROUPS*

Type	Varieties	Number
Pueblo	Hopi Hopi-Tewa Zuni Acoma	4
	Keresan Tewa Southern Tiwa	
	Northern Tiwa Jemez	5
Yuman	Cuchan Cocopa Mohave Yavapai Walapai	
	Havasupai Maricopa	7
Piman	Gila Pima Papago Lower Pima Tepehuan	4
Cahitan	Yaqui Mayo	2
Tarahumaran	Tarahumara Warijio	2
Seri	Seri	1
Athabascan	Navajo Western Apache Mescalero Apache	
	Jicarilla Apache	4
Paiute	Southern Paiute	1
Mexican	Rural Norteño Urban Norteño Hispano	
	Mexican-American (Chicano) Mennonite	5
Anglo	Mormon Texan Black Urban Anglo (Jewish)	
	Urban Anglo (Gentile)	5
Asiatic	Japanese-American Chinese-American	2
	Total	**42**

* Basic references for some of the groups listed are as follows: *all Indian groups* (Spicer 1962); *Pueblo* (Aberle 1948, Dozier 1954 and 1970); *Yuman* (Spier 1933 and 1936); *Piman* (Joseph, Spicer and Chesky 1949, Hackenberg 1955); *Cahitan* (Spicer 1940 and 1954); *Tarahumaran* (Fried 1969, Plancarte 1954); *Athabascan* (Goodwin 1969, Kluckhohn and Leighton 1946); *Mexican* (Galarza, Gallegos and Samora 1969, González 1967, McWilliams 1949); *Anglo* (Bailey 1950, Vogt 1955a, Vogt and Albert 1966); *Asiatic* (Heizer and Almquist 1971, Spicer and others 1969).

The Criteria of Ethnic Classification

By way of understanding more clearly the basis of the list, let us consider the criteria employed. In some cases language is a primary criterion, though language alone cannot be used for classifying the phenomena of ethnic distinctness. But it is a curious fact that if only language were considered, the number of groups recognized would come to nearly the same number. Thus all but one of the Indian groups—the Hopi-Tewa, who are Tewa-speaking—would still be recognized, but the Gila Pima and the Papago would be merged as a single group. In the list the Hopi-Tewa are considered distinct from the New Mexico Tewa, because of their very different historical experience during the nearly 300 years from the time of the Pueblo Rebellion of 1680 until the present. Taking up residence among the Hopis after the revolt, these residents of First Mesa have been altered in custom and integrated through marriage and a special "protecting" relationship with Hopis, to the extent that they differentiate themselves from and are differentiated by the Tewas who have continued to live in the Rio Grande Valley (Dozier 1954). We have therefore made use of historical experience as a significant factor in defining the sense of identity. Similarly, we have differentiated the Papagos and the Gila Pimas because of their quite different experiences during the past 150 years, resulting from Anglo creation of separate reservations and consequent profound differences in contacts between them and the Anglos. While the languages of the two groups are classified by the Indians themselves as merely different in dialectal degree, their institutions and their views of themselves in relation to Anglos and others have become sufficiently different to justify regarding them as distinct ethnic groups. In general, however, difference in language remains fundamental as the basis of differentiation among the Indians, despite these exceptions.

This presents a contrast with the Mexican and Anglo varieties of ethnic groups. In the case of the Hispanos, Norteños, and Chicanos it can be said that there are small dialectal, but not basic language, differences, and there is no question of mutual intelligibility of these "dialects." Yet again the historical experience of each has been profoundly different. The Hispanos lived

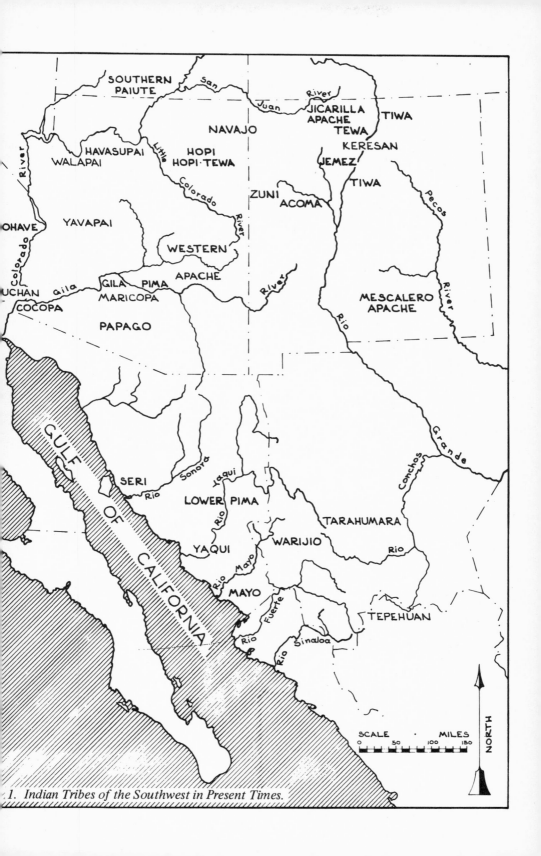

1. Indian Tribes of the Southwest in Present Times.

for only a few years under the political system of the Mexicans, and there has been no identification of their past with Mexico and certainly none at all with the Norteños. The Chicanos have, like the Hispanos, lived within the political framework of the Anglos, but under totally different circumstances; they have been immigrants and a landless proletariat for the most part, so that they have no land base as part of their system of identification.

Similarly we have differentiated Mormons, Texans, Blacks, and urban Anglos on the basis of differing experiences within the Anglo political framework. The unique events following on the Mormon development of a new religious denomination have resulted in a sharp differentiation from the Blacks, whose language and institutions are of the general type of all Anglos, and this sense of distinctness has even attained expression in the world view and theology of the Mormons. Texans and Blacks also, despite close similarity in dialect, clearly differentiate themselves from each other as sharply as from any Indian group.

In summary then it should be clear that we have placed heavy reliance on language and historical experience, using neither one exclusively in preparing this list. It would be desirable to include the moral valuation criterion, or meaning, of ethnic identity, but it is not possible to do so because of the rather spotty information available. It is probably true that such evaluation structures identify systems in important ways, and should provide the best basis for comparison of types of identity systems. However, in the absence of comparable data, we must reserve more adequate classification until the information becomes available.

It was suggested above that the named groups in our list possibly do not all constitute the same sort of entity. It seems doubtful, for example, that the Hopis may be regarded as playing the same role in the total system as the Chicanos or the Texans, or that we can regard the "group" in each case as having the same kind of social structure or identity system. The Hopis, the Yaquis, and probably all the Indian groups possess an identity anchor which is lacking in the case of Anglos and Spanish-speaking peoples. This is the sacred land concept, which is fundamental in the identity systems of "traditional" Hopis and Yaquis and all the rest, though perhaps weakest for the Yuman-speaking peoples. Even for those who have adopted secularized views of their past, lacking the rigid sacred meaning, the fact of possession of land long preceding the entrance of Anglos and Spaniards gives a special quality to the sense of identity. There is further a distinctness of language, and the fact of the absence of a long-established tradition of writing, which for all the Indian groups puts them in a special category; it is not only that the dominant societies attach importance to these matters, but there is also a feeling on the part of Indians about a certain kind of skill possessed by the Indo-European language users which gives them a special advantage. These differences are correlated with other characteristics which make each Indian group, as listed, the equivalent of the total Anglo or Spanish-speaking type, rather than the equivalent of any of the "varieties" listed.

Why, then, have we not lumped together all the English-speaking groups or all the Spanish-speaking groups? We have not done so because, despite many common traditions, including a written language, and a sense of relative transiency on the land, it does not appear that, for example, Hispanos feel a solidarity with Chicanos or Mexicans vis-a-vis any of the Anglo groups, regardless of how hostile towards Anglos they might feel on a given issue. Similarly we do not believe that Blacks, Mormons, and Texans feel closer to one another than to any of the Indian groups with which they come in contact. In short, the position is taken here that common culture elements and even some common identity system features are not decisive with respect to ethnic distance felt and acted on. While, therefore, it is perfectly justifiable to classify all the Anglo varieties listed as "variants" of a common type, if one is interested in cultural traits and complexes, it is not justifiable to do so if the focus of interest is the system of relations among ethnic groups. Implicit in our listing scheme is the view that we are concerned with and trying to isolate vital features of a system of mutual valuation, not merely a set of cultural elements which constitute the regional stock of traits. It is indeed the mutual valuations which constitute the "forces" impelling the dynamics of the kinds of relations we are analyzing. However, it should also be emphasized that we are here positing relationships for which there is very little systematic evidence. It is just such a question as Hispano sense of solidarity with Chicano or Mormon solidarity with Black which requires good research for the answers.

Here the criterion given the greatest weight in our classification would seem then to be that one about which we know the least at the moment, namely, the mutual valuation aspect of the identity system. The list points this up.

A Review of the Past

One hundred years ago a list of the ethnic groups would have appeared very similar. There would have been two major differences: (1) the smaller size of all groups and especially those of the Anglo type, and (2) the presence of at least two Indian groups which have since become extinct as recognizable cultural entities. These are the Yuman-speaking Halchidhomas, who through warfare in the Colorado River Valley and other factors disappeared during the mid-19th century, and the Opatas of Sonora. The Opatas were a large group at the time of Spanish entrance, numbering perhaps 30,000. By the beginning of the 20th century, however, processes of assimilation had proceeded so far that they were beginning to lose their identity. By the 1960's they had merged entirely, studies indicated, with the Norteño rural Mexicans of Sonora (Hinton 1959). It is a striking fact that complete extinction of native peoples in the Southwestern region is an unusual occurrence, and we have authentic evidence of the phenomenon only in the case of two or three other groups during the period since first contact with Europeans: perhaps the Piro-speaking people of the middle Rio Grande Valley, a small culturally Puebloan group; the Conchos and associated small tribelets in what is now northern Chihuahua and whose history is very obscure; and possibly a Piman group, the Sobaipuris of the San Pedro Valley.

If we consider the region 200 years ago, in the 1770's, the list of ethnic groups would be somewhat shorter and considerably different, indicating a simpler kind of ethnic system. The five Anglo varieties, the two Asiatic, the Mennonite, and the Chicano would be wholly absent, thus reducing the total number by nine. There might be some doubt as to whether the rural Norteño had differentiated by this time, but in all probability there were two distinct socioeconomic classes of Spaniards and, of course, the already well-established Hispanos of New Mexico. The not-very-satisfactory data hardly enable us to recast the Indian listings. We

37

may venture that there were only three Piman groups, Upper, Lower, and Tepehuan, thus reducing this category by one, but we should have to add the Opatas, as mentioned above, and the Halchidhoma, bringing the total number of groups to about 34.

Moving back 300 or 400 years further we are not on very safe ground in estimating numbers of groups in the terms in which our table is cast. About all that we can say is that about 1500 there were none of the Spanish-speaking types present, and the Indians may have numbered a few, but only a few, more than at any other period. In short, it is a fairly safe generalization that the number of ethnic groups in the region has increased somewhat during the past 500 years and that most of this increase has been a result of the coming into the region of European invaders, who have in the few hundred years of their residence differentiated into some ten different ethnic groups. The Indian groups have been reduced in number very slightly, nearly all of those who were present in 1500 being still present in 1970. Probably the losses in numbers of distinct Indian groups have been made up by the differentiation of new Indian groups such as the Hopi-Tewa, as well as by the recent comers from Europe.

Thus considering numbers alone there has been a certain stability of ethnic system in the region, but numbers do not constitute the only important feature of the system of ethnic relations anywhere. We are actually dealing with two very different phases in the development of the system between 1600 and 1970. Until the 1700's one kind of system prevailed; since then a quite different system of ethnic relations has developed. Before the arrival of the Spanish the Southwestern region was characterized by the presence of people everywhere living at the level of integration of simply the local community. Peoples of all the cultural types, whether pueblo, ranchería, or roving band, lived in politically and economically autonomous local units. The state was not present and there was no conquest, one exception possibly being that of the agricultural economy based on an extensive irrigation system at the site of modern Coolidge and Casa Grande. Ethnic relations were tribal relations, with no one group politically dominant or seeking such dominance. Undoubtedly there were some groups which had more influence than others in the region and consequently one could speak of some degree of cultural dominance, but this was not coupled with political and military dominance.

The Impact of Invasion and Occupation

Since the 1700's when the Spaniards, in alliance with the Pueblos, gained a degree of military-political dominance in the Rio Grande Valley of New Mexico, there has been the steady development of what we are familiar with today, namely, the subordination of all Indian groups under the political dominance of either the Mexicans or the Anglos. The present situation is characterized by groups which are in many ways dependent, rather than autonomous politically and economically, on one another. There are two political systems, the Mexican and the Anglo, each independent of the other, which have assumed political control of the people of the region. This type of system has been imposed on the preexisting ethnic system of autonomous communities and consequently there has been a readjustment of all ethnic relations in response to the official system required by the two states. It is not our intention to go into the historical development of the new system, but merely to characterize it broadly. This we shall proceed to do in what follows.

The roles of Spaniards and later of Anglos have been very different. The Spaniards began a program of "reduction" as soon as they entered the Southwest. This meant the concentration of all peoples who did not already live in compact communities like the Pueblos. The peoples of Chihuahua were generally a widely scattered population composed of very small bands of gathering and hunting people or of somewhat more compact rancherías like those of the Tarahumaras. The Spanish campaign resulted in greatly reducing the numbers of the small nomadic bands. Here, chiefly in eastern, central, and northern Chihuahua many groups with names for themselves were extinguished, either by actual depopulation or by consolidation with some other group. The more densely populated but still scattered rancherías of the river valleys along the Gulf of California coast were consolidated into mission communities, but there was little extinction except among the few nomadic coastal groups of Sinaloa. The process here was reduction in the number of separately identified groups through consolidation into fewer but larger settlement areas. The process in Chihuahua was one primarily of reduction of population and total elimination of many units which had formerly had a separate existence and sense of identity.

The Anglo actions, as indeed to a lesser extent the Mexican also, had different results. Far from reducing the number of named and identified groups, the American policy tended to stabilize the number at the level roughly of the period of the end of Spanish dominance. North of the international boundary there has been during 150 years only one extinction, the Halchidhomas. All the other Indian groups in existence and recognized by the Spaniards by the end of the 1700's are still in existence and generally with larger populations. The nature of the American program which stabilized the number of groups and encouraged population growth will be considered in some detail below. It will be enough here to say that the reservation system of landholding and administration has been a major factor in this stabilization of the Indian groups. In Mexico there have been two moves in this same direction, but much less structured than in the United States. The Yaquis in Sonora have land defined by executive order for exclusive Yaqui possession, but no corresponding administrative apparatus. The Tarahumaras have been provided services of various kinds through an administrative agency set up exclusively for their benefit, but without land ownership limitations.

The Nature of Ethnic Identity Systems

It must be emphasized that our listing does not at all imply a homogeneity within the groups named. The facts are quite otherwise. Every ethnic group named exhibits in its members wide variation with respect to cultural traits, awareness of the group's history, and intensity of feeling about relative evaluation of their own and the other groups. The Hopis are a well-known example of deep and emotion-fraught schisms within the group; the range is from absolutely rigid devotees of a revealed religion honoring *Masau'u* and consciously struggling to fend off American dominance, to placid housewives who have accepted the ritual of the Mormons and are unconcerned about "traditionalism" or any other of the distinctive Hopi issues (Thompson 1950). The fact is that this range includes people who do maintain some feature or combination of features of the Hopi identity system, and that this remains an important if not the most important element in their identities. Moreover, the children of the Mormon Hopi are much more interested in a more traditionalist-like identity system than their boarding school parents. Thus the range from deepest Hopi to American-like cannot be taken as a model of a process of assimilation. The developmental process must be represented quite differently.

Nearly all the other groups, if not all, are of similar varied composition, individuals exhibiting a wide range in cultural traits, historical awareness, and sense of moral superiority. The Yaquis are this way, the Mormons are this way, the Blacks are this way, the Chicanos are this way. Hence our listing must be taken as a classification of individuals who are characterized only in some degree by acceptance and understanding of one of the distinctive identity systems of the region. There is no question that there *is* a Hopi identity system which cannot be mistaken for the Navajo or the Hispano system. Moreover there is no question whatever that there are individuals in the Southwest who know nothing whatever of the Hopi identity system, who if they do learn of it can attach no intelligible meaning to it and simply cannot therefore accept it even on an academic, impersonal basis. One might engage in endless classification of individuals, and this would have some profit for understanding processes, but what we are concerned with is really the nature of whole identity systems, that is, with common symbols with their meanings. It is only in thought that they are discreet. In reality the degree of participation in them varies greatly among individuals. A classification of individuals with respect to their dual participation or their various degrees of participation would be important, but we shall not attempt that task here.

I am tempted to think in terms of two major kinds of identity systems, even though I realize that thinking in terms of binary systems of ideal types can be very misleading. What I see, first, are identity systems that have as an important element the symbol of roots in the land—supernaturally sanctioned, ancient roots, regarded as unchangeable. I believe all the Indian groups have this element in their identity systems and thus have a strong

41

mythological sanction for their Southwestern residence and rights. In this respect, there is great contrast with the Anglos and Mexicans, whose views and feelings about the land are coupled with a mythology of force and conquest and relative strength of military power. They argue for land rights, not in terms of God-given responsibilities—although this has begun in a very general way to creep into Anglo thought in recent years— but in terms of utility and power, human qualities. They are secularized with respect to land until the threat of war begets some sacred attitudes.

This basic difference regarding a component of the ethnic identity system ramifies into many other differences, which I suspect are important in the dynamics of the ethnic system. The Anglos and Mexicans are transients (very definitely so conceived by Hopis in relation to themselves) and foreigners to the Indians. The Indians, to the Anglos and Mexicans, begin of course from an unintelligible premise, which is branded as nonrational, un-progressive, and obstructive of the individualism which they consciously further. There is here a dichotomy among the ethnic groups which makes it easy to put them into just two classes, on this basis of the meaning of the land in the identity system. We shall explore this matter further in an effort to see whether there are any other correlates with this seeming fundamental difference in the primary phenomena with which we are concerned.

Ethnic Policies and Programs

It is not customary for dominant society members to think of nondominant ethnic groups as having "policies" with respect to ethnic matters. The term "policy" is usually associated with apparatus for attaining objectives—in short, with power—but there seems no good reason to confine the concept to the sphere of effective political or administrative organization. Benjamin Franklin was happy to use the term to designate guiding prin-ciples for individuals in their dealings with other individuals. We shall use the concept similarly in the broad sense of guiding principles for action, without reference to whether or not the group believing in them has the effective power to put them into action. We shall regard each ethnic group in the Southwest as having its own ethnic policy.

Frequently, as in the United States in the past decade, a dominant ethnic group in a modern state discovers with surprise that the ethnic policy which it has been trying to further with all good will is not accepted by the nondominant ethnic groups to whom it applies. Dominant groups have a predisposition to regard their objectives as self-evidently desirable goals and hence to make unilateral decisions in important ethnic matters. The dominant group tends to remain unaware that there can be justifiable points of view other than its own. Our position is that all ethnic groups, including the dominant one, maintain ideas as to what are the advantageous and desirable relations between themselves and other ethnic groups in their milieu. Policy, in this sense, is one of the universal dimensions of ethnic groups and must always be considered if we are to get a clear idea as to the nature of any multi-ethnic situation.

The ethnic groups of the Southwest differ with regard to the extent to which they control social machinery for maintaining or effecting their policies regarding one another. They also differ with respect to the definiteness with which they have formulated what can be called a policy. To consider the latter point first, we may illustrate by contrasting the Hopis of Arizona and the Opatas of Sonora at the beginning of this century. A majority of Hopis, according to Anglo estimates, supported a statement made to the United States Indian agent that they did not want their children to be sent to boarding schools. They said that they had an educational system of their own, that they did not think it was necessary to send children away from home to learn English, although they agreed it was good to learn English. Here was a Hopi educational policy, well-formulated in the light of information about the United States system for Indians and in awareness of the traditional Hopi educational policy, but there was definitely a group position and a statement of issues. There was also at this time a land policy clearly formulated, as well as policy positions on many other aspects of group relations.

In great contrast, we find it very difficult to locate any information indicating the formulation of policy by Opatas of

Sonora in the early 20th century. There is no doubt that 100 years before these people had a sense of identity, and that they were also identified as Opatas by Mexicans. By the early 1900's group consciousness had disintegrated and persons of Opata descent in large numbers were adopting the identification of the rural Norteño of Sonora. In short, an extensive process of assimilation, not just of individuals, but of the whole group, was going on. This has continued to the present, just as the well-formulated Hopi ethnic policy has also persisted to the present. In our survey we shall point out details concerning the range of definiteness of policy formulation and suggest some of the factors accounting for the differences. At this point we may offer the generalization that both those groups who have control of state apparatus for programming an ethnic policy and those whose policies are at odds with the dominant policy develop the most definite formulations.

The other factor mentioned in terms of which ethnic groups in the Southwest differ is with regard to control of state machinery for enforcing an ethnic policy. As we have just pointed out this influences clarity of policy formulation. The Norteños of Sonora and the urban Anglos of Arizona are characterized by definite ethnic policies. In both cases there are two levels of policy formulation. There is a national level affected by non-regional factors and a local level affected by face-to-face contacts and by state legislation. National and local levels are sometimes in opposition and there is consequent instability of ethnic policy at the state level. In both countries efforts of Indians and others to play off national against the local policies have given them some leverage and have helped to influence ethnic affairs.

Anglo Ethnic Policies

We shall deal first with the policies of Anglo groups, with stress upon that of the urban Anglos of today. It should be understood that this policy is not concurred with by all Anglo ethnic groups. Thus the Mormons must be regarded as having, as an organized group, a somewhat different policy from other Anglos with respect to Indians, and also to Blacks. It is a notable fact that Mormon senators have been prominent in opposition to prevailing national policy. Texans, as represented by rural residents in New Mexico and Arizona, do not usually act in accord with national policy respecting either Indians or Blacks or Chicanos. Blacks, I would guess, generally accept dominant policy regarding Indians, but their leadership frequently exhibits great ignorance of the nature of this policy. It should further be pointed out that it is at the level of national administrative apparatus and court systems that national policy is effective; outside the officials of these institutions there is a very different policy, frequently expressed in newspaper editorials and letters to the editors. With respect to Indians it cannot be overemphasized that the institutionalized national policy in schools, courts, and reservation administration is the dominant influence. Focused through established institutions, it is not uninfluenced by the local level, but it has so far been at the national level that the plural interests of Anglos have been controlled.

Akzin (1966) has characterized the United States with respect to ethnic policy as a "relaxed, liberal, integrationist state." He means that there is a notable absence of pressure, in contrast with some other nation-states, to eliminate the languages and cultural patterns of nondominant ethnic groups. While in a sense this characterization holds good, it must be pointed out that 50 years ago officials of the United States government were far from relaxed. They rounded up Indian children to put them in boarding schools against the will of their parents. The children were assigned to different Christian sects, and Indian languages were prohibited at any time in classroom or dormitory or playground. While the practices are not now so brutal as they once were, neither is the resistance so great after 60 years of no alternatives. At present we are in a phase in which there is more than a relaxed tolerance; there is indeed in some schools encouragement of expression of linguistic and cultural difference with respect to Indians, to Chicanos, and even Blacks. This is a tendency, but a spotty one. Instruction in Spanish, for example, is generally recognized only as a means for the better learning of English. There are suggestions of readiness on the part of some Anglos to go further. This has been important in connection with Office of Economic Opportunity programs, such as the Navajo Rough Rock Demonstration School and the new Community College on the Navajo Reservation. There Navajo history, language, medical knowledge and practice, and other aspects of Navajo culture are formally taught, the funds being provided by the federal government, the Navajo Tribe, and private foundations.

Despite these trends and recent changes, Anglo ethnic policy is strongly "integrationist," in the sense that Akzin uses that term. Akzin (1966) points out that states of this type seek the "weakening and ultimate abolition of ethnic distinctions." There is no question that this has been the dominant trend of Anglo policy towards Indians and that institutions for furthering it are still dominant. Government policy for at least 85 years was very specifically oriented to erasing Indian ethnic characteristics and replacing them with Anglo ones. It may also be said that, without actually isolating the concept of identity system, the Anglos sought to replace Indian with Anglo identity by teaching the children in federal, public, and mission schools only the symbols of U.S. history and national being, omitting nearly all facts concerning Indian leaders and Indian development. This has also been true of ethnic policy regarding all other groups, for example, Chicanos, Hispanos, and Blacks. In the 1950's the state of New Mexico withdrew the regulation ordering the use of both Spanish and English in legal notices and transactions, English thus becoming the single official language of the state.

The elimination of ethnic differences has been associated with the objective of integration. This has meant acceptance of all individuals of whatever ethnic background on an equal basis into the society dominated by the urban Anglo ethnic group. The basic assumption is that all should accept and live by the values and customs of this ethnic group. It means that no other ethnic group within the society is recognized as a distinguishable legal or political entity. No national law, and in New Mexico and Arizona since 1948 no state law, is written in any way to make distinction among individuals of varying ethnic background. However, there is national Indian legislation, for example, the Indian Reorganization Act of 1934 which speaks of Indian lands and Indian political jurisdiction, in distinction from those of all other ethnic groups. There is here clearly an aspect of Anglo ethnic policy inconsistent with the body of that policy. Nevertheless its legal basis survives attack year after year in the arena of national congressional committees.

We may sum up the general character of Anglo ethnic policy. It is probably currently in a phase of change, having moved from an aggressive, coercive integrationism to a present somewhat tentative and permissive experimental pluralism. For Indians, the present tendency is in the direction given by Congress in 1934, but only in part. That legislation encouraged Indians to organize politically; the current trends do not do this. The current phase is permissive in that within the still dominant integrationist policy, ethnic groups are permitted to develop some degree of cultural pluralism. The fact however is that in the institutions in which non-Anglo individuals take part—schools, legislatures, for example—the officeholders and employees are predominantly those who were trained in the previous phase when Anglo dominance was taken for granted and only monocultural conditions were conceived. Schoolteachers, federal agency personnel, and Anglo citizens generally are at odds with the slight moves in a different direction. They are in general like the modern Homesteaders, a community of Texans in New Mexico, as summed up by Vogt (1955a: 139): " . . . the Homesteaders regard themselves as superior to the 'Mexicans,' Pueblos, and Navajos—all of whom they regard with contempt—but manifest orientations of inferiority and insecurity toward 'city folks,' and regard . . . Mormons with ambivalent feelings of admiration and envy, tinged with . . . contempt for their religion . . . "

Mexican Ethnic Policies

The other dominant group in the region, the Norteños of Mexico, is currently in a phase of ethnic policy toward Indians which shows some marked similarities to that of the urban Anglos in the United States, and is essentially the integrationist policy usual in the modern nation-state. Since Mexico's independence from Spain, Mexican policy has moved through two major phases and is now in a third. The first and longest phase was one in which there was no recognition of Indian societies as any kind of entity. In contrast with the United States, not only was there no legal definition through legislation or courts as to Indian status, but also there was no effort until the 1920's to set up any sort of governmental machinery to "integrate" Indians into the nation. It was assumed at first that the announcement of

47

social and political equality would automatically bring Indians into the state, but this happened only here and there. The process was left up to the large landholders—the *hacendados*—through economic and other forms of coercion to effect the "integration." There was no conception of a pluralistic society being formed. Insofar as there was a concept of the kind of society to be aimed at, it was a culturally homogeneous one. The Indian contribution was conceived as having already been made. This became the dominant view just following the 1910 Revolution under the influence of Vasconcelos and his concept of *la raza cósmica* (the cosmic race). In this second phase, the integrating institution was seen as being the federal rural schools, in which no distinction was made between Indians and others, in contrast with the United States. The phase in which Mexico now is began to shape its outlines during the Cárdenas administration in the 1930's, contemporaneous with the shift toward pluralism for Indians in the United States.

Essentially the current phase of Mexican ethnic policy still rests on the assumption that the desirable objective is a culturally homogeneous society. It is said that a few minor differences, as in craft arts or even dress, are desirable, but in all basic elements of culture there will be homogeneity, the attainment of a common evolutionary level. The process by which this is to be attained is through choice by Indians, by their own leadership, in the absence of all direct coercion—in short, the relaxed position, as conceived by Akzin, which aims nevertheless at the elimination of ethnic differences. No important contributions are expected to come from the Indian cultures to the dominant Mexican culture except as folk dance, craft art, and perhaps folk literature.

Within this general frame, so different and so like the Anglo policy, there are several features of application in the Southwest to which we shall call attention. In contrast with the United States, Indian-owned lands are included like all others in regional development plans and organization. This is an important principle in Mexican policy; there should be no separate political or economic units. Thus the Indians are merged with Mexicans in *ejidos*, in schools, in municipal organizations. Mexicans in this way seek to avoid the tensions which arise when, as in the United States, there are separate economic and political units for Indians.

However, two other features of policy must be mentioned, which suggest a slight tendency towards a pluralistic policy. In 1939, President Cárdenas departed from precedent on one of his grass-roots journeys to Sonora. He sat down with officials of the eight Yaqui towns, listened to their discussion of land problems past and present, went back to Mexico City and issued a decree, ordering that all territory then held by the Yaquis was to remain their exclusive possession, thus giving special status to Indian land similar to a U.S. reservation but without any administrative machinery to match. This decree has not been consistently successful in keeping land out of non-Yaqui hands, but is still on the books.

A second action by the federal government indicating a distinct ethnic policy for the Yaquis was the plebiscite held under government auspices in 1959. President Ruiz Cortines and the federal Department of Resources and Development were anxious, as was the state government of Sonora, to bring Yaquis into the municipality-state system of political structure, which the Yaquis had not accepted. The President proposed a plebiscite by Yaquis in the homeland area on the issue of whether to retain their essentially colonial Spanish type of local government or adopt the modern municipality type. The vote was decisively for continuance of the older system. It continues to the present, having been sanctioned by both federal and state government. No other Indians of the region have had such a showdown with the federal government.

To sum up, it is clear that the dominant objective of the Mexican government is to uniformize institutional interaction and participation of Indians. But it is also clear that it does not propose to force such uniformity, but insists on Indian choice. At present conflict goes on in Chihuahua, where federal policy is challenged by the state government.

Indian Ethnic Policies

Probably all Indian groups in the United States can be said to have ethnic policies, although some of these are sketchy and are formulated only in crisis. The very small and less organized groups, such as the Camp Verde Yavapais and Tonto Apaches, may not be very clear or far-sighted with regard to objectives in their relations with Anglos and others. Nevertheless, inspection of the consistencies in their behavior over long periods suggests that there is policy, even if not very consciously formulated at any time. Because of difficulties in maintaining any sort of overall political units of their own, probably some Indian groups in Sonora and Chihuahua do not formulate or become conscious continuously of any "policy." The Lower Pimas, the Opatas during the 19th century, and possibly at present most of the Tarahumaras may be in such a category. In general however there can be no question about the existence of fairly well-worked-out policies which are the result of specific experiences with other ethnic groups and which have become part of group points of view. Good examples of the nature of highly developed Indian policies are those of the Navajos and the Yaquis.

Just as it is distorting to look only at the present phase of dominant society policies, so it is misleading to talk only about present phases of any one of the Indian group's policies. The dynamics of the ethnic system are promptly illuminated if we seek a little time perspective. Let us take the Navajos and their ethnic policy as it has developed in the past 100 years. One hundred years ago they had just returned from incarceration in Fort Sumner, where they had undergone the bitter experiences of being prisoners of war, of living under totally unaccustomed conditions with respect to food, work, and housing, plus total domination by soldiers. Something like a policy took form immediately. They were ready and willing to accept aid in the form of sheep from Anglos, but the dominant policy actuating nearly everyone was withdrawal from contact. The former aggressiveness and raiding complex were dead; they had experienced defeat and could envision further bitter experience if they broke their promise to remain peaceful. There was withdrawal and a spreading out into a wide expanse of territory. They became devoted to sheep raising. There was another part of the policy, an active rejection of forced contact, as for children in school. Very few Navajo parents at this time in the late 19th century wanted schools. The 1867 treaty obligated the United States government to furnish schools; the Navajos proved that they were interested hardly at all in forcing the government to live up to its promise.

At Round Rock some resisted forcible school recruitment. The policy was one of staying as far away as possible from all contact and becoming as independent as they possibly could. They accepted economic aid in developing a blanket market, in setting up their herding again, but for the rest it was an isolationist policy.

In the past 60 years there has been a slow and steady shift in Navajo policy which has been accompanied by the growth of much formal organization. This organization has been able in successive phases of change to formulate and express general objectives. Anglos, rather slowly, forced schools on the Navajos, boarding schools within their country, mission schools on and off reservation. In the 1950's the Navajo Tribal Council set up a $10,000,000 scholarship fund for Navajos who wished to go on for higher education. In the 1960's Navajos established and began to manage a junior college and an experimental school laboratory. Their former policy of isolating themselves, coupled with rejection of such institutional linkage as schools, has altered profoundly. They had, often only under duress to be sure, cooperated with Anglos in their program of assimilating and changing the ways of Navajos through institutionalized means, chiefly the school and the Tribal Council, both instituted by Anglos. These powerful instruments for cultural development had been gradually accepted and Navajos had learned to use them. By the 1960's there had been a complete reversal of policy. The Council was instituting industries in Navajo country and encouraging business enterprise. Thus a new policy of cooperation with Anglo change agents and adoption of new organization had replaced the earlier policy of withdrawal and rejection.

Now, however, a new phase of Navajo ethnic policy has taken form. This is manifest in many ways, in statements made repeatedly by Navajo officials and by common men, as for example, in letters to the editor in the *Navajo Times*. We cannot go into these statements at length, but we can suggest a major trend in present Navajo policy by means of the following quotation from a memorandum of the Navajo Community College on April 21, 1970:

Navajo Community College was established to bring higher education to the Navajo Reservation. About this there is no question but the most important area of demonstration and innovation is Indian control over Indian education, specifically Navajo control over Navajo education.

The college must never lose sight of its responsibilities in this area. At this college the traditional relationship must be reversed. . . . The Anglos should not be in the driver's seat. They should not be the ones directing and controlling this college.

The success of Navajo Community College in realizing local and ethnic control (Navajo and Indian control) is one of the most important contributions this college can make not only to Navajo education but to American education. If this objective is consciously sought by the college, it should be recognized that the pathway will not be easy. Most Anglos will find it very difficult to be satisfied in a relationship which places them in an advisory capacity and not in a decision making role.

This kind of policy is apparent in the behavior and thought of many organized bodies on the Navajo reservation—the Navajo Tribal Council, where it has emerged steadily into prominence over a 40-year period; the Office of Navajo Economic Opportunity, where such independence has been encouraged by the U.S. government by a new kind of contract structure unknown in Navajo affairs before the 1960's; and elsewhere as in the Navajo school board of the Rough Rock Demonstration School.

The quotation is so clear and pointed that we need say no more to indicate the nature of the direction which Navajo ethnic policy has taken. Over the past 100 years as policy has moved from withdrawal, to acceptance of help, to insistence on the "driver's seat," the Navajo role in the Southwestern ethnic system has altered correspondingly.

There is fortunately an abundance of material for describing the ethnic policy of the Yaquis during the past 150 years. As in the case of the Navajos there has never been unanimity among the Yaquis. Apparently it is inherent in the nondominant situation that different viewpoints are generated within the group. Nevertheless these differences are variations on a single theme, on a set of issues characteristic of each ethnic group; in short, there are issues which are issues only to members of that ethnic group. To cease to recognize these as issues means to cease to have an identification with that group. When one begins to say that "they" should forget old grievances one is undergoing assimilation, that is to say, change of identity. Yaquis differ and have differed, but let us consider the issues that have been important to Yaquis whatever the degree of intensity of their Yaqui identification.

We may compare Yaqui policy of the mid-19th century with policy at the time of the close of the 1910 Revolution and at the present time. Our sources for knowledge of Yaqui policy in the middle of the last century are records of peace negotiations, statements by military and civil leaders, oral history accounts, etc. We shall consider only one aspect of policy in order to keep the discussion within bounds. Repeatedly it was pointed out to Mexican military commanders, especially victorious ones, that Yaquis as represented by their elected governors were seeking the elimination of Mexicans from a territory which they regarded as their sacred possession, or, better perhaps, their trust obligation from God. There seemed to be no compromise on the part of the organized Yaquis with this position. Yaqui military commanders of ability, like Cajeme, bowed to this deeply-believed-in principle. Other relations with Mexicans could be worked out, but there was no compromise with the principle of "no Mexicans in Yaqui territory in any official capacity." Many Yaquis continued to give their lives in the name of this principle until the time of the 1910 Revolution. The Revolution and the shift of power in Mexico seemed to bring no change in the Yaqui land policy. Ex-President Obregón was held prisoner by Yaquis in 1927, because they maintained that he had not lived up to a promise to restore Yaqui land to Yaquis.

The facts of history have changed the situation in such a way that Yaquis have had to modify the principle. First, being forced to allow, as a result of military occupation of their land in 1928, garrisons of federal soldiers and officers of municipal government in their towns, they came to modify their land policy. They held during the 1940's that the resident police commissioners of the municipal government were present to manage the affairs of non-Yaquis, such as mestizo land leasers now living under the wing of the army in the Yaqui country. The municipal system was regarded as outside the proper system of Yaqui local government. In the plebiscite of 1959 they affirmed again their policy of Yaqui local government by Yaquis. Under duress, as they see it, they continue to live within a dual system which includes their own and the Norteño local government. Land issues have now in part been converted into issues of jurisdiction in law and order, authority of the National Ejidal Bank and the Regional Irrigation Commission, and the management of the cattle cooperative. One can see Yaqui policy changing character under the influence of imposed conditions affecting the Yaqui use of land and federal bureaucratic controls on persons who use the water. Yaqui policy exists nevertheless and both state and national governments have to reckon with it.

Ethnic Boundaries and Tensions

The most difficult operation in the study of ethnic groups is gaining an adequate and usable concept of boundaries. Perhaps "boundary" is not the best term to use, because of its connotations of territorial limits, of barriers which may not be passed or passed only with difficulty, and of objective physical things which have continuous existence regardless of the coming and going of individual humans. Yet there is something of all these meanings which we must attach to the concept of ethnic boundary, although no one of them need be universally included. Hence we do not propose a different term.

Ethnic Boundaries as Situations

The boundaries of ethnic groups in the Southwest cannot be represented on a map as territorial limits within which all the members of a group carry on their life activities. The boundaries are not necessarily tangible barriers of some sort; persons who are and continue to remain members of ethnic groups may move back and forth across the boundaries, and persons who seek different identities may move across the boundaries never to cross back. Ethnic boundaries are actually *situations* in which individuals are stimulated to consciousness of ethnic differences between themselves and others. The situations may be marked by physical objects, such as the signboards which occur at Indian reservation limits or by the clustering of particular types of dwellings, such as hogans or "ranch style" suburban houses or Pueblo mud-and-stone multistory dwellings. The situations may be marked by language differences on a city street, where a Spanish-speaker suddenly begins to hear English all around, or vice versa. The situation may develop in a public meeting where the language does not change, but speakers begin to use the name for their ethnic group and to make statements embodying planks in a particular ethnic policy. It is situations of interaction among people which constitute the actual ethnic boundaries—situations which have a location, are characterized by the use of artifacts, and in which roles are activated and ideas expressed. The ethnic boundaries are those situations in which the sense of identity receives some kind of expression and where individuals align themselves in some manner as members of one ethnic group or another. There may be physical markers in some situations, but, as in the case of fences around reservations or street signs in a city barrio, such markers are merely one part of the bounding situations, and it must be emphasized that, as in the case of the public meeting, there are situations in which there are no physical markers whatsoever.

Like a range fence, ethnic boundaries must be maintained. The processes of maintenance can only be identified in the situations of interaction which we have illustrated. The urban Anglo resident of Arizona or New Mexico usually has a characteristic and recurrent comment whenever he passes a reservation signboard as he drives along the highway. The range of reaction is wide because of the internal diversity of the urban Anglo group— all the way from "You can sure see they don't use their land right" to "Isn't it a shame the government doesn't take better care of them?" Such comments are events in the process of boundary maintenance between Anglos and Indians. But the process cannot be fully described without also noting the response of Indians as they drive by the same signboard. Processes of boundary maintenance might also be illustrated by describing meetings of neighborhood area councils in cities which have instituted Office of Economic Opportunity programs in which members of Mexican-American, Black, Anglo, and various Indian residents of the city customarily make speeches expressing the attitudes and statements of objectives of their respective ethnic groups. The processes of maintenance go on constantly in city council chambers, in elementary school classrooms, among clashing boys' gangs in urban areas, in Bureau of Indian Affairs conferences, in tribal council meetings, in sessions of the members of the Federal Alliance of Land Grants in New Mexico, in meetings of a Sonora Yaqui town council, etc. The sense of urgency about maintenance of boundaries varies greatly from year to year and situation to situation for the members of any ethnic group, as does the ability of leaders in the maintenance process. The fluctuations in the intensity of interest in boundary maintenance are a significant index to changing states of ethnic interrelations.

Problems in the Understanding of Boundary Systems

With the introduction of the subject of ethnic boundaries we are at the heart of our subject. We shall not in the course of this short section attempt to sketch the nature of the boundaries of all the ethnic groups of the Southwest, but rather to suggest what appear to be vital problems in connection with understanding this aspect of Southwestern life. We shall as a beginning mention three sets of problems which appear to be of primary importance:

First, how can we define these boundaries so that we may know and predict where the limits of ethnic groups are, so that reasonably accurate counts of their membership may be made and also surveys of their cultural characteristics? In short, how can we determine the demographic features of ethnic groups so that we may reach an understanding of changing interrelationships based on something other than impression and estimate?

Second, how stable are such boundaries? If they are, as seems to be the case, regularly and frequently crossed, then what are the functions of the boundaries with reference to the ethnic groups which they bound? What kind of continuity of features is to be found in the boundary systems of ethnic groups from one generation to the next?

Third, is the ethnic status, as Barth (1969) suggests, a kind of master status determining the combinations of social roles of

ethnic group members, somewhat as sex and social rank statuses
are master statuses? Do individuals constantly identify themselves as members of ethnic groups or only, as it were, when they
come up against the bounding situations? Is the identity system
of an individual, and of a group, something which is discontin-
uous and evanescent or deep-rooted and of central importance in
cultural and personality orientation?

Features of the Southwestern Boundary System

Having mentioned these focal problems for the understanding
of any system of ethnic boundaries, we shall turn to an effort to
characterize in broad terms, and in broad terms only, the nature
of the Southwestern system of ethnic boundaries. There are at
least four major characteristics of this system which should be
stressed:

Differential Awareness of Boundaries. Knowledge of ethnic
boundaries, and hence of the nature of ethnic groups in the
region, is nonexistent or of very low intensity for members of the
dominant groups—the urban Anglos and Norteño Mexicans.
(There are specialists in ethnic affairs for whom this does not
hold.) Because of the relatively large numbers of the Anglos and
Norteños, most of their associations are with one another and
significant contact with other ethnic groups is exceptional. This
condition, together with their traditional belief that all citizens
of the state are or will eventually be like themselves, brings about
an insulation from reality. They do not meet members of other
ethnic groups very frequently, if at all, and when they do they
are almost always in situations in which they, as members of the
dominant group, are superordinate, so that they tend to dom-
inate the interaction. Thus they do not perceive or do not understand the signals in the situation with reference to ethnic boundaries. On the other hand, the nondominant ethnic group members
are generally in frequent contact with members of the dominant
groups; Indians and Chicanos, for example, are daily involved
with government officials, traders, or school teachers of different
identity from their own. Awareness of at least the boundary
between themselves and the dominant Anglos is built into their

existence from childhood. This differential in awareness of boundaries is an important feature of the total system, contributing in several ways to tension and conflict in the milieu of differing ethnic policies in the region.

Fluidity of Boundaries. There is both a reality and an ideal of fluidity, of boundarylessness, among the ethnic groups of the region. There is a reality in the sense that boundaries are easily crossed, that change of identity on the part of individuals happens constantly and frequently. There are certain mechanisms built into the social system which individuals use freely for learning the necessary behavior characteristics of the dominant groups and so moving out of a group in which they began life and adopting the identity of the dominants. The public school system may be used in this way and frequently is. The open occupational structure was much used in the recent past, but is less used at present to accomplish such ends. It must be pointed out, however, that the school system, whether in Mexico or the United States, has been a one-way mechanism, that is, it has operated only to facilitate change of identity from nondominant group to dominant group. It must further be emphasized that when color is one of the identifying ethnic characteristics of the nondominant group, crossing the boundary into the dominant Anglo group has remained difficult, to say the least, for Blacks and some Indians and Chicanos. This one-sided fluidity is a reality which tends to reinforce the dominant groups' beliefs that there are no ethnic boundaries, or that they are steadily disappearing, or that there ought not to be any ethnic boundaries.

The ideal of fluidity, which is generally strong in the world view of the dominants, is rooted as we have indicated in the assumption that everyone ought to identify with and live like the dominants. But this ideal, which sanctions, for example, the monocultural orientation of school curriculums, rests on an assumption which is not always accepted by members of the nondominant ethnic groups. As nondominant group members have learned increasingly during the past century through school and occupational experience what the value orientations of the dominants are, there has developed a reaction against the dominants' ideal regarding cultural homogeneity and uniformity of ethnic identification. This reaction is now the source of new developments and change in the total ethnic system.

Languages as Boundaries. Only a tiny handful of Anglos and even fewer Mexicans or Chicanos speak any Indian language. On the other hand many Indians are bilingual in Spanish or English and an Indian language. In fact, only a tiny percentage of Indians on either side of the international border are not bilingual, and some are trilingual, using English and Spanish as well as an Indian language. Moreover many Indians speak two or more Indian languages. There is thus a barrier of language which excludes members of the dominant ethnic groups from participation in and hence understanding of Indian cultural worlds, a barrier which no longer exists for Indians with respect to Anglo and Mexican life. It is in the family and religious life of the Indians that this barrier is most strongly maintained against the dominant ethnic groups.

Beyond this, there is a basic dichotomy with respect to language which is of far-reaching significance in the relation of the ethnic groups. This is an essential part of the ideology of dominance which plays such an important role in the whole ethnic system. The Indian languages, of which the Indian groups are very conscious and which constitute a vital part of the real world in which they live, are not recognized as languages by the dominant institutions, whether schools, libraries, governmental record keepers, or literary persons. Up until about four years ago they were never taught even in specialized courses in the universities. Only the Bureau of Indian Affairs made any effort to give them recognition in schools and tribal records, and this effort was steadily choked off by Congress. Indian languages have continued to exist only as oral and not as printed written languages, with the exception of Navajo, which attained the status of a written language through the efforts of the Bureau of Indian Affairs and a few missionaries. The dominant Anglos in the United States and the Norteños in Mexico make, as it were, a distinction between Indo-European languages and Indian languages, lumping the latter all together and acting as if the Indian languages did not exist. The effects have been not the disappearance of the Indian languages, but the maintenance of nearly total ignorance of them by the dominants. Another effect has been the encouragement of a dichotomous view of education among Indians. Formal education has become associated only with English or Spanish, while Indian languages have remained associated exclusively with oral tradition and relegated to a lower valuation accordingly.

Indian Reservations as Boundaries. The Southwestern region is distinctive in the United States, and in part also in Mexico, with respect to a special form of ethnic boundary, namely, the Indian reservation. In the U.S. Southwest about one-fourth of the total land area consists of Indian reservations. These are areas defined in and sanctioned by the U.S. legal system as for use exclusively by Indians. An ethnic definition of land ownership is to be found in U.S. law only in connection with Indians. Although reservations exist in other parts of the United States, only in the Southwest do we find such large areas in which there are contiguous Indian communities not interspersed with Anglo or other communities. In Oklahoma there are nearly as many Indians, but no reservations. In the Dakotas there are large reservations, but they are "checkerboarded" with non-Indian holdings. The reservation system has established boundaries which have given a special direction to the development of Indian life, as will be discussed below. In addition, however, they have given rise to persisting tensions between Indian ethnic groups on the one hand and Anglo and Hispano groups on the other. Reservations of the type to be found in the United States do not exist in Mexico, but the Yaquis do hold land somewhat similarly by government sanction.

We may think of Indian reservations as part of a system of social relations, having as one important aspect legally defined territorial boundaries. The reservation system should be thought of as including not only these boundaries but also the functionally related consequences of the spatial boundaries in the form of political and other relations. The central feature is simply a form of corporate land ownership, not in itself unique in the United States, but modified by a governmental trusteeship which does make it different. It is like standard forms of ownership which involve corporate title to land. It is unlike them in that the title remains not in the hands of the corporation or a private trust, but with an official of the federal government, namely, the Secretary of the Interior. Title may not be transferred or holdings removed from the trust except through act of Congress. There are thus three parties to the ownership, and none may take action unilaterally. Federal statutes and judicial precedents exist which require the three parties to act jointly. This arrangement could, of course, be broken by Congress if it so chose. However, it has not chosen to do so, but has acted in terms of existing precedent.

The origin of the reservation system is rooted in 200 years of experience with Anglo aggression and Indian lands. Previous actions of Congress, of the executive arm of the federal government, and of Indians have resulted in great losses of land to Indians, which have given rise to sentiments among all three that special protective measures are necessary in order not to repeat such losses. Segments of the Anglo public and more recently individual Indians have opposed the arrangement, but it has existed for more than 70 years. Here in the Southwest, in contrast with some other parts of the country, Indian landholdings under the system have increased rather than decreased.

There is widespread misunderstanding of the nature of the reservation system on the part of Anglos, Indians, and all other ethnic groups. This persists, no doubt, partly because of the unique features which make it different from other landholding arrangements under United States law. It is important therefore that we make clear its essential features. The laws which define it have nothing to do with individual persons. It in no way restricts Indian mobility with reference to the land; Indians may move freely on and off reservations and reside wherever they please. What is defined in the law are the boundaries of the land held by an Indian group as a corporate entity. These boundaries are precisely described on the basis of treaties made with Indians by the U.S. Congress or of executive orders by the President of the United States. Other national legislation prescribes jurisdiction within the defined areas by Indian corporate entities known as "tribes." The jurisdiction includes the maintenance of law and order respecting resident Indians (with certain exceptions regarding crimes under federal jurisdiction), taxation, and other governmental functions described in tribal constitutions. The reservation system then, in effect, gives legal sanction for the territorial base of Indian ethnic groups acting as political entities within the United States with regard to domestic matters.

The membership of the political bodies is defined as all those persons on tribal rolls, and the tribes are given the power to authorize the rolls. Ordinarily the qualifications include some degree of "Indian blood," that is, descent from Indian ancestors, and may specify residence. However, tribal rolls ordinarily are not limited to residents of the reservation areas, so that jurisdiction extends over persons resident anywhere in the United States. Nevertheless Indian officials do not exercise powers over Indians outside the reservation, even though nonresident Indians may share in benefits accruing to the tribal body and may vote in tribal elections. There remains therefore a fuzzy area with respect to "tribal rights." This is all the more difficult for most persons, Indian or otherwise, to be clear about, because Indians since 1924 have been full citizens of the United States and may vote and hold office in state or national bodies. There is obviously a dual political membership for all Indians who are tribally enrolled.

The dual character of the political system under which Indians live affects their lives in many ways. In political activities within the reservations they are dissociated from all other ethnic groups. Even though Anglos, such as traders and numerous federal employees, live permanently on reservations, they may not vote or otherwise participate in tribal political affairs. The local governments of Arizona and New Mexico maintain no formal relations with the local governments of reservations. There is therefore a sharp separation between Indians and others in political life. In the Southwest, however, this is not so sharp as it was 15 years ago. A few small tribes have invited county law and order officials to operate within their reservations and, more important, a number of school districts under county authorities have been formed on Navajo, Apache, and Papago reservations, in which all residents, both Indians and others, participate and hold office. State highways through reservations also have resulted in state highway patrols maintaining authority within the rights of way. Thus the dual system still operates, but new political jurisdictions have recently been formed which overlap with tribal jurisdictions.

Despite such developments, Indians in general in the Southwest and especially Indians in official tribal government roles repeatedly and strongly state their support for maintenance of the reservation boundary system, stressing the importance to them of the collective title to land. Indian commissioners who have come into office since the 1950's have found that they have had to state publicly that they do not favor "termination," the policy adopted for a short time during the Eisenhower administration, which resulted in loss of tribal titles in Oregon and Wisconsin. Indian and non-Indian public opinion at the national level in the long run backs the reservation system.

Nevertheless at the state level there is constant tension over the reservation system. Segments of the Anglo and Hispano populations regard the system as anomalous and a source of special privilege for Indians. Among them there is a great deal of misunderstanding of the nature of the reservations. Over and over again editorials and letters to editors complain about nonexistent features of the system, such as government "doles" to Indians and exemption of Indians from taxation. Over and over again other letters correcting the misconceptions are printed, as are interviews with informed persons seeking to correct the misinformation. The misunderstanding is perennial and is an indicator of the tension to which the system gives rise. The tension continues in part because there is no institutionalized source of good information about Indians at the state level. For example, schools, except for a course or two at university level, do not provide knowledge of the Indian situation, and so the Indian world is, even for many Indians, surrounded by a world of rumor. This leads to efforts in state and national legislatures to make new laws pertaining to Indians which aim at "setting Indians free," or some other chimerical goal. Indians generally sense that the reservation boundary system is not accepted by most Anglos and that it may be attacked at any time in Congress. There is tension on their side of the boundary which gives rise to distrust of

Anglos and to a pervasive feeling of insecurity. At present among a few Indians who have studied Anglo law there is beginning to be recognition of a need for developing a less assailable foundation in law for the system.

A full discussion of ethnic boundaries would deal with occupational segregation, where it exists; with residence grouping and its cultural consequences; with membership in voluntary associations; with the selection of spouses; and many other areas of life. It would be highly desirable to have the information which would enable us to offer the view of the ethnic world of the Southwest which representative members of each ethnic group maintain. Members of the groups, of course, know where they draw lines with regard to identifying with others. Wherever there is a sense of identity there is a sense of propriety regarding what one should and should not say and do as one maintaining that identity. No studies of this sort have yet been made in the Southwest except for an incomplete description of a generalized Arizona Yaqui viewpoint from the early 1940's. This is out of date, but could be used to indicate what is required (Spicer 1953).

Intercultural Exchange

A considerable amount of information is available concerning the results of the borrowing of ideas, techniques, and customs among the people of the Southwest. Over many centuries Indians have borrowed from Indians, with a consequent enrichment of religious life, the crafts, and oral literature. For a shorter period Hispanic and Anglo peoples have borrowed from Indians in the areas of the dance, architecture, agriculture, and personal ornamentation. Indians have, of course, in turn borrowed much from Hispanic and Anglo peoples: forms of government, housebuilding, alphabets, metal tools, religious ideas and rituals, and many other cultural elements. Anglos borrowed extensively for a century from the Spanish-speaking peoples, especially those of Texas, learning the whole economy of cattle raising with its accompanying accessories of costume and artifact. More recently, the tide of cultural drift has turned and Anglos appear to be the people most borrowed from by Mexicans, as well as Mexican-Americans and Indians. Borrowing and the accompanying processes of modification and fusion of the borrowed elements always take place in some degree and fashion when people of different cultural backgrounds come into proximity. The Southwest is no exception in this regard.

Some Questions on the Desirability of Cultural Diversity

In this final section I wish to raise several questions in connection with the universal phenomenon of intercultural exchange, as it manifests itself in the Southwest. The first is a question which is implicit, if not directly expressed, in almost all discussion of such matters as Indian education, bilingualism, Black and other forms of militancy, and a host of other public issues. This is the question of the desirability of the coexistence of different cultural traditions within the same political, or the same regional economic, system. Is cultural diversity desirable or not? In the Southwest there are many advocates of positions on both sides of this issue. Among dominant Anglos in the United States and Norteños in Mexico probably a majority are convinced that cultural diversity is undesirable. They arrive at this position by a variety of arguments: the natural law (or inevitability) argument; the belief that cultural differences undermine political solidarity; the view that existing power arrangements justify conformity to the ways of the power holders.

The other position on the issue is also supported by a variety of arguments. There is the argument from history, that periods of contact among different peoples have been creative and fruitful, while isolation, as in the case of the Australian aborigines, has resulted in static sterility. There is the argument in terms of freedom of choice as an absolute good; this leads some people to the view that no state policies should favor or force the reduction of choices open to people regarding ethnic traditions, or, positively, that educational and other systems should be organized to encourage the maximum of ethnic choice.

Answers to this question have a bearing on public policy, particularly on the ethnic policies of the United States and Mexico. Answers are often given on the basis of wishful thinking or total ignorance, whereas they could be based on real information. The information already available could be used to some extent, but it would have to be reordered to help in the answering of the questions so far raised. As soon as we attempt to specify the information needed to support or refute the arguments just mentioned, we see the sort of guidance that our original question can give to help turn the existing body of information into a body of knowledge.

For example, what is the evidence for the inevitability of ultimate cultural homogenization in the Southwest? It appears to be that there is very little, that on the contrary the weight of evidence is in the other direction. There is certainly greater diversity at present than there was 200 years ago. But is this a proper interpretation of the facts about the number of ethnic groups and their differences? Has not a recent trend set in which points to homogeneity increasing as a result of the nature of, for example, the school systems? Is not mass production of material goods eliminating basic differences in ways of life? And so on? Usable concepts of the processes alluded to here can be developed under the stress of trying to answer these interesting and important questions.

Similarly, if we ask the question about creative growth resulting from cultural contact, what sort of evidence is there from the Southwest? Austin (1924) was excited about the fascinating panorama of three distinct cultural traditions meeting and merging, but remaining distinct, and wrote persuasively about the desirability of vigorously encouraging this process. But where precisely are the points at which creative growth is taking place? We can identify points of cultural fusion, as in the Southwest Indian school of watercolor painting and other new syntheses in some of the arts, but are these not extremely minor? Do they or do they not contribute to the mainstream of development in Western art? And is that the test? In either a short-term or long-term view, can we say that anything other than progressive domination and assimilation by Anglo and Hispanic peoples in important areas of culture has been going on? What, in short, is the evidence for the kind of creative growth which advocates of diversity talk about?

I believe that these questions are important. I believe that they are not dealt with in sufficiently explicit form to advance our understanding of the bases of ethnic policies. I believe that making them explicit requires guidance from cultural theory and that attempts to answer them honestly will in turn contribute to the theory of cultural process. As a preliminary to such effort I wish in this paper merely to survey briefly the range of data that must be studied in the systematic examination of intercultural exchange. I regret that the length of the paper already makes it necessary to give a sketchy and incomplete presentation.

Current Fusion in Southwestern Graphic and Plastic Arts

There are certain relatively well-known intercultural influences which I should like to touch on briefly before we go on to less well-understood developments. I refer first to painting and the craft arts (Tanner 1957, 1968). It is well-known that a fusion of Indian and European ideas and techniques has taken place during the past 40 and 50 years in painting. The Indian ideas have come from several cultures, most notably Navajo, Eastern and Western Pueblo, and Apache. What may be called a school of Southwest Indian painting, although not actually a unity, has produced work which has taken its place in American painting generally. It is distinctive, and moreover it is constantly developing. Most recently a special impetus has been given to this development through the establishment of the Southwestern Indian School of the Arts at Santa Fe, where this fusion of techniques and concepts is being strongly encouraged, not only in painting but in all the graphic and plastic arts. A process of cultural fusion is being nurtured here which has been at work in the Southwest since the 1930's and even earlier, namely, the process of dominant society encouragement of Indian arts by establishing contact between the national market for art products and Indian craftsmen. The Indian Arts and Crafts Commission introduced this technique during John Collier's administration of Indian affairs; at Santa Fe it is being augmented by dominant society subsidy of specially prepared teachers to encourage and train young artists. This process goes on through formal institutionalization by the dominant Anglos at the same time that the extensive tourist trade for Indian craft arts generates the same process under less controlled conditions along highways and in "curio" shops. The process in its two different aspects is well-established; the interiors of Anglo homes at all class levels constantly exhibit its effects, as do the techniques and standards of Indian craftsmen.

Emerging Fusion in Southwestern Verbal Arts

Let us now consider how the language boundary discussed in the preceding section is crossed with resultant intercultural exchange. Anglos north of the international boundary and Norteños south of it, the dominant ethnic groups, tend strongly to be monolingual, in contrast with Indians and with Spanish-speaking people north of the border. But one should not jump to the conclusion that this means there is no influence on Anglos, for example, from Indian literature, thought, and philosophy—the verbal arts. On the contrary, there is a persistent and interesting influence here. The urban Anglos have developed specialist groups who learn Indian languages. Aside from reservation traders' children and the handful of other Anglos who grow up under conditions adequate for learning an Indian language, there are chiefly two groups of specialists who become competent in varying degrees in Indian languages. These are missionaries and anthropologists. There are very few of these; no one has counted them, but probably in the two states of Arizona and New Mexico they do not today number as many as 50. There have never been more than this, but they have through 100 years played an interesting role in bringing Indian verbal arts into the purview of some Anglos. They have recorded and translated much oral literature: poetry, myths, legends, fiction, historical narrative and comment, and some autobiography. Up to now the greatest body of such literature has been Navajo (for example, Wyman 1970), but also some Eastern and Western Pueblo literature has become available, as well as a lesser amount of Apache, Mohave, Yaqui, Pima, and Papago. Some specialists have recently accepted into the Western category of philosophy and ethics some materials from Navajos and Hopis (Brandt 1954, Ladd 1957). All told, there is a large amount of such material in English and much of it is very carefully and accurately translated. It still remains a tiny proportion of what might be translated. The fate of this material so far has been that of all specialized scholarly products; it is consulted by other specialists, only occasionally inspiring some exceptional Anglo to try to relate it to educational or artistic activities in Anglo or Indian societies.

It appears at present that the techniques employed by the Anglo specialists are being increasingly used by Indians—techniques for recording, for controlled translation, and for linguistic analysis. There are now a few Southwestern Indian linguists and anthropologists trained in these techniques and more nonspecialists who are able to use them. The recording of texts and their translation may be expected to play an increasingly important role in formal education of both Indians and Anglos. The way is being pointed by the work done in preparing curriculum materials in the anthropological tradition at Rough Rock Demonstration School on the Navajo Reservation, at the Navajo Community College, and as projected at the Hopi Cultural Center.

It appears to me that these developments could be of importance in stimulating a real fusion in the verbal arts, but the specialists cannot themselves bring about such a growth. Those who can do so, utilizing creatively the materials provided through the specialized techniques, are the thousands of bilingual Indians. There can through them be developments in this direction in either or both English and the Indian languages. The most immediately important fusion will probably be in English, led by bilinguals. We may remember that it was after the near extinction of Gaelic in Ireland that the great Irish Renaissance began in Anglo-Irish literature. Whether or not the Indian languages persist with important functions, it is quite likely that an Anglo-Indian literature with distinctive qualities is already in process of emergence. It depends on the bilingual Indians and the tools which specialist Anglos have provided.

One may see this process at work among the bilingual Chicanos in the Southwest. Very recently, within the past five years, and with the assistance of private foundations, there has come into being a Chicano literature which is in a peculiar way a bilingual literature, if such a phenomenon may be admitted. This is not confined to what we have arbitrarily delineated here as the Southwest. Its focus, although not its only source, is in California. The best examples come through the Quinto Sol publishing house, a quarterly journal called *El Grito* and an anthology of verse and prose, *El Espejo* (Romano 1969). In these publications there are articles, verse, and fiction by Chicanos in Spanish, in English, or sometimes in a combination. They follow no formula, but range from clear Anglo literary patterns to expression which is clearly neither Anglo nor Mexican. There seems to be something here obviously in process of formation, and the spirit which activates it is vigorous. The point to be made is that we see here the growth of a distinctive literature in the hands of bilinguals and influenced by the literary traditions and mythologies of both Mexico and the United States.

In connection with the verbal arts it must be noted that there is detectable a current of revitalized interest among younger Indians and also among younger Spanish-speaking persons in the United States in the languages of their ethnic groups. This is not a phenomenon with a single cause. One rather practical factor has been that during the 1960's an increase in the number of jobs available in reservation communities resulted from federal funds. This brought back to these communities many individuals who had taken up residence away. Inevitably life among speakers of Indian languages has stimulated interest in the languages among these people. This is not the basic factor however. A new climate of attitude toward ethnic characteristics has rather suddenly come into existence. In schools and in a variety of federally subsidized programs modification of policies with reference to the Anglo conformity principle, or "melting pot theory," of 20 or 30 years ago has played a role. I am inclined however also to believe that the simple fact of achievement of bilinguality by so many members of non-English speaking ethnic groups has led to a recognition that the English language is merely a tool and not a way of life. There has also been a tendency to devaluate the estimates of Anglo culture which teachers and other Anglo spokesmen have promulgated. One might consider the generalization that the creative process of fusion in the verbal arts takes place only among people who are forced to or voluntarily cross the language boundary.

Fiestas, Ceremonials, Fairs, and Rodeos

Intercultural exchange is much affected by social structures in which members of different ethnic groups customarily interact with one another. Let us consider first a type of structure which has a long tradition in the Southwest, namely, the intertribal fair or ceremonial gathering. There are numerous ceremonials sponsored by one ethnic group to which persons of many other ethnic groups come. Two of the largest ones existing today in the Southwest are the annual saint's day fiesta of Laguna Pueblo in New Mexico and the annual celebration of the day of St. Francis of Assisi at Magdalena, Sonora.

Laguna draws chiefly other Pueblos, Navajos, Chicanos, and Anglos (Vogt 1955b). The participation of those not from Laguna Pueblo is as buyers and sellers of goods and as audience. Several thousand attend annually and become acquainted or reinforce their acquaintance with the particular kind of ritual which characterizes Laguna saint's days. There is no record of what ideas they take away with them which might influence the handling of their own ceremonies. We know only that they exchange jewelry, pottery, blankets, and other crafts, as well as some tools, food, and other goods. It is not apparent that there is interchange in areas other than material goods. However, it should be pointed out that there is much evidence that the religious activities of all the Pueblos and the Navajos, although not the Apaches, are characterized by many borrowings of small items of ritual and of larger complexes of ceremony and ritual concept. It may be that today this kind of interchange is not so vigorous as in the past, despite the existence of such mechanisms as the Laguna fiesta where it could take place.

The Magdalena fiesta of St. Francis every October 4 in Sonora is another example, on a much larger scale, of this type of multi-ethnic gathering (Dobyns 1964). Again a saint's day occasion, it is attended by as many as 10,000 persons from Arizona, Sonora, and Sinaloa, and probably other places. Mayos, Yaquis, Tarahumaras, Papagos, Pimas, Norteños of all varieties, urban Anglos, and probably members of other ethnic groups come regularly. Yaquis and Mayos seem to be the only groups which take advantage of the occasion to present some of their secular ceremonies and to make money from such presentations. There is extensive trade of foods and goods of various kinds, but again there is no record that cultural ideas and customs are exchanged under these circumstances. Aside from the interchange of trade goods, they seem rather to be occasions at which a common supra-ethnic group interest is affirmed, namely, veneration of the powerful saint, and to some extent the ethnic boundaries are reinforced. This latter process takes place as members of various ethnic groups segregate themselves from others in camping spots and speak their language among themselves, rather than the common language which nearly all know, namely, Spanish.

A somewhat similar, more recent kind of gathering, purely secular, is sponsored by the dominant urban Anglos in Arizona and New Mexico. Usually chambers of commerce have taken the lead and the interest is primarily commercial. These are "pow-wows" or "ceremonials" or "festivals" which have the avowed purpose of making Indian dance and song available to non-Indians under conditions controlled by the Anglo sponsors. The one of this type of longest standing in the Southwest is the Gallup Ceremonial in New Mexico Navajo country. Attendance by Indians is on about as large a scale as by Anglos and other tourists. Its focus is a three-day presentation of Indian songs and dances by groups of Indians from all over the Southwest primarily, but now also from the Plains and other parts of the United States. The dances and music are taken out of their cultural context and put into the context of Anglo performances or "shows." This involves a kind of fusion of traditions affecting both Anglos and Indians. In addition it is clear that some borrowing of costume, dance step, music, and other elements has gone on extensively among annual performers. Plains Indian dance costumes, steps, and music have been adopted by Navajo boys' clubs and other Indian groups in the Southwest, even as far from Gallup as Topawa on the Papago Reservation. There is in this respect a borrowing and fusion chiefly among Indians which has had far-reaching influence in the Southwest. The influence is strong also on Anglos, who have developed clubs and special associations for carrying out Indian dances and performing Indian music.

The Gallup Ceremonial has also become a great center for the exchange of Indian craft arts. In this capacity it has been a major influence on the development of those arts, because of demands made on the craftsmen if they are to sell their goods in the predominantly Anglo, but also Indian, market, and also because design elements and techniques of manufacture are interchanged among Indians. This kind of interchange goes on, but the distinctiveness of each Indian group's crafts also continues; it is details rather than total patterns which are exchanged.

The Gallup Ceremonial is only one among several such annual gatherings which might be mentioned, including the Flagstaff Pow-wow, the Tucson Festival, the Casa Grande Aw-awdam Tash, and others. Some, especially those in the Rio Grande Valley, go in for elaborate pageantry and emphasize the enactment of historical events. Most, however, are confined to dances isolated from context and to craft fairs. This kind of gathering has as a major function the reinforcing of ethnic boundaries, as different Indian groups compete with their distinctive dances and songs, but at the same time they afford opportunities for interchange of material goods, some ideas regarding dance and song, and craft techniques.

Of increasing importance on the U.S. side of the international border are events which seem to be strictly according to the Anglo pattern of the county and state fair. Rural and urban Anglos and Mormons have, ever since their arrival in the Southwest, developed this kind of an organized annual display of all kinds of material products and skills. The pattern has been adopted by Indian groups, either as a large-scale tribal effort, as in the case of the annual Navajo Tribal Fair at Window Rock, or as an adjunct of an annual rodeo, as in the Papago Rodeo at Sells. In any case, these differ from the pow-wow type of gathering in two ways. On the one hand, they are not sponsored by Anglos but rather by the Indian group itself, and, on the other, there tends to be a wide-ranging and balanced exhibition of products that all segments of the group are proud to display. The exhibits and preparations for them are integrating mechanisms with respect to the Indian ethnic group and also between the Indian group and the dominant urban Anglos, who usually play an important role as advisors and organizers, as well as interested audience.

The fairs are a result of the many-sided effort of urban Anglos to change Indian ways during the past century. Many other Anglo introductions into Indian societies could be pointed to in the areas of agricultural activities, youth clubs, women's clubs, church organizations, etc. Through the aggressive initiative of Anglos working for the many Protestant churches, the Catholic Church, the Bureau of Indian Affairs, more recently the Agricultural Extension Service, and other agencies, Anglo technology, forms of organization, and patterns of thought have been introduced and accepted by Indians, as in the instance of the agricultural fair. These introductions were not asked for at the beginning, but have been steadily presented by active change agents. A very wide range of such patterns have been accepted in all areas of Indian life, and they are now being organized by Indians themselves. We are at present in what appears to be a second phase of this interchange, in which Indian control is resulting in modification of the adopted patterns under influences from each of the Indian cultures in which they have become embedded.

This important aspect of intercultural exchange may be seen as a special relationship between urban Anglos and all the Indian groups. It has been characterized by the establishment of social structures, and hence lines of communication, between many specialized segments of Anglo society and the Indian societies. During the past century these have become steadily more efficient as communication lines. They have become more efficient in two ways. On the one hand the Anglos for the most part have learned slowly how to communicate cross-culturally; this has involved some small degree of acquaintance with viewpoints and customs of Indians. On the other hand, it has now become apparent that Indians are learning to use the communication lines, not just as passive recipients of messages, but now as active initiators. In other words, they are demanding that they be listened to with regard to introductions desired and methods of introduction. This has already influenced the Indian Division of the U.S. Public Health Service, the Bureau of Indian Affairs, and some churches. The communication lines have slowly become two-way channels.

This sort of communication and the intercultural exchange resulting, it should be noted, have been focused on the relations between Indian groups and the dominant urban Anglos. Nothing comparable to it has been developed between Anglos and Spanish-speaking people, among the various Anglo groups, or among the Spanish-speaking groups.

Intercultural Exchange in Mexico

In conclusion, let us glance at some features of intercultural exchange on the Mexican side of the international boundary. It appears that the processes are moving in a different direction there than they are in the United States. In the absence of dominant society sanction of Indian ethnic boundaries, to the extent that they are sanctioned in the United States, it appears that the national integrationist approach dominates. The federal rural school teachers, the officials of the regional irrigation commissions, the bureaucrats of the Agricultural Credit Bank, and similar persons in contact with Indian groups are trained in the viewpoint that modern Indians must integrate into the mestizo society which dominates modern Mexico. The Indian contribution to Mexican civilization, they say, has already been made by the Aztecs and Mayas, and modern Indians must become "civilized." This view is implicit in the textbooks used by both Norteños and Indians. The ranchers, the bureaucrats, and the citizen Norteños generally maintain views about modern Indians which are quite comparable to the prevailing views of Texans in New Mexico. They use either derogatory terms, such as *indio crudo*, or somewhat condescending terms, such as *indito*, to refer to them. There has been no real growth of Indian "militancy" as in the United States, nor of effective Indian utilization of the municipal-state governmental structure. Consequently the dominant processes with respect to Indian-Norteño relations appear to be: (1) withdrawal from cooperative contact on the part of hard-core traditionalist Yaquis, Mayos, Seris, and Tarahumaras, and (2) individual assimilation to Norteño culture which is taking place widely in Sonoran and Chihuahuan cities and towns.

There is nevertheless an interesting cultural exchange which involves the Yaquis of Sonora. The traditional Yaqui deer dancer, who in a ceremonial context imitates deer movements in a stylized dance form, to the accompaniment of archaic Yaqui poetry and Yaqui music, has become an important symbol of the state of Sonora and also of the Mexican nation. In Sonora the deer dancer occupies an important central position on the official coat of arms of the state government, and representations of the deer dancer are to be found in innumerable contexts in the popular and commercial art of the state. Its meaning seems to share features of that of the Plains Indian warrior in the United States. The deer dancer in tense and dramatic pose suggests the formidable fighters which everyone knows the Yaquis once were; it is a symbol of the strength and courage of a respected people now passing out of existence. At the national level the deer dancer has become a tremendously popular figure in the *Ballet Folklórico*, which has modified the dance and its spirit to fit the romantic quality and the technology of effective stage shows for city audiences which characterize this group. The deer dancer has thus been brought into Mexican culture at the national level, where it stands for the powerful, uncontaminated spirit of the primitive Indian, which is regarded as an element in the modern national character.

The Norteño Variety of Mexican Culture: An Ethnohistorical Approach

Miguel León-Portilla

The expression *norteño* (northern), as applied in Mexico to human groups, to their forms of culture, and to a vast geographical region of the country, has had different meanings. In fact, in the various stages of Mexican history, what has been thought and said about the North poses very different questions. Many of them become meaningful when we realize that, with the passage of time, knowledge of the area and of the different northern cultural realities has also varied. But perception of the differences did not succeed in eliminating, in the numerous appraisals of what the North is, a series of definitive traits that appear as constants. In Mexico, the North has always been thought of as a physical and cultural frontier, and also very frequently as a country in which, if indeed there may be wealth, development of human life is not easy. And despite the obviously relative character of what has been understood by "North" in different moments, these traits are mentioned time and again, as though in contrast, beside the multiple differences.

The Meaning of the North in Mexican History

In the days before the Spanish conquest, the Nahua peoples of high culture regarded the North, the frontier of their civilization, as a country of "broad plains and rocky lands." (This is the meaning of the expression *in ixtlahuacan, in texcallan,* which very often appears in different native chronicles to describe the northern lands.) In the North lived the Chichimecs, people of the bow and arrow, who always threatened the Mesoamerican world. But also in the North were located *Chicomóztoc* (the place of

77

the seven caves) and Aztatlan (the place of the herons), mythical regions whence the ancestors had come. Although in those northern places many wonders had occurred, life there was extremely difficult. Only the Chichimecs had remained in the North. In some epochs the limits of Mesoamerica, that is the area of the high civilizations, had been extended toward the North, but in others pressure from the Chichimecs had forced it to contract. This was further proof of the hostile nature of those regions and of their inhabitants, the northern groups of rudimentary culture.

During the centuries after the conquest, the North, without ever losing its character as a physical and cultural frontier, was conceived as a field open to expansion. Penetration was always difficult. In the North, where there were no large towns nor great kingdoms to conquer, it was not a simple matter to obtain cheap labor for the mines or for the cultivation of the land, as had been the case in central and southern Mexico. However, an ultimate echo of some medieval myths, strangely parallel to those of the prehispanic era, claimed the existence there of lands of fabulous riches where, instead of seven caves, seven marvelous cities should exist. With much greater success than the prehispanic Mesoamericans, Spanish military forces, missionary friars, and all kinds of people desirous of profit and adventure, penetrated the North and broadened the area of dominion, pushing the frontier outward time after time.

In the years that followed the conquest of the Aztec capital, infiltration began by way of Michoacán and Colima, until Guadalajara was founded in Nueva Galicia; then penetration continued via Sinaloa and Sonora. Also, northward from the central region of the country, as far as Zacatecas, settlements and mining towns were established. Durango was opened up during the same 16th century and, in a flash, the exploration of New Mexico began. In the 17th century there were already missions, Spanish towns, haciendas, ranches for the raising of cattle, and forts (the well-known "presidios") in what was called Nueva Vizcaya, in Sinaloa, Sonora and New Mexico. The peninsula of Lower California, which had been the object of multiple projects, began to be a land of missions toward the end of the 17th century. In the last century of the colonial period advances into the northwest were the establishment of missions in Upper California, with a series of subsequent explorations into territories where the Russians and British had already appeared. In the northeastern portion of New Spain, also in the 18th century, the colony of Nuevo Santander, today Tamaulipas, was founded; this, along with the expansion into Coahuila and New Mexico, strengthened the foundations in Texas.

Recollections of the difficulties that had to be overcome in some of those undertakings became the titles of well-known classical works written about the northern penetrations and settlements. The *History of the Triumphs of Our Holy Faith Among the Fiercest and Most Barbarous Peoples of the New World* was written about the middle of the 17th century by a Jesuit missionary who had served for several years in Sonora and Sinaloa, Andrés Pérez de Ribas (1944). And from the epoch of Father Kino comes the report entitled *Light Shed on Unknown Lands in North America and Diary of the Explorations in Sonora*, by Captain Juan Mateo Mange (1926).

As a result of the triumphs achieved in those regions during the colonial period, the northern frontiers, at the time of independence, were far removed from central Mexico. The northern domains, then known as the "Interior Provinces," comprised the so-called "Governments" of the two Californias and New Mexico; Texas, which formed part of the intendency of San Luis Potosí, which also included the provinces of Coahuila, Nuevo León, Nuevo Santander or Tamaulipas, and San Luis Potosí itself; the intendency of Durango, formerly called Nueva Vizcaya, which included the present states of Chihuahua and Durango; and, finally, the provinces of Sonora and Sinaloa, which formed the so-called intendency of Arizpe. Together the "Interior Provinces" and the "Governments" of New Mexico and the two Californias formed a territory of more than three million square kilometers, about six times the area of France.

But by that time those lands conquered, and to varying degrees colonized, by New Spain no longer had only "barbarous tribes" on their frontiers. In 1819, two years before the consummation of Mexican independence, Spain had signed a treaty with the young Anglo-American nation whose desire for expansion had already brought it into contact with the most northerly settlements of New Spain. The 1819 Treaty of Onis was ratified in 1832 by Mexico and the United States. In it the northern boundaries of Mexico were fixed in the following manner: beginning at the mouth of the Sabine River on the Gulf of Mexico, following its course to parallel 32; from there in a straight line north to the degree where the Red River of Natchitoches enters and then, following its course, to the point where the 100th degree of longitude west of London crosses said river; from there in a straight line northward to the headwaters of the Arkansas River at parallel 42; from this point the border was established by said parallel to the Pacific (O'Gorman 1966: 214-218).

By virtue of that treaty, the North acquired a new type of physical as well as cultural frontier, internationally recognized, and no longer open to subsequent forms of expansion. The border had been established opposite an Anglo-American state of tremendous vitality which emulated the old Spanish expansion. Mexico, during the decades that followed its independence, struggled in the midst of frequent revolutions which prevented it from achieving any kind of political stability. Under those circumstances, it could give very little attention to its northern provinces.

In obvious contrast to that situation, penetration by people from the United States began to make itself felt. In 1836, only four years after ratification of the boundary treaty, the Anglo-Saxon colonists in Texas proclaimed their independence, an act which culminated in the annexation of Texas by the United States in 1845. This event, together with the U.S. attitude of "manifest destiny," brought with it, first, a war with the United States and, later, the establishment of a new frontier in 1848 to the south of New Mexico and Upper California.

As a consequence, the concept and reality of Mexico's northern lands had to be drastically altered. For Mexico, the rapid colonization by U.S. citizens of Upper California, the territories of Arizona and New Mexico, and the state of Texas, meant the presence, much nearer, of a physical and cultural frontier with a powerful country whose goals of further expansion and other forms of influence were much to be feared. In this context, we may recall the Gadsden Purchase, the acquisition by the United

States of the territory of the Mesilla in 1854, and likewise proposals aimed at obtaining Baja California and portions of Sonora and Chihuahua (Rippy 1931: 126-167).

What has been said up to this point confirms, in a general manner, that throughout Mexican history, over and above multiple differences, there are some constant features in evaluating the significance of the North. Among them is the recognition of its great geographical extension, conceived as a possible source of riches. But there is also the idea that these riches are not easy to acquire, since cultural development must overcome obstacles in the North not present in other places. Further, and always, beyond what has been colonized, there exists a hostile frontier both physically and culturally speaking. With regard to the latter, for the Mesoamerican peoples this frontier was composed of inhospitable lands, the dominion of the Chichimecs. In the days of New Spain, garrisons guarded the frontier against the so-called barbarous tribes. In independent Mexico, the presence of the Anglo-Americans also fixed a new type of frontier in which a distinct culture and the threat of its expansion were regarded as a constant danger. These characteristics that we have pointed out as an introduction permit us to discern a first substratum common in the attitude of those who penetrated the North from central Mexico.

The Scope of This Study

To pass on to an analysis of what possibly constitutes a northern variety of Mexican culture, it is first necessary to define the scope of this study. It has been written, in conjunction with other studies, to aid in understanding a region pluricultural in the past and in the present.

Geographical Extent and Cultural Affinity

The region is that which some North American investigators designate the "Greater Southwest," a term coined by Beals (1943) to embrace the geographical and cultural realities of the southwestern part of the United States and a portion of what in Mexico is called the Northwest. But the reality of the "greater

Southwest" varies according to different points of view. It is not the same for archaeologists, ethnologists, or historians of the colonial period. Most commonly, within an ethnohistorical frame, it is thought of as including the U.S. states of Arizona and New Mexico and the Mexican states of Sonora, Sinaloa, Nayarit, Chihuahua, and Durango. In the case of Mexico, some of these states form part of what is traditionally designated as the "Northwest." In fact, in speaking of the Mexican Northwest, one ordinarily thinks of Baja California, Sonora, Sinaloa, and also, at times, Nayarit (for example, Mendizábal 1930). But since in the United States the designation of the Southwest does not always include Upper California, which is sometimes described as the "Far West," it seems advisable here to exclude from our direct field of attention the Mexican peninsula of Baja California. Reference will be made to it solely in determined cases, either to emphasize its relations with other entities of the Mexican Northwest, or to point out, by contrast, some important differences.

Keeping in mind that there has been an ancient cultural interrelation in the area that concerns us, we will insist briefly on the matter of its geographic designation. Within what, at the end of the 18th century, were called the "Western Interior Provinces" and the "Government of New Mexico" the following territories were included: Sonora, Sinaloa, southern Arizona; Nueva Vizcaya (Durango, Chihuahua, southern New Mexico); the "Government of New Mexico," embracing much more than the territory of this state today, that is, a considerable portion of what is now Arizona. As may be seen, the "Western Interior Provinces" together with the "Government of New Mexico" almost coincided with what has been called "the Greater Southwest."

Spicer (1962: viii) acknowledges the fact that to describe this vast region, which today belongs to two nations, as the "Greater Southwest" implies a certain North American ethnocentrism. According to Spicer, it is also improper to apply the adjective "Greater" to the term "Southwest" in historical and anthropological studies of this region. He prefers to wait, as he expresses it, until someone coins a more adequate name for this vast region as a whole, in which diverse forms of culture have appeared and to different degrees have coexisted. It should be remembered that other expressions have been introduced to describe portions of this area or of even a larger expanse of this part of the North American continent. "The Spanish Borderlands," with an obvious colonial connotation, was the favorite designation in the works of the historian Bolton (Bannon 1964). To emphasize, on the other hand, the differences both cultural and geographical between ancient Mesoamerica and the North, Jiménez Moreno (1958: 35-36) has coined the term "Arid America." Only as a suggestion, to define the field of our study, I here propose a new expression: the "Mexican-American West." Thus, reference is made both to the geographical area and to the ancient cultural affinity between what in the United States is understood by "Southwest" and in Mexico by "Northwest," with the somehow artificial exclusion of the Californias.

The Need for a Historical Approach

The vast region described here as the Mexican-American West has been the scene of complex and varied historical processes. In them, as well as in its equally different physiographical, climatological, and ecological characteristics and in its varied natural resources, are found the antecedents without which it is impossible to understand the contemporary multicultural reality. But despite the existence of a certain number of studies, made from the standpoint of both the natural and social sciences, relative to this region or to certain areas within it, it must be acknowledged that much remains to be done. This is particularly true with regard to the Mexican portion that we call the "Northwest." Here the field is open to every kind of study, not only those directed to its possibilities of development, but also those of an archaeological, ethnographical, or historical character.

These circumstances explain the need for an approach which, on the one hand, takes these historical antecedents into account as a whole, and, on the other, recognizes the numerous difficulties involved. Both things, need and problems, oblige us to delineate a historical sketch of the region in an almost impressionistic form, so as to have at least a frame of reference. In it we will emphasize some aspects and moments which seem of particular interest as subjects for more intensive research in connection with the various cultural processes of the Mexican Northwest.

The Times Before the Spanish Penetration

The territory in which the pluricultural evolution which we wish to describe took place presents itself as a plurality of "physiographical provinces," that is, of geographical areas with distinct and well-defined characteristics (Vivó 1958: 48-49). We therefore begin our approach to the cultures of their most ancient inhabitants attending to those "natural provinces" which totally or partially integrate the Mexican Northwest. In preparing this overall account of the prehispanic inhabitants of this region, works by the following scholars have been consulted: Beals (1932), Jiménez Moreno (1943), and Spicer (1962); studies of the following groups have also been used: the Tarahumara (Fried 1969), the Huichol and the Cora (Grimes and Hinton 1969), the Pima, Opata, Papago, and Seri (Hinton 1969), the remnant Indians of Baja California (Owen 1969), the Southern Tepehuan and Tepecano (Riley 1969), the Northern Tepehuan (Service 1969) and the Yaqui and Mayo (Spicer 1969b).

The West Coast Corridor

Let us first concentrate upon the region that Bolton (1947) called the "West Coast corridor"—that is, the zone bounded on the east by the Sierra Madre Occidental and on the west by the coasts of Nayarit, Sinaloa, and Sonora, including the low, sub-tropical lands to the south, the semidesert plains and fertile valleys in the lower basins of several rivers, and the region known as the Sonoran Desert. In this physiographic province, before the conquest, lived the ancestors of various Indian groups that have survived to the present. With regard to the designation "West Coast corridor," archaeological research has demonstrated that through it there was an early diffusion of cultural elements of Mesoamerican origin. That explains why, at certain periods, the frontier of the high cultures of Mesoamerica succeeded in extending itself throughout Nayarit and northward into Sinaloa, reaching its northern limit at the river of the same name. With only two exceptions, the Seris and the Yuman-speaking peoples, the rest of the Indians who inhabited different parts of this area at the time of the conquest had important affinities, despite their numerous cultural differences.

The Upper and Lower Pimas as well as the Opatas, the members of the Cahita group, the Yaquis and Mayos, and farther south the Coras, all spoke tongues belonging to the Uto-Aztecan linguistic family. Likewise, they figured among the more developed groups within the Mexican-American West, surpassed only by the Pueblo Indians of New Mexico. All of them practiced agriculture and manufactured pottery. With respect to their settlement patterns, they had some common characteristics. The Pimas lived in relatively scattered communities, preserving at the same time a certain mobility, for, notably in the north, they came down from the mountains to the valleys during the winter to cultivate corn, beans, and squash. To the south, the Opatas, the Yaquis, and the Mayos had their *rancherías*, some of them already incipient towns, in the river valleys. This sometimes happened in the upper course of the rivers (Opatas), or downstream in the vicinity of the coast (Yaquis and Mayos). The forms of social organization of these groups were more complex and allowed not only for the presence of shamans but also for an incipient kind of priesthood. Finally, with respect to the Coras, many of whom, as today, lived in the mountains of the Sierra Madre, it can be said that they were particularly exposed to Mesoamerican cultural influence. In fact, the small states or *cacicazgos* of the Jalisco region maintained different forms of contact with them.

The two exceptions referred to above, the Yumans, who lived in the valley of the Colorado River in the vicinity of its mouth, and the Seris of Tiburón Island and neighboring regions on the Sonora coast, belonged from the linguistic standpoint to the entirely different Hokan family. The culture of the Yumans, although less developed than that of the Pimas, resembled it in some respects. The case of the Seris, on the other hand, constituted an example, unique within the region, of considerable primitiveness. Integrated solely as bands of hunters, gatherers, and fishermen, they had no agriculture and led an extremely precarious existence. Their cultural level may be compared only with that of the Lower Californian Cochimis or Peninsular Yumans, with whom, at least linguistically, they had certain bonds. In any case, the enclave of the Seris constitutes an exception, worthy of attention in this physiographical province.

We may add that, just as during the prehispanic epoch Meso-american influences made themselves felt in varying degrees throughout this corridor, something similar would occur later. From the first half of the 16th century, the earliest form of Spanish penetration in the Mexican-American West began through the West Coast corridor.

The Sierra Madre Occidental

Another physiographical province, to the East of the fore-going, is that of the Sierra Madre Occidental, the most important mountain range in Mexico. In its northern part lived the Tara-humaras, the Varohios and the Conchos, and, farther south, the Tepehuanes, the Acaxees, the Xiximies, the Huicholes and most of the Coras. All of these groups, like the great majority of those in the West Coast corridor, spoke tongues of the Uto-Aztecan group. Their ways of life included *rancheria* settlements, al-though in general these were much more widely scattered than those of their western neighbors. In varying degrees, they also engaged in agriculture. The Tarahumaras, the Varohios and the Conchos, for example, cultivated small cornfields in the little valleys on the slopes of the mountains, and came down during the winter to the plains or took refuge in caves. Like the Tepehuanes, Coras and Huicholes, they also supplemented their diet by hunting and gathering. In the particular case of the Coras and Huicholes, it is interesting to anticipate that they were to resist, for many long years during the colonial period, the pene-tration of the Spaniards and any permanent contact with them.

Ethnohistorical research carried out in relation to the Tara-humaras and the Tepehuanes leads us to assume certain forms of contact, during the centuries before the Spanish penetration, between them and the somewhat more developed groups of the western slopes of the Sierra Madre and the West Coast corridor. This very probably occurred to the cultural benefit of the tribes living in the Sierra. It seems, on the other hand, that these groups, with the exception of the Coras and Huicholes, had not received a significant influence of the Mesoamerican cultures. To become convinced of this it is sufficient to recall that between most of them and the Mesoamericans stretched a vast territory inhabited by those generically known as the Chichimec nomads.

The Northern Plateau

The third and last physiographical province, partially included within the area of the Mexican-American West, is that
composed of the plains of what in Mexico today is known as the
Northern Plateau. This is valid specifically with respect to the
territory situated on both sides of the lower Río Grande. Within
this region is included the northeastern zone of the state of
Chihuahua. Here lived Indian groups completely different from
those of the Sierra Madre or of the West Coast corridor. They
were Apache tribes that spoke tongues of the Athapascan family:
the Lipans, the Mescaleros, and others. Apparently they had been
present in these regions for a relatively brief period of time after
an immigration from the northeast. In the zone they had penetrated, they did not yet have fixed places of residence. Notwithstanding their nomadic life, they already practiced agriculture to
a limited degree, although they chiefly obtained their food from
hunting and gathering.

The various Apache groups, who made incursions to distant
places after their acquisition of horses, were regarded during the
colonial period as true barbarians, the source of every kind of
danger and misfortune (Forbes 1960). It was doubtless a surprise
to the Spaniards to discover that, still farther north, lived other
Indians, the so-called Pueblos, who proved to be the possessors of
the most advanced culture in all the northern territories. They
will not be discussed here as they fall outside of what is now
Mexico.

Ideally, from the standpoint of what in Mexico is designated
as the Northwest, we might also discuss here another "physiographical province," the peninsula of Baja California. However, as
already stated in defining the zone to be covered, we abstain in
view of the accepted geographical limits for the Greater Southwest or Mexican-American West.

This brief description of the cultural levels characteristic of
the different Indian groups within these three physiographical
provinces, brings us to formulate certain considerations. Undeni-
ably the Indian tribes, both as an antecedent and because of the
present survival of many of them, constitute a first reality that
cannot be ignored in a search for the pluricultural physiognomy

of the area. The Indians who inhabited, and inhabit, the different physiographical provinces of this vast region were much less numerous and much less developed culturally than those of Mesoamerica. At the same time they presented differences among themselves, despite some characteristics in common. The way of life of those with permanent settlements, and who engaged principally in agriculture, differed greatly from that of tribes who lived in vaguely defined areas and depended chiefly upon hunting, gathering, or fishing. It is important to stress, also, the absence of a lingua franca, as Nahuatl had become in central and southern Mexico.

Facts like these must be taken into account as they conditioned the forms of contact, first between the tribes themselves, and then with the Spanish conquerors, colonizers, and missionaries. The new structures created by population centers and missions during the colonial period, and the kinds of enterprises organized to take advantage of the Northwest's natural resources, are also to be understood in relation with this tribal substratum. Doubtless most of what has just been mentioned requires more ample research. The Indian presence in the Northwest, both as an antecedent and a reality, which although modified has not disappeared, must be studied profoundly as one of the very significant elements within the pluricultural context of this vast area.

The Colonial Period

For the Spaniards, to penetrate into the North was a radically different experience from that of conquering central Mexico. Hernán Cortés had required only a little more than two years to conquer the Aztec capital and to destroy its hegemony in vast portions of Mesoamerica. And, despite the resistance of the Indians there to accepting new forms of government and Spanish institutions, a different order of things began to be implanted with relative efficacy and promptness. Because a true civilization existed within the confines of Mesoamerica, it had been possible in the processes of change to make use of elements of the old social, political, and economic structure. With respect to the North, it was known from the outset that other kinds of peoples lived there, devoid of any cultural refinement. However, from shortly after the conquest, rumors had also circulated about the existence in very remote northern regions of other kingdoms with towns and cities at least as rich as those of the Aztecs. Such fables, and the fact that some years later precious mineral deposits were discovered in the North, awakened the interest of the old conquerors and of a great number of new explorers and adventurers.

The Penetration of the North

As early as 1522, Cortés sent one of his captains, Cristóbal de Olid, to Michoacán and Zacatula. A little later, Gonzalo de Sandoval led an expedition in the direction of Colima. In 1529, Nuño de Guzmán, already famous for his excesses as president of the first *audiencia* and for the atrocities he had committed in the Pánuco region, penetrated westward through Michoacán, and in a short time he established settlements in what was to be called Nueva Galicia. So rapid was his advance through the western corridor that, in 1531, only ten years after the conquest of Mexico, he established the Villa of San Miguel de Culiacán in Sinaloa (López-Portillo 1935). Some of his men advanced even farther, though only on exploratory missions, to the Yaqui River in Sonora.

In spite of the ruggedness of these territories and the proven hostility of the tribes that inhabited them, their attraction increased constantly. Beginning in 1532, Hernán Cortés, with the royal licenses he held for discoveries in the "Southern Sea," sent out a series of maritime expeditions which, touching the coast of Nueva Galicia, culminated in the discovery of the peninsula of California. And although he could not find there the riches he coveted, he did not abandon his projects relative to those regions (Rubio Mañé 1959 Vol. 2: 246-332). The first viceroy of New Spain, Antonio de Mendoza, encouraged by the news brought by Fray Marcos de Niza, dispatched new expeditions (Aiton 1927). In 1540, Hernando de Alarcón sailed northward up the Gulf of California and into the mouth of the Colorado River. About the same time Francisco Vázquez de Coronado set out overland and after crossing through Sinaloa and Sonora reached Arizona and

New Mexico, and even explored beyond (Bolton 1948). However, neither the emissaries of Cortés nor those of Mendoza were
able to discover the fabulously rich towns and cities they sought.
They could only verify that in those enormous, and often arid,
expanses lived warlike tribes whose ways of life could not be
compared with those of the Indians of central and southern
Mexico. In fact, by that time, violent encounters with wild tribes
had already occurred in Nueva Galicia. Particularly serious was
what is known as the Mixtón rebellion in 1541, which had to be
suppressed personally by Viceroy Mendoza (López-Portillo 1939).

These first attempts to stretch the ancient frontiers of Mesoamerica by way of the western corridor certainly did not achieve
their purpose. The most effective expansion followed another
route. The triumph over the rebellion of the Mixtón in 1541
permitted penetration from Nueva Galicia in the direction of
Zacatecas. There, in 1546, the first justification for the determined efforts to penetrate the North was found, when mines of
precious metals were discovered. From that time on, Zacatecas
was the great center of attraction, and also a point of departure
for undertaking new conquests (Powell 1952). As a result, what
was to become known as the "Road of Silver" was born. To
assure communications between Zacatecas and Mexico City, the
authorities began to establish new towns, missions, and forts.
Soon, too, new deposits were discovered where other mining
centers were established: Guanajuato in 1555, Sombrerete in
1556, Fresnillo and Mazapil in 1568. Frequent assaults and
rebellions on the part of the Chichimecs, although they were
subdued time after time, made constant precaution and defense
necessary. However, the zeal to exploit the gold and silver deposits from that time on prevented the abandonment of what
had been achieved and, furthermore, impelled new attempts at
penetration.

The Institutions of the Frontier

It is not our intention here to summarize the history of that
long process which during the centuries of the colonial area
resulted in the ultimate conquest of the various northern provinces; an overall treatment may be found in a work by Navarro
García (1964: 1-46), and further details in the studies of Saravia

(1940-56), Mendizábal (1930), Alessio Robles (1931), Gallegos (1960), and Bolton (1917, 1936). Rather, we are interested in the basic characteristics of that penetration and in the forms of life and culture that developed in the different kinds of settlements established in the conquered regions. Actually we believe that many of the cultural traits typical of the Mexican North have their roots precisely in what occurred there during this formative stage of colonial New Spain. We will recall here only some of the subsequent processes of expansion from the moment when, as in a triangle, Mexico City, Guadalajara and Zacatecas found themselves in communication with each other and ready to undertake new conquests.

About 1563, the famous Francisco de Ibarra advanced from Zacatecas and again extended the limits of the frontier, founding Durango and Nombre de Dios. Ibarra then crossed the Sierra Madre by way of Topia and went down into Sinaloa, for the first time joining the western corridor with the regions of the "Road of Silver." With Francisco de Ibarra, Nueva Vizcaya was born (Mecham 1927). Later on expansion continued, making possible the definitive penetration of New Mexico and other regions of the northwest, such as Sinaloa and Sonora, as well as of the northeast, in the direction of Saltillo, in Coahuila. The forms of life that began to develop in those vast territories, inhabited before only by tribes of limited culture, were to become consolidated and further expanded in the following centuries.

From the founding of Zacatecas in 1546, the march toward the North had attracted an increasing number of people of very different types. First were old conquerors or their descendants, as well men more recently arrived in New Spain, desirous of emulating past exploits and, above all, determined to make themselves rich. They were followed by others more or less familiar with mining operations, adventurers of every kind, and soldiers of fortune. Almost always compelled, groups of Indians, frequently former Tlaxcalan allies of the Spaniards, also marched northward in the role of servants or auxiliary troops. New mining towns and forts for their defense against the wild tribes were organized. Part of the people there began to devote themselves to agricultural pursuits and stock raising, indispensable as a nearby source of supply for those who worked in the extraction of minerals. Thus the first northern farms and haciendas came into being, and also some towns and future cities which were to rival the mining centers.

Not less important were the missionaries, Franciscans and Jesuits, who participated in the various northern penetrations and settlements, often from the beginning. To the Franciscans was due the creation of many missions, beginning in Zacatecas and then more extensively in New Mexico (Arlegui 1851; Ocaranza 1934, 1937-39). To the Jesuits was due the spiritual conquest of a large part of Sinaloa, Sonora, Durango, Chihuahua, southern Arizona, and Baja California (Pérez de Ribas 1944; Alegre 1956-60; Dunne 1940, 1944, 1948, 1952, Decorme 1941).

Without doubt there was great diversity in the purposes and behavior of people so different among themselves—the missionaries, the royal officials, the captains and soldiers, the miners and *hacendados*, with their peons and Indian servants. But despite the differences, all had to confront in their own manner the realities that characterized the northern lands. Those vast expanses were a frontier country. To create any form of settlement there was always difficult in the extreme. Lack of means of communication, especially in the beginning, meant isolation. In one way or another, contact with the so-called barbarous tribes of the several regions appeared to be both dangerous and necessary. In that context, throughout the colonial period, many of the cultural characteristics of the Mexican Northwest developed. Traits common to the great majority of new arrivals were determination, courage in the face of danger, and a will to work. All this implied physical strength. Perhaps as a result of the survival of the fittest, the Indians native to these regions appeared to a certain degree endowed with similar qualities. Confrontation and conflict among peoples like these was inevitable.

The Northwest, as a frontier land, knew every type of violence on the part of those who entered it, as well as rebellion on the part of the Indians. At the same time it was also the scene of profound, though slow, transformations, brought about by the implantation of Spanish institutions, more or less adapted to new circumstances. And this was carried out basically through the establishment of the mining towns, forts, villages, ranches and haciendas, and the missions. A brief description of these forms of settlements will bring us closer to the cultural reality that emerged there (Spicer 1962: 281-333, as well as other sources cited here on missions and mining towns).

The chief incentive in the northern penetration was to exploit the gold and silver mines that were discovered there (Powell 1952, West 1949). But from the entrance into Zacatecas, together with the soldiers and adventurers appear the Franciscan missionaries, determined to broaden their field of action. This was concisely described by the Franciscan chronicler Arlegui: (1851: 12) "Captain Juan de Tolosa having then news of the silver mines that existed in Zacatecas and its environs, held by the barbarous heathen, he entered with men of war, accompanied by four religious. . . . And on September 8, 1546, he established his camp on the slope of a high peak, today called La Bufa, where the Indians of the Zacatecan nation had their stronghold. . . . " There, while the work in the mines began, the friars devoted themselves to converting the Indians. Arlegui, who was interested primarily in missionary work, insists upon the importance of the mining towns that were soon founded in Durango, the Sierra Madre, and southern Chihuahua as centers of attraction and cultural contact. His *Crónica*, in this respect, could almost be regarded as an introduction to the development of mining in northern Mexico (Arlegui 1851: 15): "At that time, with the news of the opulence of the mining center, many Spaniards gathered there, attracted by the magic of silver, as effective in stirring men to action as the magnet is in attracting steel."

In speaking of the Sombrerete, Parral, and Santa Bárbara mines, Arlegui (1851: 121) repeats that the creation of the mining camps came to be the motive for the arrival of still more people and opening up new work possibilities:

> It is the case with all the rich mineral deposits that are discovered that a multitude of people immediately flock to the vibrant echo of silver, from as many places as there are in America. And since the spot where the mines are discovered is often unproductive of the necessary sustenance, the farmers and stock raisers of the surrounding country sell their grain and animals, and since they alone cannot supply

the crowd that gathers, others see themselves forced, by necessity or greed, to discover new occupations and stock ranges with cattle, even on lands in greater peril from the barbarians. It is God who disposes by this means that, even though the mines may fail, the surrounding lands remain with new enterprises and well-stocked haciendas, and with sufficient trade between the inhabitants.

What Arlegui describes so piously as a result of the providence of God, namely the multiplying of large landholdings, haciendas and ranches, became an extremely significant institution in the North. This meant differences with what had already taken place in central Mexico. There, civilized natives often had been entrusted in *encomiendas* to work for the conquistadors. In the North, on the contrary, the so-called primitive Indians were entrusted to the missionaries, whose task it was to gather them into newly created villages. The Spanish captains, governors, explorers, and *adelantados* could expect there, instead of Indian serfs, more generous grants of land to develop agriculture and, to a larger degree, to raise cattle. Indeed, this was the beginning of the highly productive livestock enterprise in the North. The vast possessions of Diego de Ibarra can be cited as an early example of this situation. He came to own the haciendas of Trujillo and Valparaiso in present-day Durango which by 1578 had more than 130,000 head of cattle (Chevalier 1956: 122).

In his scholarly article "The Formation of Large Landholdings in Mexico," Chevalier (1956: 123-130) discusses other similar cases. They show clearly how the economy of the North was transformed by the introduction of cattle raising on a large scale. On the other hand, the rapid multiplication of the horse and the cow deeply influenced the way of life of the Norteños. Herding, tending cattle, and horsemanship became common professions—arts present in a man's everyday life. At fiestas a man's horsemanship was highly admired, as was even more the case when he had to fight barbarous Indians. Many of the latter soon learned how to ride horses as well, and to increase their herds of horses and cows was one more valid reason for raiding any Spanish ranch or settlement. The large-scale introduction of cattle raising influenced the North's physiognomy to such an extent that more than one contemporary historian has ventured to speak of the "cow and horse" culture of northern Mexico, a part of which was to become the present Southwest of the United States.

These conditions became general in a relatively short period in the enormous area ranging from Zacatecas to New Mexico. The nuclei of Spaniards and mestizos were growing and expanding with more people, among them the Indians brought as allies from central Mexico, as well as Negro slaves and mulattoes. In turn, the missionary work, first of the Franciscans and, later, of the Jesuits, increased and channeled the contacts with the various groups of natives. In some cases evangelization was carried on from the mining settlements, where monasteries were established, or in the vicinity of the haciendas and ranches. This occurred when the Indians of the region had become obliged to depend upon the new Spanish centers, with generally lamentable consequences. Some of those natives had to work in the mines almost in the role of slaves; others had to make their living on the haciendas (Zavala 1968). And it must have been no rarity, in those circumstances, that the soldiers of the garrisons and other adventurers forced themselves upon the Indian women, giving rise to a limited amount of *mestizaje*.

New penetrations, and the misfortunes their subjugation signified for the tribes, provoked the many rebellions described in the chronicles and in reports of the colonial authorities. This, in turn, resulted in the establishment of more garrisons and the creation of new forts, situated at strategic points. In fact, the forts marked lines of defense that were moved constantly farther north throughout the colonial era. Exploitation of the mines, in periods of bonanza, meant easy acquisition of wealth for the big impresarios, and for the royal treasury as well. It explains how some of the mining settlements came to be converted into towns and cities with sumptuous buildings, churches, palaces of government, shops and stores, and mansions for the richest inhabitants. But many times, when the veins were exhausted, the decadence of those centers made itself quickly felt. Then, as we have seen from Arlegui, the situation of the *hacendados* and farmers was better, for on the vast lands they possessed they came to have thousands of head of cattle, as well as crops not to be despised.

In one way or another, agriculture and stock raising, in addition to trade, and of course mining enterprises, were marking the transformation of the country.

The mission, an institution purposely set apart from the Spanish centers, whose function it was to Christianize and civilize the natives and to save them from imminent destruction, was an extremely important element in this historical process. The Jesuits, who labored among many different groups, introduced methods and criteria that merit study. In the Northwest, their work embraced the regions of Chínipas, the Tarahumara in the Sierra de Chihuahua, Sinaloa, Sonora, Nayarit, and Baja California. Their aim in each case, as circumstances permitted, was to bring about the concentration of the Indians around the mission. There, the church, the missionary's house, the school, the storehouses, and more or less scattered dwellings for the Indians were constructed. A parallel concern was the search for means of subsistence. This was achieved, thanks to agriculture and stock raising, and also to limited forms of trade. The system of government placed authority in the hands of the missionary, who in turn obeyed his religious superiors and maintained contact with the royal officials. From among the Indians, he chose the governors, mayors, judges, treasury agents, teachers, and catechists. When a mission was successfully developed, arts and trades like ironworking, carpentry, brickmaking, and weaving were introduced.

The Jesuits repeatedly insisted that the only manner of preventing the Indians from being absorbed and destroyed by the new structures of the mining settlements, the haciendas, and the towns, was to keep them isolated from their fatal influence. In certain cases, as on the peninsula of California, isolation was almost total. At some places in Sonora and Sinaloa, the proximity of Spanish haciendas, mines, and towns brought with it interminable conflicts. Frequently the Jesuits were accused of exploiting the natives for their own benefit, and of trying to create a kind of autonomous state within the Spanish provinces of the North. In fact, these accusations were to constitute one of the causes of their expulsion in 1767.

It would be difficult to attempt to evaluate here the missionary work of the Jesuits in the Northwest, but one point will

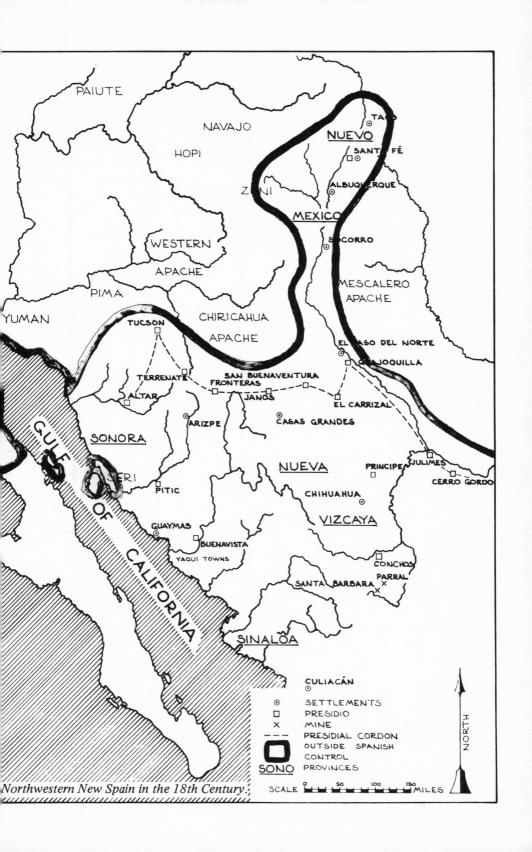

PAIUTE

NAVAJO

HOPI

NUEVO

TAOS

SANTA FÉ

ZUNI

ALBUQUERQUE

MEXICO

WESTERN

APACHE

SOCORRO

PIMA

MESCALERO
APACHE

YUMAN

CHIRICAHUA

APACHE

EL PASO DEL NORTE

TUCSON

GUAJOQUILLA

TERRENATE

SAN BUENAVENTURA
FRONTERAS

ALTAR

JANOS

EL CARRIZAL

ARIZPE

CASAS GRANDES

SONORA

SERI

NUEVA

PRINCIPE

JULIMES

PITIC

CERRO GORDO

CHIHUAHUA

GUAYMAS

VIZCAYA

BUENAVISTA

YAQUI TOWNS

CONCHOS

SANTA BARBARA

PARRAL

GULF OF CALIFORNIA

SINALOA

CULIACÁN

⊙ SETTLEMENTS
□ PRESIDIO
× MINE
--- PRESIDIAL CORDON
◻ OUTSIDE SPANISH
CONTROL
SONO PROVINCES

SCALE   0   50   100   150   MILES

NORTH

Northwestern New Spain in the 18th Century.

be mentioned that seems to count in their favor. In spite of everything, the missions left imprints that have not been erased. To the Jesuits must be attributed the birth of towns and cities that in the beginning were only mission headquarters. On the other hand, it must also be attributed to them that in many cases the tribes survived within a world of vested interests and frequent violence. If in Baja California the cultural changes introduced by the Jesuits, together with a series of epidemics, determined the gradual disappearance of the Pericú, Guaycura, and Cochimí, in Sonora and Sinaloa, by contrast, the Mayo, Yaqui, Opata, and Pima escaped annihilation. When the exodus of the Jesuits occurred, other missionaries such as the Franciscans, who already had experience in the area, took over their tasks. However, under the new circumstances their work meant only a temporary postponement of the deterioration that was to mark the end of missionary activities.

The Isolation of the North

It must not be thought that the population of the North ever reached large proportions. Estimates based on reports and accounts of the epoch indicate that about 1760, or two centuries after the penetration was initiated, the number of inhabitants, excluding the uncivilized Indians, totaled only some 230,000 individuals. Navarro García (1964: 405-406) cites the estimates of Teodoro de Croix, according to whom, by 1778, the Interior Provinces had an approximate population of some 220,000 inhabitants. He compares this figure with the estimates given by Bishops Tamarón and San Buenaventura who, on the basis of reports received from the various parishes and missions, had assigned to the same provinces a population of 233,600 in 1760. While there are discrepancies, the various regions agree in relative position (See Table I).

The Spanish settlements continued to be islands of a sort in the western corridor, in the Sierra Madre, and along the "Road of Silver." In spite of the existence in the North of organized provinces, with more or less defined boundaries and with working Spanish administrations, those who lived there continued to suffer from isolation. Aside from the rudimentary schools, established in monasteries or in mission enclosures, there were no other centers of higher education. Nor did the majority of those dedicated to work in the mines, to labor in the fields, to stock raising, or to trade have a marked degree of cultural refinement. Unbridled greed and the zeal for power made violence frequent. The presence of unconquered tribes, furthermore, held numerous towns in a state of constant anxiety. All this shaped the way of life, the psychology, and the culture of those who lived in the North.

TABLE I

THE POPULATION OF THE INTERIOR PROVINCES IN THE LATE 18th CENTURY*

	Around 1760	Around 1778
TOTAL	233,600	220,400
Nueva Vizcaya	117,200	100,000 +
Sonora	89,000	87,600
Nuevo México	20,400	20,800
Coahuila	4,600	8,000
Texas	2,400	4,000

*All figures from Navarro García (1964: 405-406).

The decades prior to Mexican independence were, for the Northwest, the period of ultimate expansion and also a time of great projects, like those of the Royal Visitor José de Gálvez, which were only partially achieved. The missions of Upper California were established, but on the other hand, in Sonora, Chihuahua and New Mexico, the situation deteriorated in many respects. The Seri Indians of Sonora revolted several times during this period, and the Apaches, regarded as the greatest menace, committed innumerable assaults and depredations.

New Spain, through its mining centers, haciendas, ranches, forts, villages, cities, and missions, exercised effective control over extensive territories in the North, from Zacatecas to central Chihuahua, in Sinaloa and Sonora, and in what could be described as an enclave in New Mexico. Other regions continued to be frontier lands, where the isolation and perils were greater than ever. It might appear that New Spain's drive of expansion had begun to weaken and could no longer make its presence felt effectively in such a distant world. This was the situation when a radical political change, the independence of Mexico, took place.

After Independence

The processes of contact and transformation which occurred in the Northwest during the centuries of Spanish rule left a deep imprint on the cultural physiognomy of that large portion of the country. As already suggested, it was then that a kind of northern variety of Mexican culture began to take shape. But following the War of Independence, other forces came to modify the prevailing situation in varying degrees. Nonetheless, the inevitable changes helped to define the Northwest's own identity even more fully.

It is impossible to analyze here the complexity of events which have contributed to molding the cultural patterns of the Northwest from independence to the present day. We shall limit ourselves to emphasizing what appear to have been the most meaningful moments and forces during this more recent period. Independence was much more than breaking away from Spanish dominion. The country, now politically free, was faced with the need to endow itself with the forms of political and social organization best suited to its own particular situation. The principles derived from the French Revolution, as well as the example of its neighbor, the United States, were to exert a powerful influence against the ideology of those conservative groups determined to preserve institutions like the monarchy and the union of church and state. A consequence of this antagonism was the series of struggles which for a long time prevented any type of political stability.

A Century of Insecurity: Apaches, Anglos, and Others

Mexico, convulsed by frequent uprisings and civil wars, could not attend to most of the problems inherent in its own organization and development. The distant northern provinces, with their relatively sparse population, fell outside the field of most immediate interest. Northern isolation increased with every passing day, and in the case of provinces like Upper California and New Mexico their link with the center of the country appeared to be chiefly symbolic. This explains the proliferation in the North of leaders who were nothing more than caciques, interested only in preserving their position of dominance. Due to the extreme weakness of the ties with the government in the center of the country, the old system of defenses, with forts standing guard against the incursions of wild tribes, was reduced to a minimum. Thus, to isolation was added insecurity, two factors which contributed to the decadence of many of the old mines, and the haciendas dedicated to agriculture and stock raising. Also, trade became rachitic, due both to diminishing exploitation of the sources of wealth and to lack of protection along the roads. Finally, the missions, which survived for some years, began to show signs of decline, a forewarning of their definitive and legal suppression.

Northern Mexico presented a very discouraging picture during the decades following independence. It would appear natural that in their isolation the northerners would cling to their own cultural tradition in hopes of better times. Soon, however, they had to face a new situation, which came to endanger their very cultural and political identity. War with the United States, followed by the occupation of several of the northern Mexican states, meant the changing of the border and the permanent proximity of a powerful nation with different traditions and language. Paradoxically, isolation from central Mexico had caused the region to draw nearer to the Anglo-American world, which, due to its expansionist drive, inevitably had to be regarded as a permanent menace. Nevertheless, contacts and exchanges with the North American neighbors multiplied. Also, in the territory acquired by the United States, there remained a population of Mexican origin and, with it, many elements of the old northern culture. This meant that, at least to a limited degree, there was preserved a certain affinity in the heterogeneity of the new frontier.

In accordance with the Treaty of Guadalupe Hidalgo, which fixed the new border between the two countries in 1848, the

United States were obligated to prevent raids by so-called bar-barous Indians in the frontier region. In practice, however, the pressure exerted by the Anglo colonists resulted in Apache bands crossing over into Mexican territory, establishing their head-quarters in various places in Chihuahua and Sonora (Rippy 1931: 172-176). The northerners' traditional hatred and fear of the Apache increased. Many ranches, haciendas, and even towns had to be abandoned due to their frequent raids. There are numerous accounts of what was, for several decades, a constant struggle against those tribes which no one could subjugate. Also, legisla-tion passed by Chihuahua and Sonora demonstrates the hostile attitude of the local governments in face of this problem (Gamio and others 1958: 57-64).

To this source of insecurity, another series of dangers threat-ened the Northwest during the second half of the 19th century. Its isolation from central Mexico, its sparse population, and the potential riches that were thought to exist in the region, pro-voked filibustering invasions originating in U.S. territory. Among such cases may be cited that of William Walker, who proclaimed the ephemeral republic of Baja California and Sonora in 1853 (Woodward 1966). Other bands of adventurers, who had been in Upper California at the time of the gold rush, also penetrated the state of Sonora, such as the Frenchman Gaston Raousset de Boulbon. But despite their extreme scarcity of resources, the people of the North again and again warded off such invasions. More than one filibuster captain paid for his greed with his life. Events like these provoked the Mexicans of the Northwest to assume an attitude of permanent defense. That, in turn, awak-ened a deeper sense of nationality, linked essentially to a deter-mination to preserve their cultural identity and the land colo-nized by their ancestors.

Accustomed to reacting against Apache raids, filibustering incursions, and what was regarded as a permanent threat of expansion by Anglo-Americans, the northerners once again dem-onstrated their capacity for resistance during the French inter-vention following 1862. The troops of Napoleon III were repulsed many times in the North. Furthermore, it was on the Chihuahua border that President Juárez was able to reorganize his government and assemble the forces which were finally to rid

Mexico of the French and put an end to Maximilian's empire. This war against the French intervention had a positive effect on the North. Then more than ever, since the days of independence, the distant regions of Chihuahua and Sonora began to feel themselves linked with the rest of the country.

The years that followed, especially those of the long regime of Porfirio Díaz, were a bonanza for many of the old upper-class families in the Northwest. The haciendas took on new life and became increasingly concentrated in the hands of a few. Northern landholdings were famed for their almost incredible size. The mining industry also revived, although now it was almost totally in the hands of foreigners. In the Northwest during this period, important gold mines were worked in Nacozari and Altar, Sonora; in Ocampo, Hidalgo; and in Parral, Chihuahua. There were silver mines in Batopilas, Arteaga, and Parral, Chihuahua; and in Copala, Sinaloa; and copper mines in Santa Rosalía, Baja California; Cananea, Sonora; Barranca del Cobre, Magistral, and Chorreras, Chihuahua. To foreign enterprises, the government granted every type of concession, including the construction of railroads, which, from the Chihuahua border and later from that of Sonora also, led to the center of the country.

However, the people on the great landholdings and in the mines still lived a very precarious existence. Indian tribes—the Yaqui case must be remembered—were often in rebellion and were dealt with violently, as though their total extinction were desired. Such was the panorama in the Northwest at the beginning of the 20th century. As in the rest of the country, development basically favored the upper classes and foreign interests. But at least one positive consequence appeared to derive from the new state of affairs: in one way or another, the ties between these distant territories and central Mexico were strengthened.

The Northwest in the Revolution

It was symptomatic that, among the various movements which presaged the Mexican Revolution, a large number of them occurred in the Northwest. There was great discontent among the working classes, especially miners and agricultural laborers. In 1906, a strike in the mines at Cananea, Sonora, clearly a movement for social justice, was repressed with violence. The people of the North, who on many occasions had demonstrated their ability to fight for their own rights, were becoming aware of the grave problems that affected the entire country. On one hand, there was the centralist dictatorship of Porfirio Díaz, which prevented any political change; on the other, the situation of the masses, who worked and lived in subhuman conditions, steadily worsened. If in the center of the country there were those who openly called attention to the necessity for radical changes, it was the men of the North who most forcefully impelled the movement that culminated in the Revolution. Francisco Madero, native of Coahuila, appears in this context as the apostle of a democracy, which, once implanted, was expected to work a general transformation. And there were many northerners who immediately seconded it, particularly in Chihuahua and Sonora.

When the Revolution became generalized and its goals more fully defined, after Madero's death, there appeared in the Northwest leaders who were to exert a decided influence on the overall state of affairs in Mexico. It will suffice here to recall the names of Francisco Villa, Alvaro Obregón, Plutarco Elías Calles, Abelardo L. Rodríguez, Adolfo de la Huerta, Joaquín Amaro, and Felipe Angeles. Together with other leaders, also from the North, including the former governor of Coahuila, Venustiano Carranza, they finally took control of the principal revolutionary forces. Later, despite their rivalries, they organized the new government, the immediate forerunner of contemporary Mexico's political system.

As Bolton (1964: 78) noted in his essay on the evolution of the Mexican Northwest, it does not appear to be mere hypothesis to relate the emergence of these revolutionary leaders with the series of processes which from colonial times had been shaping the cultural physiognomy of the regions from which they came. In the Northwest, the hostile environment, isolation, and the necessity of being ready to defend oneself, had often resulted in the appearance of individuals aware of their rights and capable of fighting for them.

For the northerner, the Revolution meant a broader consciousness of his own problems, now conceived in relation to those of the entire country. For the first time, large numbers of them, the revolutionary troops of the northern states, came into direct contact with the realities of central and southern Mexico. Among its many other consequences, the Revolution brought about in this way a rapprochement of men who traditionally had lived at a distance from each other. A tangible proof of the great differences which had existed before was simply the appearance of the northern troops, compared with that of southern revolutionary forces such as the Zapatistas. Among the latter, Indians abounded, the descendants of Mesoamerican groups, now led principally by men of mestizo extraction. In the northern armies, however, it was common to find descendants of the Spanish farmers and miners of colonial times, people from the old haciendas and ranches. They were excellent horsemen, ready to mobilize, and to use their skill in the revolutionary cavalry. Indians were rare among them, with the exception of the famous Yaqui battalions, and the Yaquis themselves were very different in aspect and culture from the natives of central Mexico.

The triumph of the Revolution definitively marked a period of northern influence in Mexico. For almost a decade following the regime of Venustiano Carranza, the presidents of the republic were all men from Sonora: Adolfo de la Huerta, Álvaro Obregón and Plutarco Elías Calles. It is not strange, then, that their plans should stress the need for attention to the problems of their native regions and for putting an end to their isolation. Between 1920 and 1930, the first steps were taken along those lines, and this initial momentum, despite every kind of setback, continued under succeeding revolutionary governments. A statistical and economic evaluation of the resources of Sonora, Sinaloa, and Nayarit published by the Mexican government is revealing (Anonymous 1928). Presented as a study of the possibilities of these states, it also pointed out the obstacles which hindered their development and their participation in national life. One of the greatest problems continued to be their very sparse population. Sonora, Sinaloa, and Nayarit, with a combined area of more than 300,000 square kilometers, had something less than 800,000 inhabitants in 1921. This meant a population of less than three inhabitants per square kilometer. To attract more people to those regions, economic incentives had to be created. The dividing up of the great haciendas was not sufficient; in addition, means were required to permit the proper exploitation of the land. The mining centers, in a state of deterioration after the Revolution and still largely in the hands of foreigners, could not serve as the basis for new development projects. Further, the Indian groups which continued to live in various parts of the Northwest were marginal entities, traditionally impoverished and even more isolated than the rest of the population.

To attend to these problems, government action was mobilized. Expropriation of the latifundia and land distribution were followed by the building of a series of large dams, utilizing the rivers descending from the Sierra Madre. Agricultural development encouraged internal immigration, which soon made itself felt. The establishment of an extensive educational system began to take the Indian groups into consideration. The state took over the means of communications already in existence—that is, the railroads—and gradually began the construction of roads for motor vehicles in those regions. It would be naive to think that these and other programs, at least partially realized, have meant a total answer to the problems and possibilities of this great portion of Mexico. From almost every point of view, the integration and development of the Northwest still leave much to be desired.

The End of Isolation

Nevertheless, it is worthwhile to note some of the changes which have occurred in the cultural reality of this area. First comes the extraordinary increase in population following the post-revolutionary years. This has been due not only to natural increase, which especially during the last two decades has been common to almost the entire country and which is now described as a "demographic explosion." Taking the case of Sonora as an example, we have the following figures: in 1921 it had a population of 275,127; by 1930, there had been a slight increase, bringing it up to 316,271 inhabitants; in 1940, demographic growth was still limited and there were only 364,176. By 1950, however, immigration from other regions of Mexico had contributed substantially to its growth. According to the Mexican Bureau of Statistics, between 1940 and 1950 those who immigrated to Sonora totaled 62,570, and the 1950 census showed a considerably larger population: 510,607 individuals. Internal migration caused the state to receive another 142,312 persons in the

1950's and the population of Sonora at the beginning of 1960 was 783,378.

The other northern states were likewise a focus of attraction for immigrants from other parts of Mexico. The following table on internal migration give the number of persons in 1960 born outside the state of their current residence.

TABLE II

IMMIGRANTS IN NORTHWEST MEXICO, 1960*

TOTAL	885,564
Northern Baja California	308,322
Southern Baja California	11,552
Chihuahua	206,022
Durango	78,281
Nayarit	62,673
Sinaloa	76,202
Sonora	142,312

*Figures supplied by the Dirección General de Estadística, Mexico

If to these figures are added the immigrants counted in the same year in other northern states—Coahuila 155,768, Nuevo León 254,521, and Tamaulipas 291,379—it is apparent that by 1960 more than a million and a half Mexicans, mainly from the central area, had moved and established themselves in the border states. This fact, clearly not a result of any type of compulsion, is explained by the attraction, fundamentally economic, which these regions have for immigrants.

Among those attractions were the opening up of great areas to cultivation, thanks to numerous irrigation projects; northern Mexico until recently has been the region most favored in this type of investment. At the present time it is there that, to a certain degree, modern agricultural technology can be said to exist. Another inducement, of great importance, has been the proximity of the United States. Many of the border inhabitants work in the United States, although they retain their residence in towns located on the Mexican side. Further, the creation of various industries in the northern states, many with North American capital, has meant greater work possibilities. These and other facts explain why in several of these states, the minimum wage, fixed officially, is higher than the average in the country.

The traditional isolation of northern Mexico is today on the verge of disappearing. Changes that have occurred there, including those derived from the intense North American influence, pose new questions related to the problem of describing the cultural physiognomy of the region. It seems necessary, therefore, to recapitulate the most characteristic traits noted throughout northern Mexico's history, to determine to what point they have persisted, at least as a cultural substratum.

Ethos and Cultural Differences in the Mexican Northwest

It might be hypothesized that northern Mexico is already losing some or many of the traits which have shaped its cultural identity since the colonial period. Improved communications with the remainder of Mexico and the immigration of people from other regions of the country might be effecting a process of national homogenization. On the other hand, the influence there of the United States might also be more manifest every day. Thus, national and foreign influences, both very complex, might appear in some respects as opposing forces inevitably affecting the cultural reality of this area.

Another hypothesis would be to affirm that the cultures of the Mexican North, a consequence of its own historical process, has been able to assimilate the various external pressures and to preserve to date many of its ancient characteristics. It should be added in this case that some elements of this Norteño culture have also persisted among the Spanish-speaking people established in what today is the U.S. Southwest.

Obviously, before accepting or rejecting any one of these hypotheses, research of many types is required, only a small part of which has been carried out. We need more comprehensive historical studies, and further field work from the standpoint of ethnology and other branches of the social sciences. Actually lack of research remains an obstacle which prevents any attempt to make a precise catalogue of "northern" traits and patterns. That is why we prefer to attack this problem from the point of view of what has been called the *ethos*, or general meaning and orientation of a culture. Recalling the historical origins of the Northwest, attention will be given to the most influential elements in the formation of its own ethos: motivations, values, attitudes, and types of relations typical of the various populations which at different times settled there.

A first characteristic almost constant in the attitudes of those who, since the colonial era, established themselves in the Northwest, seems to be a determination to confront all kinds of dangers and difficulties in order to obtain the riches and advantages which supposedly or really exist there. It is this determination which launched the various movements of penetration, including perhaps those of the early indigenous arrivals. It then led to the creation, from their very roots, of the original colonial settlements in which one had to work strenuously in order to subsist. Such was the case in the mining camps, the haciendas, the ranches, and new towns.

In the midst of his isolation, the Norteño settler found himself in the presence of Indian tribes from which he could expect little benefit but, on the contrary, great danger. Missions and forts were the two types of reply to the question posed by the tribes. The missionaries sought the concentration of the Indians, their conversion, and better means of subsistence, isolating them as completely as possible from any outside contact. For their part, troops stationed in the forts had the task of repelling the unsubdued tribes, the so-called barbarians. In one way or another, missions and forts functioned as institutions that, finally, separated the natives, or kept them at a distance, from the new centers in which the Spanish-Mexican population established itself.

Thus, in the Norteño, a different attitude from that which prevailed in central Mexico was firmly fixed. Since in the North it was so difficult to make use of the labor of the uncivilized tribes, it seemed best to repulse them or concentrate them in the missions. This probably explains why, even today, within the

Mexican-American West there still exists a well-defined pluri-cultural reality. At present, groups like the Tarahumara of Chihuahua, the Yaqui, Seri and Pima of Sonora, and the Mayo of Sonora and Sinaloa continue to live apart, preserving much of their ancient culture. Furthermore, in the 19th century—and even in the 20th—uprisings on the part of some of these tribes did break out. The case of the Yaquis of Sonora offers no doubt the best example of a militant resistance which produced not a few rebellions. All this explains why, for the Norteño, ideologies like Indianism often seem to be romantic postures of no practical significance. On the part of Indian groups, the answer to such a situation has been distrust and almost perpetual complaint against the wrongs and exploitation of which they have been the victims, as is also the case in the United States.

The ethos of the Norteño has been shaped, thus, in his isolation from the Indian world and in his attitude of confronting danger, dedicated to any work that would permit him, if not to secure the coveted riches, at least to achieve a better way of life. Stock raising, particularly, was for the Norteño not only a significant source of income but an institution that coloured his way of life. Horsemanship was, and still is to a considerable degree, an art practiced by the male in innumerable circumstances. The Norteño feels proud of his skill and shows it in his fiestas and rodeos. In those activities and always when he works on the ranches he wears the traditional attire of the vaquero. It can also be recalled here that both the traditions and attire of stock raising came to exert a powerful influence on the famous cowboys of the U.S. Southwest.

The Norteño's isolation and the accentuated need for protection produced a greater family cohesion and a more persistent preservation of the ties of kinship. To date, in several northwestern states, the family, as an institution, displays greater stability than in central and southern Mexico (Borah and Cook 1966). In fact, both in colonial times and more recently when other migrations began to take place, those who arrived in the North frequently came accompanied by their wives and children.

The ethnic configuration of the northern population also presents other characteristics worthy of consideration. As has already been mentioned, *mestizaje* with the tribes that lived there was very limited. A good percentage of the early colonists were of Spanish extraction. Many were *criollos*, persons born in Mexico of Spanish parents, and others were mestizos of predominantly Spanish culture. Almost the only Indians who mixed with the Norteños were from central Mexico, chiefly those of Nahua-Tlaxcaltecan filiation who had gone north as companions and servants of the Spanish. At any rate, the result was the implantation there of New Spain's culture in formation. To date, and regardless of the more recent migrations, old cultural habits and elements have been preserved in the Northwest. Thus, in the Spanish language, as it is spoken in the North, numerous archaic expressions persist, and what is known as a Norteño accent is clearly perceived in the speech. In diet, also, differences exist. The use of wheat-flour tortillas, rather than corn ones, shows a Mesoamerican influence assimilated in their own manner by people of predominantly Spanish extraction. Up to now, the consumption of meat and vegetables is also higher in the North than elsewhere in the country. The examples mentioned only anticipate what a systematic investigation will be able to discover in this order of differences.

Some of the most important decisions adopted by the people of the North, throughout Mexico's independent life, also would seem to be explained on the basis of their ethos. Although, in general, the doors to a higher education or any other species of cultural refinement had not been open to the northerner, he developed qualities that enriched him in a very special manner. Among them was his great capacity for adaptation, his attitude of resistance to the threat of losing what he regarded as his, and an ever stronger consciousness of his Mexicanism. Proof of this is found in several facts already mentioned. There is the belligerence of the North during the war with the United States, in dealing with invasions by filibusters, and also at the time of the French intervention. These forms of participation in the life of the country, in turn, determined a desire for stronger ties with the integral reality of Mexico. Perhaps this explains, too, the decisive role of the North in the Mexican Revolution, when, in several of the border states, leaders emerged who effectively opposed the dictatorship. They also fought to put an end to the alienation represented by the great landholding, the mines, and other concessions in the hands of foreigners. From another point of view, this ethos helps to explain the preservation of determined cultural values and elements among the Spanish-Mexican groups that continue to live in the U.S. Southwest.

Our brief account of significant historical events, from the times before the Spanish penetration down to the present, has already demonstrated the appearance of some different and peculiar traits in the Mexican Northwest. To have pointed out the isolation and the types of motivation of those who settled there, aids probably in explaining the arising of an ethos, distinct to a certain degree, within the broader context of Mexican culture. We believe that, despite the stronger ties now linking those regions with the center of the country, and in spite of the undeniable influence of the neighbouring United States, the Northwest has preserved a great number of its old features and values.

We regret not being able to continue our description of the ethos of the Norteños further. Due to the absence of ethnographic studies one would have to depend largely on the insight of certain authors of literary works portraying life in the North. Novels and accounts about the Revolution in northern Mexico, personal reminiscences, diaries, and even poetry should be included in the list. Mention can be made of the works of Martín Luis Guzmán, Rafael F. Muñoz, and little known works such as *Four centuries of life of an hacienda* by Saravia (1940-56).

In this paper we have pointed out some aspects of the many that remain to be investigated. It would be dangerous to forget that all of the Mexican-American West continues to be a vast, pluricultural region. The presence of the diverse Indian groups living there cannot be ignored. Research in this as in other fields is urgent, both on the early native antecedents, studied by means of archaeology, and on the contemporary situation of the often-neglected Indians. The future of the Indian tribes cannot be clearly foretold. The Mexicans, who obviously are at home in the Northwest, on the other hand are a minority in the border area of the United States. With regard to the future of these minority groups, a prediction is likewise impossible.

Beyond doubt, the possibilities of the Mexican Northwest and the U.S. Southwest are great. In both cases, enormous extensions of land are involved, with natural resources utilized only in part. Their populations, although culturally heterogeneous in many respects, nevertheless participate in a common tradition. North Americans, Mexicans, and Indians of several different tribes necessarily have to live there in permanent contact and interplay. The pluricultural reality gives rise to reciprocal influences. These, many times, can be positive and, as such, contribute to overall improvement. Incomprehension and, worse still, feelings of superiority of one group with respect to the others signify the contrary. The area that concerns us continues to be an open field for the study of situations of cultural contact and interaction. These and other problems have been merely touched upon here. In summary, our purpose has been to reflect on what is already known in order to point out the wealth and complexity of the subject and the fact that much still remains to be investigated.

The Mormons: Church and People

Thomas F. O'Dea

The Mormons, more properly the members of the Church of Jesus Christ of Latter-day Saints, are one of the many diverse groups which are part of the complex society of the Southwest. To understand them, it is necessary to know their peculiar history and to be aware of their religious beliefs. Indeed, in a brief but eventful history they developed into a people with distinct traditions and a highly articulate sense of their own unique identity. They represent a religious group which developed into something resembling an ethnic group with respect to certain strategic characteristics of their group consciousness and group life. With that development and its consequences, and with its present significance in the region, we shall be concerned. It may be helpful, however, to begin with a brief consideration of the characteristic ethnic structure of the nation as a whole and to indicate how the Southwest differs from it in significant ways.

The Special Significance of Ethnicity in the United States

The development of American society took place in close relationship to a large and long-lasting immigration of newcomers to our shores. From 1820 to 1930, 37,762,012 immigrants came to this country, 32,276,346 of them from Europe. Most of these people were not well off and entered the ranks of the working population, although most of them were not in such dire straits as the Irish immigrants fleeing famine at home in the 1840's, or many among the so-called "new immigration" which began in the 1880's from southern and eastern Europe. As a consequence of this mass immigration significant differences among subgroups in the American population came to be based not simply upon differentially evaluated function or the embodiment of esteemed values. That is to say that social class was not the only basis for the existence of significant distinctions among people in America. With the coincidence of economic development and mass immigration, religion and nationality took on a strategic social significance. Ethnic and religious designations became in America status designations intertwined with occupational and class designations. In this situation, social mobility, acculturation, and assimilation became interpenetrating sociocultural processes. Consequently, religious and ethnic groups became interest groups merging with—and at times cutting across—class distinctions, and became involved in the competition for power and influence characteristic of an industrial society which is to some degree occupationally open and politically democratic.

Limits to Assimilation

American society emphasized the importance of assimilation both as part of its official and unofficial ideology and as built into its occupational structure and its opportunities for social mobility. Most immigrant groups indeed moved toward such assimilation, but at the same time they showed strong tendencies to maintain significant elements of the older heritage and older identity. The result of this "double response" to the American situation was that considerable "Americanization" took place, but much ethnic identity remained. Long after mass immigration from Europe stopped, Glazer and Moynihan (1963) have shown the significance of Jews, Italians, and Irish as ethnic groups in the life of New York City, while the Germans, formerly of great importance, have disappeared there as a separate ethnic phenomenon.

In short, in America, religion, ethnicity, and social position became closely intertwined. While the general pressure for acculturation and assimilation prevailed, and while the immigrants and their descendants often met pronounced hostility (for example, Billington 1938), there resulted a situation combining assimilation up to a point with considerable ethnic identity and separateness. The hyphenated American came into existence, and Christopher Columbus, John Barry, Chaim Solomon, Pulaski, Kosciusko, Junipero Serra, and a host of others have joined the

American pantheon together with Washington, Jefferson, Lincoln, and the rest. The trend toward homogeneity involved a considerable degree of separate identity and of separated social life. Nowhere, perhaps, is this more dramatically evident than in the case of the Catholic Church, which long maintained its own separate educational and cultural structure, while Catholics also participated in the general secular institutions of the country (O'Dea 1970: 39-67).

Moreover, in America political causes involving the "old country" became significant issues in domestic politics. In the 19th century when the "Irish Question" was the great disturbing problem for a complacent Great Britain, Irish immigrants in America (and Australia) took an active part in the politics of the old homeland and made its concerns an important element in the political life of America (for example, Brown 1966). Today Jewish groups are active in support of Israel, "the new-old country," in these her times of peril. Further, in the reactions of various groups in this country to our present domestic turmoil, we see the emergence of an "ethnic" opinion into public view, revealing the continuing vitality of ethnic identities.

The combination of assimilation and acculturation, together with the preservation of an older religious or ethnic separation, remained characteristic of much of the American scene, although with marked regional and local variations, until after World War II. It was suggested in the 1950's however, that in much of the country, and especially among the middle class, ethnicity as a significant mark of identity and loyalty was giving way to religion. In addition it was noted that Protestantism, Catholicism and Judaism were evolving as the "three great religions of democracy," membership in which meant that one belonged to the general American community (Herberg 1955). Though there is a good deal to be said for this thesis, it is undeniable that ethnicity remains a visible and significant part of the American picture. As we enter the 1970's the religious situation in America is greatly changed. Post-conciliar Catholicism and increased ecumenical relations between Catholic and Protestant religious groups and institutions represent a genuine breakdown of the older separatism. Mass higher education carries assimilation and acculturation forward to an unprecedented degree. Change of a significant kind is obviously taking place. Today the relationship of ethnicity and religion to social structure and stratification is in transition and merits close and careful study (Gordon 1964: 51-54).

There are three groups in the American population who are conspicuous because they did not become a part of the many-sided processes of incorporation into general American life with the degree of success and depth of involvement experienced by most of the descendants of immigrants from Europe. Most obvious are the Blacks, but important also are the Mexican-Americans and the Indians. Indeed the Indians live today as reminders of the human costs exacted by the westward expansion of American society (Billington 1949). At least two of these groups are strategic to the ethnic structure of the Southwest. Moreover, as is pointed out elsewhere in these papers, these groups now tend to repudiate the older policy of assimilation combined with a degree of maintenance of older identities and allegiances—a policy that never worked for them—and to demand a kind of separatism within the general structure of the American commonwealth. Whither such policies will lead we do not know.

Ethnic Relations in the Southwest

With the Indians and the Mexican-Americans we deal with groups whose history stands apart from the general ethnic history of America. Indeed, in the Southwest it is the "old-stock" Americans who are the newcomers. Here they are still dominant, but they are not old stock. The Indians obviously are the old stock, but the Mexican-Americans are hardly newcomers. Moreover, in this conference we have dealt not simply with the "Southwest" as North Americans have understood it, but with a larger area which crosses the international border. Sonora and Chihuahua together with Arizona and New Mexico represent a region with significant common characteristics as well as diverse components and distinct histories. To this region the Mormons came in two or three encounters; in this region they worked out their peculiar destiny. They came to be recognized as distinct from the general run of Anglo-Americans, and in settling south of the border they sought to escape prosecution by the federal government.

In the Southwest, Spicer has identified 42 separate ethnic groups, many of which have long been part of the area. Most of them did not arrive through the process of the "westward movement," as did the Anglos, the Mormons, and the Blacks. Nor is the status of assimilation among them similar to that of the descendants of 19th-century European immigrants. The different Pueblo groups have been here the longest; others like the Navajo came many centuries ago from the North. The various Spanish-speaking groups represent the thrust of population northward from Mexico, and earlier from New Spain. Here we have a different kind of ethnic history and consequently a different kind of ethnic structure. Today these groups are part of a complex social situation in which the interests of each and of all are deeply and complicatedly involved. Spicer characterizes this situation by suggesting that "there is a subsystem of the whole society which may be understood as a system of ethnic relations maintained by definable social and cultural processes and which changes in response to factors both within and outside of the system." We are concerned here with understanding the structure and dynamics of this ethnic system in the Southwest.

Societies are constituted by reciprocal attitudes, memories, responses and activities, out of which there come to be significantly shared and reciprocal elements. Of these components of a social structure evaluations occupy an important place. In seeking to understand a system of ethnic relations, we seek to understand what Spicer calls the "vital features of a system of mutual valuation." He has suggested three basic elements involved in this evaluated ethnic identity: (1) a cultural content associated with significant activities, (2) a common historical experience, and (3) an image or self-conception vis-a-vis other groups. I shall return to a consideration of these conceptions later. Let us now turn to the Mormons, one of the groups found both in the U.S. Southwest and the Mexican Northwest.

Who Are the Mormons?

The Church of Jesus Christ of Latter-day Saints considers itself to be a new foundation or reestablishment of the "Church of Christ in these last days . . . by the will and commandments of God" (*Doctrine and Covenants* 20: 1), and by that token neither Catholic nor Protestant. Although its members were long known as "Mormons," there is a tendency at present for that term to be regarded as quaint and to use instead the term "LDS" as the popular designation. The church was founded on April 6, 1830, in upstate New York by Joseph Smith, Jr. and a small band of followers. Smith, who became the Mormon prophet, claimed divine visitations and in 1830 published the *Book of Mormon*. This book is believed by Mormons to be an American scripture, a native American "bible," recording the dealings of God with Hebrews who came to the New World. It recounts the story of three Hebrew migrations to the Western Hemisphere, the subsequent history of the groups involved, and the final darkening of the skins of the surviving remnant as a punishment for their apostasy. The *Book of Mormon* became central to the new church. Thus was America provided with a sacred history and an explanation offered for the origin of the Indians. Religious enthusiasm in upstate New York had given rise to a new church, a new scripture, and a new prophet destined to play a significant part in American religious history.

Early Expansion and Persecution

In 1831 the new church expanded outside of New York with the founding of a Mormon community at Kirtland, Ohio, and from then on until Joseph Smith was murdered in Illinois in 1844, the church grew, migrated, was persecuted, saw considerable internal dissension, and was embroiled in conflict with hostile outsiders. In these few years four attempts were made to build a separate Mormon community that would embody the group's peculiar ideals and establish the existence of the Mormons as a people apart from the general run of the unregenerate. At Kirtland, Mormon efforts, which involved the building of the first Mormon temple, ended in financial disaster. In Missouri, two more attempts were made, one at Independence and one at Far West, but in each case after some initial success their efforts attracted the hostile attention of the Missourians and the Saints were driven out in violence and bloodshed. They were driven from Independence in the winter of 1833-34 and went into Clay County, but again, they were soon asked to leave. They then founded Far West, from which they were also expelled. It was estimated by Joseph Smith that the losses incurred by his followers in Missouri amounted to $2 million. The expulsion from Far West was the occasion of a small-scale "Mormon War" which cost the lives of 40 persons, all but one or two of them Mormons.

While the treatment of the Latter-day Saints in Missouri was another example of the intolerance and violence which has characterized all too much of American history, nevertheless from the point of view of the social scientist studying social processes it might almost be deemed inevitable. The initial successes of their endeavors, their New York or Yankee manners, their religious beliefs which seemed peculiar if not perverse to more orthodox or at least more conventional Protestants, their open declarations of their intentions to make the area a holy land, their favorable attitudes toward the Indians, and the rumors of abolitionism which derived from an initially favorable attitude toward Negroes—all these combined to elicit marked hostility from the Missourians.

When they were driven from Far West the Mormons moved to the east again—the only eastward move in their long odyssey— and established another community at Nauvoo, Illinois. Here they achieved great success, both economically and politically. The state legislature granted them the famous "Nauvoo Charter," which made the city almost a state within the state, with its own government and army, while diligent enterprise soon brought into existence an attractive city of some 15,000 inhabitants on the east bank of the Mississippi (Flanders 1965). But the old pattern of success, hostility, and expulsion had not been thrown off. To the fears which Mormon size and power aroused before in Missouri, there was now the added suspicion aroused by rumors of plural marriage. Moreover, Mormonism was becoming a national issue. On September 4, 1842, the *New York Sun* declared (Flanders 1965: 271): "Should the inherent corruption of Mormonism fail to develop . . . sufficiently to convince its followers of their error, where will the thing end? A great military despotism is growing up in the fertile West, increasing faster, in proportion, than the surrounding population, spreading its influence around, and marshalling multitudes under its banner, causing serious alarm to every patriot."

The growing tension resulted in a second "Mormon War," and in the events that followed Joseph Smith and his brother Hyrum were murdered by a mob in the jail in Carthage, Illinois. After prolonged tension and some open fighting in which artillery pieces were actually used, the Saints were again driven out (Flanders 1965: 271): "By 1845 the civil authorities in county and state were either unwilling or unable to protect the city from the rising tide of depredations. . . . " In September, 1845, the Mormons announced that they would abandon Nauvoo the following spring. They sold their lands to French utopians, and in subzero weather the following February, they began their evacuation. By the next fall the city was all but deserted.

Settlement in the West

With the prophet dead there followed a time of discouragement and internal dissension. Several groups broke off from the main body; the most important of these later became the Reorganized Church of Jesus Christ of Latter Day Saints. Into the leadership vacuum left by the prophet's assassination stepped Brigham Young, pushing aside his most likely rival, Sidney Rigdon. Young was a man of great energy, intelligence, and organizational ability. He pulled the disheartened group together and organized their migration across Iowa to the banks of the Missouri River, where he set up winter quarters. After a season of severe hardship, Young organized the Mormon migration to the West. On April 7, 1847, 17 years and one day after the church's founding, Brigham and a party of 148 left for the valley of the Great Salt Lake. They arrived July 22, and two days later Young himself, who was ill, entered the valley. This marked the beginning of the Mormon settlement of the intermountain West. Thousands came in the following decades, at first by wagon train, then by handcart, and finally by railroad.

The Mormons developed their settlement on a planned basis and the existence of a centralized church government enabled them to carry out a rationally conceived effort. The church "called" settlers to go as a religious duty to establish communities in the irrigable valleys throughout the region. By the time of Brigham Young's death in 1877, there were 357 Mormon settlements with a Mormon population of 140,000. In 1861, the church called 309 families to establish the town of St. George at the confluence of the Santa Clara and the Virgin Rivers (Anderson 1966). Settlements were set up from Provo to Las Vegas to make a highway along what Young foresaw as a "Mormon corridor" to the sea (Werner 1925, Hunter 1934). Expansion in that direction was however later given up by the Mormons. Settlers were pulled back in the 1857 "Mormon War," which saw 2,500 troops under the command of Albert Sidney Johnston come into Utah to meet oblique but genuine Mormon resistance. Yet overall expansion continued. After Young's death, new settlements were established along the Little Colorado River in Arizona and adjacent areas in New Mexico, and in Mexico and Canada.

Mormon efforts succeeded in the intermountain West. True enough, hostility still continued on a national scale, especially from the federal government, but expulsion was now out of the question. The long Mormon-Gentile conflict, which together with material success and growth marked Mormon history in the West, crystalized around two issues—Utah's admission to the Union, and the status of plural marriage. While polygynous marriage had been practiced secretly in Nauvoo, following 1852 it was practiced openly in the western settlements. It elicited a decidedly hostile reaction from American public opinion and from the government. Congress acted more than once in the matter, and the federal courts in Utah enforced the new laws.

In 1863, during the Civil War, Congress passed the Morrill Law, outlawing plural marriage. This statute was found constitutional by the Supreme Court in 1879. Then in 1882 the Edmunds Act was passed, followed in five years by the Edmunds-Tucker Act. These laws were stringent and even harsh, the latter disestablishing the church as a legally existing corporation, which involved a seizure of assets by the federal authorities. The small non-Mormon group in Utah supported the federal government in the fight. A Mormon underground was established and great efforts were made to defend and support the institution of plural marriage (Young 1954: 380-409). Mormon leaders were seized by federal agents and jailed for "cohabitation." But after the death of President John Taylor, who was a bitter-ender on this issue, the new president of the church Wilford Woodruff, acted to renounce the practice of polygamy. There ensued in the church a covert struggle and during that time additional plural marriages were contracted in the Mexican settlements, to which people were sent from the United States for that purpose. In the end, however, the antipolygamists won and the church genuinely gave up the practice, though theoretically always holding it to be the ideal.

At the constitutional convention in Utah in 1887, the Mormons, with some 200 members in jail, capitulated and supported the outlawing of polygamy. In 1896 Utah was admitted to the Union. There followed a period of accommodation to the ideals and values of the general community as the church strove for and achieved a new respectability and acquired a new conservatism. Yet real religious peculiarity remained, and the Mormons continued as a distinct group. Mormonism's most impressive accomplishment, after survival and growth under difficult and adverse conditions, was the successful settlement and economic development of the intermountain West (for example, Arrington 1958). This accomplishment finds its most appropriate monument in the establishment of irrigation, for which the Latter-day Saints possessed the requisite social discipline and cooperative attitudes.

Recent Developments

Since World War II two significant developments affected the Mormon Church. The church continued to grow. In the 1960's the Mormon church reported a 74 per cent increase in membership, which came to total 2,815,000. It had taken the church 117 years to reach the figure of a million members, and another 16 years to reach two million. In this last decade the church also saw its greatest territorial expansion. In 1960 there was only one stake of the Mormon church (a territorial subdivision roughly comparable to a diocese but much smaller) outside the United States and Canada. Now there are 37. When the decade began there were a total of 290 stakes, now there are 496. Now a majority of the church membership live outside Utah. Moreover, Utah has become urbanized and to some extent industrialized, although the church has traditionally preferred agriculture and the Mormon Zion in the mountains was always conceived as based upon farming. Yet by the 1960's more than half of Utah's income was derived from nonagricultural pursuits. There was also a migration of Mormons to southern California, as well as to the Middle West and East. Thus there has arisen a Mormon urban middle class of size and importance.

What Do the Mormons Believe?

The Mormon church considers itself to be the product of divine revelation, which began with Joseph Smith and continues through the institutionalized agency of the church presidency. The *Book of Mormon*, the *Doctrine and Covenants*, and *The Pearl of Great Price*, all alleged revelations to the Mormon prophet, are accepted as sacred scripture in addition to the Old and New Testaments. The *Book of Mormon* claims to be a precolumbian American scripture. The *Doctrine and Covenants* contains revelations believed to have been given to Joseph Smith for the governance of the church and the solution of its problems; it includes the revelation on plural marriage (Sec 132). *The Pearl of Great Price* contains what are alleged to be lost parts of the Pentateuch, some of which were transcribed and translated by the prophet from papyri found in mummy wrappings, some writings of Joseph Smith, and a statement of articles of faith. It is this work which is utilized to justify the discriminatory practice which denies Negroes the Mormon priesthood (Book of Abraham 1: 21-27).

Mormon doctrine denies an *ex nihilo* creation and instead posits a finite developing God in an uncreated developing universe. God is a demiurge who organizes already existing matter. Moreover, the Mormon understanding of the Trinity tends to become tritheism. Mormonism believes in a God who is developing increasing mastery over the uncreated elements of the universe, and it sees man as made in His image and therefore also involved in an adventure of increasing mastery of his own. This extra-Christian evolutionism, which Joseph Smith introduced into Mormonism in Nauvoo if not before, sees God as a material being located in space and time. It sees man as having had an existence before birth, as destined for infinite progress after death, and the earth life as being one episode in such an eternal process of development. These religious conceptions emphasize the practical side of man's life. The eternal development central to these doctrines was originally seen as closely related to plural marriage and numerous wives and children. The present life is seen in the light of Mormon teachings as a time of probation and trial during which men, by their own effort and with God's help, experience a new kind of environment and by their struggle to master it hasten their own development to God-like status.

The emphasis upon development, effort, activity, and mastery finds concrete embodiment in a set of mundane virtues comprising what has been called "the work, health, recreation, and education complex." This complex provides significant guidelines for the everyday life of the believing Mormon. It represents values that become deeply internalized in Mormon socialization, both in the family and in the church. This developmental ethic is combined with an insistence upon a highly active membership in the church and a faithful observance of its ordinances. In the course of its history Mormonism was transformed from a congregational type of religious organization to one characterized by authority, hierarchy, and centralization. Obedience to the church's teachings, as well as to the church's general authorities, together with the values of the work, health, recreation, and education complex and active participation in the great variety of church activities, are the basic characteristics of the Mormon way of life. For the believing Mormon, "life is more than a vocation, more than a calling; it is an opportunity for deification through conquest, which is won through rational mastery of the environment and obedience to the ordinances of the church" (O'Dea 1957: 143).

The *Book of Mormon* is quite obviously a book Christian in content and in tenor. It bears a clear relationship to the milieu of upstate New York, and the influence of the religious enthusiasm of that "burned-over district" is palpable enough. From that source came the emphases upon millennialism and upon repentance so central to Mormon religious thought. But this Christian side of Mormonism, which is its original content and still ex-

126

tremely important, even central to it, has not been explicitly integrated with the newer extra-Christian evolutionary elements introduced later by Joseph Smith. It is true that, in interpreting and transforming the doctrine of salvation through works found in the *Book of Mormon* as the doctrine of deification through effort in a process of eternal development, a degree of integration is achieved. But the fact is that the two disparate religious world-views exist side by side in the Mormon belief system and are held in that kind of juxtaposition by Mormon believers. No genuine theological attempt to reconcile the two has been made. The belief system of the Mormon church displays a number of traditional Protestant positions: the traditional belief in atonement by Christ, an Arminian emphasis upon salvation through works and free will, and a revival emphasis upon repentance. It is also characterized by such innovations as the doctrine of human preexistence, a developing material deity, baptism for the dead, marriage for time and eternity, and in former days plural marriage. Mormonism has been characterized as a heightened and theologized form of the secularized outlook of an almost ex-Protestant middle class—a resacralization of secular values and attitudes. It emphasizes optimism, self-improvement, hard work, and respect for the law. It values recreation as a means to health, makes health a theological virtue, places great emphasis upon the family—even the extended family in the larger context of the church—and enjoins abstinence from liquor, coffee, tea, and tobacco.

Mormonism and the Question of Ethnicity

We have already noted the special significance of religious and ethnic groups as identity and interest groups in America, and the way in which immigration and industrial development combined to produce a mixture of religion, ethnicity, and social stratification in this country. In the Mormon case, however, we have a unique phenomenon in America. The Mormons are a religious group and central to Mormon identity is membership in the formally organized church and its auxiliary organizations. But that is only part of the picture. For family and kinship are basic to Mormon values (O'Dea 1957: 141-142):

127

The family is a very important institution to Mormons. This refers to both the nuclear family of husband, wife, and children, which is, of course, the basic social unit, and larger kinship groups . . . there is great emphasis upon extended kinship relationships, and large-scale family reunions, which may have as many as a thousand persons in attendance, are common to Mormondom during the warmer part of the year. The Mormon consciousness of group accomplishment fits in with an awareness of family contribution to the larger tasks of the Mormon people throughout their history. The formal structure of the church is penetrated and supported by strong ties of extended kinship both of blood and of marriage. The official church emphasis upon temple work, with its vicarious rites for the dead, increases family awareness and reinforces family loyalties.

This interpenetration of church and family is further sacralized by the institution of the Mormon priesthood which admits all "worthy males," and which continues to have a certain degree of quasi-patriarchal character. The male head of the Mormon family is a priest in the church. To all this must be added the social and political isolation which was so characteristic of the Mormon historical experience. From the beginning the Latter-day Saints sought to set up their own separate community. In Nauvoo, they achieved for a time what almost amounted to political independence. In the West, they tried to establish the State of Deseret, on a much larger scale than the present state of Utah. In this respect Brigham Young continued the tradition set in the Middle West. Deseret would in fact be a Mormon homeland, but it would also be a state within the American federal union. This conception was of course rendered obsolete by the Civil War, but Congress would never have agreed to it in any case, as is evidenced by the rejection of the Mormon proposals. In the West, isolation and the fact of being the majority of the population within a large geographical region gave the Mormons the kind of separation necessary to solidify their peculiar identity and to link it to a geographical territory—to a homeland.

Even though complete separation did not occur, the Mormon experience has nevertheless been cited to illustrate the processes which tend to transform a sect into a nation (Park and Burgess 1921: 872-873):

> Once the sect has achieved territorial isolation and territorial solidarity, so that it is the dominant power within the region that it occupies, it is able to control the civil organization, establish schools and a press, and so put the impress of a peculiar culture upon all the civil and political institutions that it controls. In this case it tends to assume the form of a state, and become a nationality. Something approaching this was achieved by the Mormons in Utah.

Moreover, to the combination of religious, familial, and geographical factors shaping the evolution of the Mormon people, we must add the element of hostility and conflict. The Mormons were treated by their fellow Americans as enemies. As a consequence the Mormon attitude toward the United States was long marked by a profound ambiguity. America was regarded as the promised land; it was dedicated and given a sacred history in the *Book of Mormon* as "a land choice above all other lands" (II Nephi 1: 5). Moreover, the democratic institutions of the United States were held to be divinely inspired. They were seen as specially prepared for the renewal of divine revelation and its propagation by the Mormon church. Yet from the start the Mormons were involved in conflict with their fellow Americans, and in Utah gentile opposition was spearheaded by the federal government. When the Civil War broke out the Saints, though preferring the Northern cause, considered it a war in Babylon out of which God had called His elect. Thus, both patriotism and a potential separatism characterized the Mormon attitude in the 19th century. Since the end of polygamy and the admission of Utah to the Union the church, as part of its accommodation to the general community, stressed patriotism as a basic attitude of the church and its members and continued to teach that the democratic political institutions of the United States were divinely inspired. However, as Johnston's army approached the Mormon country in 1857, there were open expressions of separatism in Utah.

It has often been observed that Mormonism is a typical American religion, originating in America, holding America to be its holy land, and enshrining as central to its teaching typical American values. It is also true, however, to state that the Mormons have a separate and distinctive history of their own, and this peculiar experience has made them a group with a strong particular identity. It is notable how often the members of the LDS church refer to themselves as "the Mormon people" both in writing and in speech (O'Dea 1957: 115-116):

> What has begun as a sectarian religious group, through its emulation of the Old Testament Hebrews in the unsettled conditions of the Middle and Far West, had been transformed into the Mormon people. The Saints had not achieved territorial monopoly of power and influence, but they more than compensated for this by the nature of their common experience, which developed in them strong group solidarity. Mormonism had indeed gone from "near-sect" to "near-nation". . . . The Mormon group came closer to evolving ethnic identity on this continent than did any other comparable group. Moreover, it was a genuine, locally and independently conceived ethnicity, born and nurtured on this side of the water and not imported from abroad.

While this quasi-ethnic character of Mormonism is not one that is formally recognized and declared by the church, there is nonetheless a genuine feeling of peoplehood. The Church of Jesus of Latter-day Saints is the formally organized core of the Mormon people—a people chosen of the Lord and gathered from many backgrounds. Mormon family structure interpenetrates with formal church structure and reinforces it. The history of the Mormon people is told in the formal teachings of the church, where it is given prominent emphasis, and in the individual family histories so cherished by many Mormons. Such teaching and telling reinforces the sense of distinct peoplehood.

Church, People, and Conflict

In my earlier work on the Mormons, I identified ten sources of strain and conflict which had been of significance in Mormon history (O'Dea 1957). I will list and discuss them briefly here, since they deal with elements of Mormonism important for our present study. Some of them are now matters of times past, but some of them are not. Indeed, some of them are as real and significant as sources of strain and conflict as ever, and all of them have had their effects upon giving meaning to Mormon history, and giving form to the Mormons as a particular group.

The Mormon Encounter with Modern Secular Thought

This is the LDS version of the encounter of religion and secularism which has been so prominent a phenomenon in the Western world in the past several centuries, and which has been intensified by the development of science and technology in recent times. In the Mormon case, the realm of education has been the chief locus of the encounter. Modern secular thought, both substantive and critical, challenges Mormon doctrines and conceptions at numerous points and thus brings into the Mormon subculture a disruptive dynamic of considerable significance. This situation is made more serious since the teachings of the church stress the importance of education. Official Mormon response to the problems involved here brought into existence the Brigham Young University (BYU) at Provo, Utah, which now has over 25,000 students. BYU is run in a highly authoritarian manner under the presidency of Ernest Wilkenson, and Mormon orthodoxy in thought, word, and deed is both supported and enforced. Yet BYU students are not without their authentic religious problems. A second response has been the development of the institute and seminary system. This system involves setting up Mormon student centers near colleges and high schools, and running an extensive program of LDS education together with social activities. Even here, however, the problems of the encounter with secularism have arisen and caused difficulty.

A structural element of the Mormon church organization enables the church to avoid these problems to some degree. The lay leadership of the church involves two significant consequences. First of all, it means that theology, as an area of intellectual endeavor which necessarily involves the confrontation of difficult religious problems in a rational manner, does not really exist in the Mormon church. Weber (1963: 30) observed that rational theology waits upon the development of a specialized priesthood composed of men who are full-time professionals. The existence of lay priesthood and lay leadership means that people from middle-class occupations—with middle-class outlooks and middle-class notions of what is and is not normative and desirable—occupy the leading influential and decision-making positions and set the dominant tone for the entire church. For such people the intellectual problems facing the church, both in terms of problems inherent in the Mormon belief system and the challenges from secular thought, are either not recognized or, if recognized, not responded to in intellectual terms.

Such leadership not only neglects rational theology, but it also tends to give little scope for the intellectuals within the church. Indeed it may fairly be said that the Mormon church has long tended to stifle its intellectuals. This tendency to neglect or suppress intellectuality is increased by the extreme activism of the church. Thus, the conflict over literalism versus liberalism in the interpretation of the scriptures finds little expression and no solution in Mormon church life.

My 1957 study found that the church is forced to hold to its latter-day revelations literally or lose the theological and charismatic basis of its legitimacy. Moreover I found dissident intellectuals of whom it was said (O'Dea 1957: 240): "Their group loyalty is strong; their pride in the accomplishments of their people, great; their respect for the values of their faith, genuine; but they are unable to accept an orthodox literal theology which for most of their fellow churchmen is the basis of all other cherished values." Thus, it was concluded (O'Dea 1957: 230): "The conservative, literalist, fundamentalist group now seems to control the church and these principles of church organization— lay leadership, seniority as the basis for promotion, selection on other bases than theological learning, and control of appointments by conservative elements—make the advancement of liberals into church leadership very unlikely in the next several years." It can safely be said that these conditions still prevail. The one major change in this respect is the appearance of an intellectual journal which is nonpartisan within the range of accepted Mormon positions. This publication, *Dialogue*, affords a medium of expression and discussion for the intellectuals and may have great significance for the church's future. It provided what has long been lacking: a regular outlet for authentic Mormon intellectual activity.

Rationality versus Charisma

This is an area of strain and conflict closely related to the encounter with modernity, but one that is inherent within Mormon doctrine itself. Mormonism has always been inclined toward practical rationality, but it has also given central significance to charismatic phenomena. This is not merely a matter of the routinized charisma of office, since the Mormons attribute to the office of the church president an unroutinized channel of communication between God and man. The president of the church is the successor of the prophet Joseph and is God's "prophet, seer, and revelator" upon the earth. Moreover private revelations are claimed, and are approved by the church so long as they are for personal guidance and make no claim to authority in the church. There is also the performance of faith healing rites, the "healing ordinances," and there is the ever-present millennialism. How does this set with the practical rationality? In the earlier rural situation it was not too difficult to put the two together, but with urbanization and higher education the two are less reconcilable.

Authority and Obedience versus Democracy and Individualism

The Mormon church began as a congregational polity and was soon transformed under the impact of charismatic leadership into an authoritarian structure. Today democratic forms remain, but they are mere forms. The church conferences in April and October vote to "sustain" the general authorities of the church, but since God guides the church through the president such sustaining votes are now taken for granted. Yet at the same time Mormonism continues to place a tremendous emphasis upon man's freedom and responsibility. It is remarkable how well the church has succeeded in involving a large proportion of its members in voluntary participation while keeping policy-making centralized and hierarchically structured. Yet this area remains a potential source of strain, and for the intellectuals it is a deeply felt one.

133

Consent versus Coercion

The problem of dissent and how to handle it has been a major one in Mormon history. Although the church has generally won consent from its members, it has at times used coercion against its dissidents. At Nauvoo when a highly articulate opposition to the prophet made its appearance, the leadership used coercion and the consequences were nearly disastrous. But the death of the prophet at the hands of outside enemies reestablished the sacredness of the official church leadership. In early Utah the Danites, a church-sponsored terrorist group, helped to keep down dissent, although it may indeed be the case that church loyalty would have preserved unity behind the leadership without such extreme measures.

Plural Marriage versus Change of Doctrine

The church made a heroic stand to defend its marriage doctrine and practice against the federal government, and although it was forced to back down there were many in the church who were in favor of not giving in. But in reality the church had to compromise and it did. It took the position that plural marriage was the ideal form of marriage but that men were not yet worthy of it, and that it had to be suspended. The church admonished its members to obey the law of the land. However, one small group—the so-called Mormon fundamentalists—broke off from the church, set up a parallel ecclesiastical structure, claimed to be the true church, and continued to practice polygamy. Erickson (1922: 77) stated that there were those "in the Church who believe that neither the government nor the Church has the right to eliminate an institution divinely established. This is the most consistent orthodox class. There are a few men of the Mormon faith who believe they have the authority to solemnize plural marriages, and consequently these marriages are still performed. A large percentage of these polygamists have been excommunicated from the Church." This fundamentalist group still survives and involves several thousand people. In 1953 a fundamentalist settlement in the "Arizona strip" on the Utah-Arizona line was raided by order of the governor of Arizona;

some 120 men and women were arrested by a force of over 100 state and local policemen. According to Day (1963: 53), the governor expressed the fear that the small sect community at Short Creek was growing so rapidly that in another ten years it "would be in the thousands."

Family Ideals versus Equality of Women

It is important to note that, while Mormonism accepted patriarchal ideals of the family with plural marriage and while these ideals were not repudiated after plural marriage was no longer practiced, the Mormons nevertheless generally accepted and advocated the equality of women with men. The idea of equality for women was apparent in Utah territorial laws, which gave women the right to vote in 1870. Women actually voted in Salt Lake City in the municipal elections in February of that year, a year before women voted in Wyoming. Wyoming is credited with having first established woman suffrage, however, since its law was enacted in 1869. In the Mormon-Gentile conflict of the period this situation gave rise to the anomaly of eastern feminists so strongly against Mormon marriage institutions, which they considered to be slavery for women, that they supported the abolition of woman suffrage in Utah. The Mormon contrariety of emphasis on both partriarchialism and on equality for women has been a source of strain in the past, but today only a vestige of it seems to remain.

Advocacy of Progress versus Agrarianism

Mormon doctrine teaches that men are both intelligent and free, and that they are placed in this world as a necessary episode in the course of an eternal progress to godlike status. The doctrine has always possessed a strong worldly emphasis, and the Mormons have generally been strongly oriented to material progress here and now, as can be seen from the history of their community-building activities. They have always been open to technological and social inventions and have always eschewed the rigidities of dress and practice characteristic of other religious groups to whom they have at times been compared. In early Utah the church itself played the central part in promoting economic development, and the Mormon people were highly motivated toward the achievement of economic growth. In his economic history Arrington (1958: 411-412) observed:

> The policies and practices applied by the Mormons in developing their desert habitat, it should be recalled, although different from those generally applied on other Western frontiers, had their origin in the cultural milieu of ante-bellum America. Thus, they had much in common with traditional American experience. If there was anything distinctive in the Mormon venture, it was the scale on which the experiment was carried out, the degree of success achieved in the face of overwhelming obstacles, and the intensity of application and continuity of policy over a long time. Above all, in an era increasingly hostile to all forms of collectivism, the Mormons demonstrated the effectiveness of central planning and voluntary cooperation in developing a large semi-arid region. As the waste involved in the short-sighted, unplanned, and ruthless exploitation of other Western frontiers became more apparent, the Mormon pattern became increasingly appreciated—became recognized as prophetic of the pattern which the entire West would ultimately have to adopt.

In this connection, I have written (O'Dea 1957: 154): "Freedom, rationality, the universe a world to conquer (a projection of the American continent to infinity), progress, self-improvement, mastery—these are the basic principles of Mormon theology. . . . Mormonism has elaborated an American theology of self-deification through effort, an active transcendentalism of achievement." However, what the Mormons sought to develop was a pre-Civil War society based upon agriculture. Here again the Mormons tended to theologize a general American preference of the time. With continued urbanization in the country as a whole, and in Utah as well, with a majority of the population no longer deriving its livelihood from farming, there has arisen a LDS urban middle class. This middle class has, however, brought from its recent rural roots a kind of agrarian mentality and ideology into city life. Lowry Nelson (1952: 279-280) has called attention to this agrarian heritage and its significance:

> The economic virtues which were associated with agrarianism and which the Mormons not only accepted but had ground into their culture by their experiences on the frontier, were hard work and long hours, frugality and thrift, getting ahead economically, and self-sufficiency for the individual and the community. Wealth-getting which was condemned by the early Christian Fathers as sinful was applauded by the Mormons. . . . The point of this discussion is that while agrarian ideas persist in official policy, the membership of the Church is largely composed of persons not engaged in agriculture. . . . In spite of these shifts of the membership the Church has taken no steps to define the relationships of men in an industrial-urban society, comparable say to the labor encyclical of Pope Leo XIII for the Catholic Church, or the statements of the Church of England, the Federal Council of the Churches of Christ in America, or the World Council of Churches.

As a consequence of this agrarian tendency in their thinking, urban middle-class Mormons tend to perceive and define social problems, and project personal ambitions and goals, in a form that took concrete shape in the context of a farming way of life. Hard work, effort, application, and initiative appear to many to be sufficient to solve social and economic problems, while measures taken by the government, especially the federal government, are immoral. As with many middle-class Americans in recent decades what may be called "yeoman values" were brought by the Latter-day Saints into urban life, but again in the Mormon case they tend to be theologized and reinforced by sacralization. I have commented previously on two results of this persistence of agrarian ideology (O'Dea 1957: 252):

> One is that it is freed from the context of the farm and even of the church and prepares the urban Mormon to take part successfully in the competitive modern society and economy. The individualism of

agrarian life is projected into the city occupations and especially into those areas where the church does not command or evoke cooperation and thus makes for an even more aggressive version of competitive middle-class mores. The second result of this agrarian ideology is that the church officialdom does not come to terms with contemporary problems in a contemporary way. Modern industrial relations, limitations of hours of work in factory and office, and the inhibition of the businessman's quest for wealth by social regulation—all brought into existence by a complex, highly differentiated, and interrelated industrial society—tend to be seen from the older agrarian viewpoint. While Catholic and Protestant bodies have concretized Christian teachings with regard to industrial society and its problems, the Mormon leadership has failed to meet this new situation.

A significant further consequence has been the political conservatism of the church leadership and of important church people. Thus, the ability to innovate and the flexibility of adaptation, so characteristic of the long Mormon history of experiment and institution-building, has largely been lost. Many Mormons are finding it difficult to handle the complexity of our rapidly changing society, with its many-sided technological and communications revolutions, and come to seek symbolic solutions or at least refuge in such right-wing movements as the John Birch Society. Four years ago Robert Welch spoke at a meeting in Salt Lake City during the April conferences of the Mormon church, and the *New York Times* reported that Mormon liberals feared that a move was afoot to give the society some kind of favored status in the church. Apostle Ezra Taft Benson, former Secretary of Agriculture and father of a leader in the society, was originally scheduled to introduce Welch to the audience of Mormon elders from across the nation. But he canceled his plans, apparently because of the expression of strong opposition from some church leaders.

Political Conservatism versus Social Idealism

This conflict is closely related to the former and is often found concretely intertwined with it. While the Mormons developed what has been called a "yeoman ethic," and while such an ethic tends to foster conservatism in the transformed industrial-urban situation, the Mormons also developed what can fairly be called strong socialistic elements in their approach to economic life. They built a cooperative community and made wide use of a variety of cooperative techniques in their successful settlement of the intermountain West. As a consequence of this interesting history, post-frontier Mormonism has exhibited tendencies toward social idealism and cooperation, as well as tendencies toward political and economic conservatism. The conservative tendency has been especially marked in the ranks of church leadership, but it is a widely diffused one in the church.

With the coming of the depression in the 1930's, there was some rekindling of the old cooperative ideal among church members. In 1939, the conservative counselor to the president of the church, J. Reuben Clark, Jr., chided those who saw in modern social programs the equivalent of the United Order in the 19th century. The United Order at one time established socialist communities in Utah and Nevada and was approved of by Brigham Young and the church leadership. With the presidency of John Taylor, however, forms of cooperation which gave a bigger role to private business were adopted. It is of interest to this study to note that the more socialistic forms of cooperation seem to have been more popular in the south of Utah and the adjoining Mormon areas. In 1939, President Clark stated (O'Dea 1957: 254): "There is a growing—I fear it is growing—sentiment that communism and the United Order are the same thing, communism being merely the forerunner, so to speak, of a reestablishment of the United Order. I am informed that ex-bishops, and indeed, bishops, who belong to communistic organizations are preaching this doctrine." By "communism" Clark probably referred to something rather less radical than the Stalinism of the 1930's.

Since World War II the church leadership has remained conservative and possibly become more so. The older cooperative spirit among the membership, which had been mobilized in a church welfare plan to meet the needs of the poor during the depression and continued long afterwards, also remained largely latent or was expressed within safe ecclesiastical confines. In the

1960's a new problem—the problem of race relations in American society—arose within the church to challenge the conservative leadership and to arouse the social idealism of its more liberal members and its more modernized youth. I shall discuss that problem and its status below.

Patriotism versus Particularism

I have already pointed out that what the Mormons developed in the settlement of the intermountain region was an indigenous ethnicity—or more accurately a quasi-ethnicity, since the forms of awareness accompanying its development did not become unambiguously and explicitly ethnic in content and character. Yet there was definitely a conception of peoplehood. Having imitated the ancient Hebrew model, the Mormons produced something like their own Israel, what they considered "a holy nation, a royal priesthood." In the course of this development they found themselves often engaged in conflict with outsiders and with the government. Their theological conceptions define them as a peculiarly chosen people. Hence there is in the Mormon outlook a central and profound element of particularism.

Yet the Mormons have also always felt themselves to be very much American, and in fact their history shows them in strategically significant ways to represent a typically American development in religion. They originated in America; their central values bear a pronounced American impression. The Mormons have long exhibited a strange dialectical relationship to America. They have been involved in profound conflict with America, but they have also not inaccurately been characterized as an "America in miniature." They have exhibited a combination of typicality and peculiarity. This ambiguity has at times led to separatism, as I have already noted. But with the end of the polygamy conflict and Utah's subsequent admission to the Union, the church has placed a strong stress on the virtue of patriotism.

Belief versus Environment

Under this heading in my original study I grouped a variety of conflicts to be observed in Mormon history. The fact that Mormons were oriented to agriculture as the proper ethical economic basis of life and were acting accordingly amidst the

potential mineral wealth of Utah brought some conflict in territorial days. The fact that Mormons in Missouri believed themselves to be peculiarly called by God helped to antagonize their
neighbors. In Utah, the Mormon stress upon large families made
it necessary for many to migrate, which in turn conflicted with
the long-standing Mormon preference to live in Zion. But perhaps
the most difficult of these conflicts is that involving the peculiar
Mormon belief about, and attitude toward, the Indians.

Basing themselves upon the *Book of Mormon*, the Latter-day
Saints consider the American Indians to be the descendants of
Hebrews who migrated to this continent. Moreover, they hold
that it is part of their own vocation and mission as a divinely
restored church to prepare for the second coming of Christ.
According to Mormon doctrine that coming will be to the New
World, and the millenial kingdom will be built here. The *Book of
Mormon* relates that Christ came to this continent and showed
himself to the Hebrews here in the brief period between His
resurrection and His ascension into heaven. Central to this complex of ideas is the status and character of the Indians. The
church holds it to be part of its mission to convert the Indians
and enlist them in the building of the kingdom in preparation for
the millennium. This is an old belief in the church and before the
LDS church left New York it had already sent out missionaries to
the Cattaraugus Indians near Buffalo. The church still believes
the statement in the *Book of Mormon* that when the Indians,
called in their fallen state the "Lamanites," are converted they
will once again become a "white and delightsome people." (II
Nephi 30: 6). In Missouri, Mormon talk about converting the
Indians and having them as companions in the building of Zion
contributed to the growing hostility of the Missourians.

In Utah, although the Mormons killed four Indian cattle
thieves at the very outset of settlement, and although they
fought the so-called Black Hawk War against the Indians in 1867,
they established better relationships with the Indians than did
most Anglo-American settlers. In the valley of the Great Salt
Lake the sparseness of the Indian population made them a cause
of little difficulty to settlers. Yet elsewhere there was considerable contact and many attempts at missionizing. In this respect
the career of Jacob Hamblin is interesting since he spent a

lifetime as a missionary and peacemaker among the Indians (Bailey 1948). In the Utah War of 1857 a group of Mormons in southern Utah attacked and massacred a wagon train of Missourians who were passing through on the way to California. In this they were joined by Indians who apparently saw this as an alliance with the Mormons to fight against the "Mericats," as they designated non-Mormon Americans (Brooks 1950).

Yet the Mormons were of general American background, and they also quickly assimilated their European converts to American attitudes. Moreover, they were pioneers, and as such could not but enter into the kinds of relationships and competition which necessarily prevail between colonists and a local population which they threaten to displace. Consequently the Mormons also developed a pioneer attitude toward the Indians, seeing them as inferior and in certain ways undesirable, which conflicted with the favorable attitudes deriving from their religious conceptions of the Indians and of America.

Some of these sources of strain and conflict remain important in Mormon life and are today characteristic of the situation of the Mormon church, while others are largely a matter of history. Yet history is the crucible out of which emerge the attitudes and orientations of the present. All of these sources of strain and conflict characteristic of their experience have conditioned the present-day outlooks, values, and ideals of the Mormons. In the issues of the encounter with secular thought, authority and obedience, progress versus agrarianism, political conservatism, and patriotism versus particularism, there is much that appears central to the Mormon belief system and very much of contemporary concern. Issues dealing with rationality versus charisma and plural marriage versus change of doctrine also possess some genuine present-day reality. The issue of Mormon attitudes toward Indians also remains of significance, especially in the Southwest.

The Negro and the Mormon Priesthood: Manifest and Latent Elements

In the 1930's, as the Mormon Church and the nation as a whole faced the depression, the church leadership exhibited a strongly conservative attitude. At that time the significant area of conflict between liberal Mormons and the conservative leadership, in addition to the more strictly religious contention of liberalism versus literalism in the understanding of the scriptures, was focused upon economic issues, especially on opposition to or support for New Deal policies. These issues possessed a profound resonance with Mormon history and Mormon values, as was seen in the discussion of political conservatism versus social ideals. While these issues remain important in new forms in our day, the 1960's brought to the fore an issue of its own. The decade began with the tremendous national struggle around the issue of civil rights, and as it went by there came the issue of the Vietnamese war. Both of these represented issues of authentic content in their own right; their manifest content was real and serious. But they were also symbolic of larger and deeper issues. Their connotations moved out into the semiconsciousness of the American public—into those areas of deeper fears, allegiances, antagonisms, anxieties, hopes, and aspirations which precede and undergird the manifest issues of political life. Beneath the manifest contents of these issues lay the latent contents of consciousness, for which they served as symbolic catalysts. This deeper level for every social group is the product of that group's historical experience, and the meaning of issues and events for each group exhibits the consequences of that history.

For Mormons too the 1960's gave prominence to the problem of race, and Mormon history and experience had already endowed that issue with a special Mormon meaning. Racial issues came to the fore at a time when Mormonism was facing its transitional problems in a new setting—the setting of being reintegrated into an American society in which rapid change and a vast communications revolution were effecting a radical detraditionalization of thought and behavior. Beneath the manifest phenomena of the church's confrontation with race lie the many half-conscious problems which seek their way to open expression around the key symbolic catalyst of that issue. There are all the problems involved in the continuing encounter with modern secular thought, which now as before challenge the fundamental horizon and basic ground of the Mormon faith. There are all the problems involved in the transition from a rural to an urban way of life, and the concomitant adaptations of attitude and outlook demanded by change. There is the intensification of all these problems by the communications revolution, which destroys so much of the spiritual isolation in which Mormonism developed. These problems, which cannot but be present in some form for many who do not and cannot formulate them articulately, are part of the latent level which church leaders and members bring to the current confrontation. Further, the history of conflict and persecution, the history of achievement and group self-confirmation, the history of defeat in the polygamy struggle, the history of accommodation and concomitant secularization that followed—all these lie behind and help form that latent level.

Some elements of the situation in which the Mormon church finds itself today are that most of its membership is no longer gathered unto Zion, that it has a large middle-class membership involved in general national problems in many ways, that the Wasatch Front—Ogden, Salt Lake City and Provo—is being rapidly urbanized, and that new attitudes are rapidly making their way into the heart of Mormondom. There are also the rigidification of church structure and religious attitude reinforced by the continuing gerontocratic rule of the leadership, and the attraction of rightist politics already noted. Salt Lake City, the historic center of Mormonism, today faces all the modern problems of juvenile delinquency, the impersonalization of urban life, religious crisis and doubt among university students, and the search of youth for new values and new identities. In these circumstances there teases at the backs of people's minds a question of a most disturbing sort—a question of legitimacy, of sense of direction, of prospects for the future. Americans begin to ask where is America going, is our way right, will we survive, and in what shape? Parallel questions are provoked by the contemporary Mormon situation concerning the church. As always in situations where history sets the stage for the eliciting of such fundamental questions, many defense mechanisms are utilized, mostly unconsciously, to avoid the pain and anxiety of the questioning: repression of doubt, displacement of issues, expression of antagonism, etc.

The Curse of Complexion

The question of the status of the Negro in relation to the Mormon priesthood is the new symbolic issue which is related in a profoundly complex and largely unconscious way with these deeper problems. The frustrations, the threats, and the confusions involved in these problems deserve the most serious study. It is these that have found an amorphous and unclear expression around the issue of the exclusion of the Negro from its priesthood, which is a central problem facing the Mormon church. This is true both with respect to its internal structure and to its external relationship to an American society, which itself grapples with the problems of race relations amidst growing violence.

On this issue Wallace Turner (1966: 218-219) has written:

> The most serious problem facing the LDS church today is the Negro question. The church has successfully become everyman's church—except it cannot be the African Negro's church. . . .
>
> The Negro is barred from the priesthood purely on racial grounds. As we untangle the theology, we must always remember that every devout male Mormon—except the Negro—is expected to become a member of the Aaronic priesthood as a boy of twelve years and a member of the Melchizedek priesthood at eighteen or twenty years. . . . But Negroes are barred from this advancement. . . .
>
> There are many positions taken within the Mormon world on these matters. The ultra-conservatives look on the problem for Negroes as just one of those things that are inflicted unhappily on other people who should accept their fate humbly—and quietly. The conservatives believe that the Lord has told them that the Africans are not to be taken into the priesthood, and that's that. The ultra-liberals take the position that this interpretation of the scriptures is absolute nonsense. The scholars attempt to reason a way out of it. The vast center of the church just accepts it without question. The apostates, who hate the church anyway, take the position that it's all to the good, that maybe the Saints will wreck themselves, and the rising aspirations of the American Negro will help shove them onto the rocks.

David L. Brewer (1968: 521-522) has explained the origin of this policy as follows:

The Negro policy was anticipated in 1830 by the *Book of Mormon*'s doctrine of the curse. The Lamanites, ancestors of the American Indians, were cursed with a dark skin when they rebelled against God. Following publication of the *Book of Mormon*, Joseph Smith published the first part of the *Book of Moses*, which declared that "a blackness came upon all the children of Canaan, that they were despised among all people."

Still later, the "Mormon Missouri Compromise" occurred, as a result of persecution by proslavery settlers. The Mormon newcomers were identified as tactless zealots, who favored the abolition of slavery. To prevent a conflict, a Mormon newspaper published in 1833 an article suggesting that members avoid controversy over the slavery issue—a reasonable request since most of the Saints were Yankees and Yorkers. But the article angered the Missourians, apparently because it also mentioned the possible abolition of slavery. To further placate the non-Mormons, the editor wrote another article, insisting his original intent had been to keep Negroes from coming to Missouri *and* from becoming Mormons. Although the editorial retreat didn't prevent trouble, it did have a significant effect upon the Mormon racial mentality.

The compromise was complete when Joseph Smith began to defend slavery. He also began translating the "Book of Abraham," used later to justify excluding Negroes from the priesthood. In this document Pharaoh is identified as a descendant of the Canaanites through Ham. Interestingly, Mormons also identified the Canaanites with Cain, and thus consider the curse of Cain as the apparatus through which a lineage was provided for rebellious spirits.

Joseph Smith subsequently opposed slavery but his later views were not sacralized in scripture. . . .

The best biography of Joseph Smith, although it was found unacceptable by the LDS church, states (Brodie 1945: 173): "The Book of Abraham in effect crystallized Joseph's hitherto vacillating position on the Negro problem. . . . Perhaps this atti-tude was merely a concession to Missouri." Although Joseph Smith died at a time when he was advocating the abolition of slavery, and when the church position itself seemed not yet definitively formed, the earlier view came to prevail (Brodie 1945: 365): "The Utah Church accepted the ideological fruits of Joseph's earlier stand, which actually had been a political com-promise, and rejected the more courageous about-face because it was merely an utterance in a political campaign."

The Current Crisis

With the short-lived bid of George Romney for the Republi-can presidential nomination, the Mormon race policy became a national issue (Harris 1967: 207):

"George Romney has precipitated a crisis in the Mormon Church that may well rank with the plague of the locusts," says a delighted Arizona State Univer-sity professor and Mormon, L. Mayland Parker. Along with other young LDS thinkers, Parker has carefully demolished most of the theology behind the Negro exclusion, including the passages in *A Pearl of Great Price*. He believes his church is stuck with a practice, not a doctrine and, like other churches, can now change without revelation. But LDS conservatives, sensing that the Negro issue is the first stage of a general de-mythology drive, resist the young men rising to demand reform.

On June 21, 1970, *The New York Times* carried the fol-lowing item:

The Mormon Church has been getting advice re-cently from members on the right and left about criticism of its practice of excluding Negroes from priesthood orders.

A widely known Mormon conservative had circu-lated an information package that attempts to equate criticism of the church with attempts to advance a Communist conspiracy.

From the liberal side has come a small book that argues that the Negro exclusion policy is not based in doctrine, but was started to meet political needs that

147

were recognized by Joseph Smith, the founder of the Church of Jesus Christ of Latter-Day Saints.

The book, "Mormonism's Negro Policy: Social and Historical Origins," was written by Stephen C. Taggart, a graduate student at Cornell University. Mr. Taggart died Aug. 1, 1969. The book was prepared for publication by his widow, Pamela. His father is Glen L. Taggart, president of Utah State University at Logan.

Mr. Taggart's book cannot be characterized as an attack on church policy. Rather, it is an examination of the historical evidence that demonstrates, as Mr. Taggart wrote, that "The Negro policy and its attendant teachings all developed on an informal basis in response to historical circumstances rather than through revelation."

. . . .

"The weight of the evidence suggests that God did not place a curse upon the Negro—that His white children did," Mr. Taggart wrote. "The evidence also suggests that the time for correcting the situation is long past due."

Meantime, from W. Cleon Skousen, a right-wing Mormon spokesman, has come a warning that Communists have set out to criticize the church and its institutions.

Mr. Skousen's statement is attached to reprints of an article taken from the Oct. 18, 1969, issue of *World Magazine*, an insert prepared for the *Daily World* and *People's World*, Communist organs.

The article reprinted by Mr. Skousen argues that Negroes are mistreated in Utah because of the Mormon numerical superiority there. It also lists some of the church's financial interests in radio and television stations, and newspapers. Pictures of politically prominent Republican Mormons are captioned "Nixon's Mormons."

. . . .

In distributing copies of this article, Mr. Skousen attached to it his analysis headed "Subject: Communist Press Calls for Attack on L.D.S. Church." The analysis called the article "a signal to the Communist 'transmission belt' to go to work."

There have been many repercussions of this issue. Black athletes at the University of Wyoming have refused to play against teams from BYU, while Stanford University has declared its intention to sever athletic relations with BYU.

The controversy has also tended to focus some attention upon the *Book of Abraham*. Three years ago parts of the original papyri from which Smith claimed to have translated the book were found in New York's Metropolitan Museum, and the *New York Times* for May 3, 1970, cautiously commented: "Examination of these originals has heightened the confidence of some Egyptologists that the Book of Abraham is not a translation." The paper also reported that Richard P. Howard, official historian of the Reorganized Church of Jesus Christ of Latter Day Saints, which rejected these and other innovations which Smith claimed in scripture and revelation, had recently published an article calling the *Book of Abraham* "simply the product of Joseph Smith, Jr.'s imagination." The author of the article, printed in the pilot issue of *Courage: A Journal of History, Thought and Action*, was said to have also written: "Whatever the intent of Joseph Smith in expounding this view of the Negro . . . it is clear that the ancient papyri from Egypt contain no such information."

The question of the Negro and the priesthood has indeed become a major controversy in the church, and on the latent level it stands in close relation to profound problems deriving from the great historic transition being undergone by both the church and the nation. The liberal elements in the church see it as a reference point for protest against the dedication to the status quo on the part of the conservative leadership. It symbolizes for them the challenge of modernity to the older conservative interpretation of Mormon teachings to which the church has generally clung in this century. It arouses not only the older concern with social idealism, the older opposition to authoritarianism, and the older desire to go beyond literalism, but also the challenge of the new—of facing together with the nation as a whole the need to stand up to profound social problems in America. The conservatives, on the other hand, find in it the symbolic issue for holding the line against the latest onslaughts of modernity and secularism. They see it as a line that must be held for the preservation of old positions on church authority, on scripture and revelation, on political conservatism, and on the quasi-isolationism of the Mormon community.

All the inchoate, obscure, and deeply disturbing feelings aroused by the present transition of the country, of the inter-mountain West, and of the church itself are involved in the problem of the Negro and the priesthood. This problem is the master symbol of the conflict between elements for and against modernity in the church. It permits and enables further coalescence of liberal religion with liberal politics and of conservative religion with conservative politics. While symbolic responses of this kind enable people to express their anxieties and insecurities, and thereby provide some catharsis and some relief, it is doubtful that catharsis and symbolic expression can help very much in untangling the complex of issues and problems which give rise to the profound malaise that requires such catharsis. Protest and resistance within the church may start with this issue, but what is required is the open examination of the deeper issues which derive from Mormonism's confrontation with modernity. Such an examination requires that the Mormon intellectuals play a more significant role in the church. The appearance of the journal *Dialogue*, and the Taggart book offer some indication that they may have begun to make some headway.

The Elements of Ethnic Identity: The Mormon Case

Spicer has suggested three categories indicating in a general way the content of those terms which are usually employed to designate ethnicity, and has suggested the possibility of a fourth. There is first a "cultural content," which often involves language although this is not necessarily the case. Second is "a sense of distinctive historical experience." Third is the image of the group "vis-a-vis all other groups, or at least vis-a-vis the dominant group."

Cultural Content

With respect to cultural content in the Mormon case, it consists first in commitment to the teachings of the Mormon church. Spicer has suggested that there is involved in this cultural content "a feeling for if not a conscious and articulated awareness of behavioral differences." He also comments, with some of the more traditional ethnic groups in the Southwest obviously in mind, that "awareness of and willingness to give high priority to traditional forms of kinship obligation, in other words to fulfill traditional behaviors, are usually of great importance in the common identification." Behavior in terms of what we have characterized as the "work, health, recreation, and education complex," together with activity in the church and its auxiliary organizations, is an important kind of identity behavior in the Mormon case. So is observance of the abstention from coffee, tea, alcohol, and tobacco commanded by the church. This has become a very important mark of good standing, although it was for many decades of Mormon history regarded as optional—as "counsel" rather than as "commandment." In a similar category we may place the practice of tithing. When I lived as a participant observer in a rural Mormon village in New Mexico in 1950-1951, the church in that village, consisting of 41 families and 241 persons of all ages, paid $8,850 in tithes to the general authorities. There were some families on church relief and some who did not tithe.

The significance of activity must also be stressed. The Mormon church is an activity-oriented organization and one that keeps statistics on its activities. Nelson (1952: 285) wrote of what he called the "tripartite division of the Church into *regulars*, *casuals*, and *nevers*. . . . " The sizes of these three classes, the kinds of interstitial individuals to be found at their edges and between them, and the ways in which nonregulars are treated by the regulars and by the church organization are important questions about which there is no data for any extended treatment. Regularity, occasionalness, and nonparticipation must be seen and characterized in relation to church attendance, tithing, abstention from the use of stimulants, and activity in the church and its auxiliary organizations. Other behavioral matters of significance are admission to the priesthood bodies and regular advancement through the various stages (which depends upon abstinence, participation, and general behavior, that is, "worthiness"), temple marriage ("for time and eternity"), and participation in temple work (vicarious baptism for the dead, a ritual which reinforces Mormon familism and strengthens ties between family and formal church organization).

Historical Experience

Enough has already been said in this paper to make it evident in the Mormon case how centrally significant is Spicer's second category. The Mormons are aware of themselves as a people apart with a special sacred history. That history is taught by the church; it is in fact a basic element in the church's formal teaching. It is also passed on in the more informal family context, where it is presented from the point of view of the family itself and of the family's part in the special sacred history of the Mormon people. In terms of the positive and negative aspects of the felt common experience of one's ancestors, the Mormon case is an interesting one. The Mormon feels this history to be something extremely positive—to be his people's participation in the divine plan calling the elect out of the unregenerate world. But the facts indicate the Mormons have actually had a difficult history and were often the victims of hostility. This experience has left a very definite residue in Mormon consciousness, a kind of defensiveness which recent commentators have observed, despite the changed conditions of Mormon life in the 20th century. For example, (Harris 1967: 207) spoke of the Mormon church as being the victim of a "persecution complex which hangs it up." However the Mormons are a particular kind of minority group; they are a minority group which became the chief settlers of an area; they are what Hughes (1943) characterized as a "charter member minority." Moreover the Mormons are a minority group who have moved from a despised and persecuted minority to an eminently respectable one (Dwyer 1941).

Self-Image

What has just been said about the Mormon sense of history is significant as well for the category of "image." The Mormons do have a definite image of themselves as a different and separate people. Like all such images, the Mormon image in part reflects reality and in part is fictitious. For example, in the 1930's the church leadership was conservative and took a strongly antagonistic position with respect to the New Deal. For the church leadership and many members free enterprise became something close to a sacred category and a religious value, and for many this remains largely true today. This conviction is intertwined with the work ethic, the insistence upon individual initiative, and the emphasis upon family responsibility. To meet the depression the church established the Church Welfare Plan, a vast cooperative enterprise, a kind of ecclesiastical socialism, established to counter the "socialistic" measures of the government. The plan provided a great quantity of food and clothing, gave work to unemployed church members, and helped the needy in other ways. For some time afterwards one often heard Mormons say that they did not need federal relief because they took care of their own. Actually, however, there were considerable numbers of Mormons on various kinds of federal aid programs and the importance of federal help in Mormon areas was great. The self-image generated by these welfare activities was only partially reflective of reality. Spicer commented that the Yaqui example shows that the "elements of the image are clearly a moral evaluation of the group in relation to others. . . . " This is true as well in the Mormon case. The Mormon self-image is that of a chosen people, participating in the mission of the true church, a people with a special history which has made them different; a people who are hard-working, honest, healthy, highly literate, who place a high value on education; a people who do not drink or smoke or otherwise abuse themselves, etc.

Sacred Homeland

Spicer further stated that "the Hopis, the Yaquis and probably in fact all the Indian groups possess an identity anchor which is lacking in the case of Anglos and Spanish-speaking peoples. This is the sacred land concept which is fundamental in the identity system of traditional Hopis and Yaquis and all the rest. . . . " It was shown earlier that the Mormons represent a case of an ethnic identity—or quasi-ethnic identity—which has emerged in a brief but intense history on this continent. Imitating the biblical Hebrews under conditions that made mimesis real, the Mormons became a "people." Part of the Hebraic notion of "peoplehood" was the idea of a "promised land," important to the Mormons from the very beginning. They had tried to build their community in Missouri, which Joseph Smith had declared to be "the land of promise, and the place for the city of Zion" (*Doctrine and Covenants*, 57: 2). Sidney Rigdon, at the time second only to the prophet in importance in the church, asked the new arrivals in Missouri: "Do you receive this land for your inheritance with thankful hearts from the Lord?" The people replied: "We do." (O'Dea, 1957: 42).

This feeling was transferred later to the intermountain West. While the church still officially teaches that Missouri is the place where Christ will return in the last days, the popular feeling of Mormons is that Utah—to borrow from a statement of Brigham Young—"is the place." Utah is seen as the true Mormon homeland —Utah and the surrounding Mormon areas of adjoining states. The Mormons feel that the text of Isaiah 35: 1 has a special relevance for them, and they have inscribed it upon the monument which stands at the place where Brigham Young and the pioneer party entered the valley of the Great Salt Lake to begin the Mormon settlement of the region: "The wilderness and the solitary place shall be glad for them; and the desert shall rejoice, and blossom as the rose." They also feel that their own efforts at God's command have fulfilled the prophecy of Isaiah 2: 2: "And it shall come to pass in the last days, that the mountain of the Lord's house shall be established in the top of the mountains, and shall be exalted above the hills; and all nations shall flow into it."

The landscape of the intermountain West takes on a sacred character for the Mormons, as can be seen in the hymnody of the church. Yet in the last three decades there has been an enormous migration of Mormons out of the Mormon country. They have gone to California, especially to southern California where they now have a temple in Los Angeles, to the Middle West, and to the East. The last four presidential cabinets have contained Mormon members, the present having two. Moreover conversion no longer involves emigration to Zion. In recent years the church has built temples outside the Western Hemisphere, indicating that one can now be "gathered" without moving bodily to the Mormon country in the West. In the 19th century, the church's Perpetual Emigrating Fund brought some 90,000 immigrants from Europe to the West. In those days one did not merely join the church; one was physically gathered unto Zion. Now there is a Mormon diaspora— again resembling the Hebrew model—but this time aspects of the

Hebrew model that are not at all salient in the earlier period. Yet Utah is still the center, for as Jewish history in antiquity demonstrated, dispersion is not inconsistent with reverence for a homeland and a holy city.

Ethnic Policies and Attitudes

In the Mormon case we have the Mormon people, an informal category whose chief basis of unity is the family, and the Mormon church—the Church of Jesus Christ of Latter-day Saints, a formal religious organization subject to formal leadership. Hence when the question of policy is discussed, it must be recognized that it has a dual application. There is formal church policy, and there are the popular attitudes of church members. Much that has been written here with respect to Mormon beliefs, the Mormon sense of a common historical experience, and the image or self-definition of the Mormon people contains implicitly a great deal that is relevant to the notion of ethnic policy. This is true whether such policy is considered on the formal level of explicit church policy or on the informal level of typical attitudes and behavior of Mormons toward outsiders.

Church Policy

As a formal organization, the Mormon church is committed to proselytization and a good deal of Mormon energy is spent in missionary effort. At the beginning of the 1970's there were 12,000 full-time Mormon missionaries serving two-year missions, largely at their own expense but with some help from their home wards at times. In addition there is local missionary work carried out by the local ward in its own area. The church is oriented to the conversion of all, but it must be noted that its conception of conversion is of a rather sectarian character. The church seeks to call all to conversion, but it does not expect to convert all. In this sense it is more like what Troeltsch calls a "sect" than what he designates as a "church." It expects its call to be heard and responded to only by the elect, who are to be called out from the midst of the nations. But the fact that these elect are sought everywhere—or almost everywhere—gives a somewhat universalistic cast to Mormon sectarian tendencies. The universalism attributed to Mormonism should, however, be qualified in two directions. First, the church has at times been more highly motivated than at others to do missionary work among the Indians, for reasons already indicated. Something of the same appears to be the case with respect to the Polynesians and the Maoris of New Zealand, where Mormon missions have registered considerable success. Second, Blacks are officially excluded from first-class membership in the church. This policy led the church to pass up a real opportunity in Nigeria in the middle 1960's.

Popular Attitudes

On the unofficial level, the Mormons exhibit a whole array of attitudes relevant to the topic of ethnic policies. It may be suggested that many active Mormons, the "regulars," tend to look upon white American Protestants and Catholics with a feeling of benign and benevolent superiority. With those less integrated into the church and its activities this attitude will be different, and actually a fair variety of attitudes will be found. With respect to the Negro, the general character of Black-White relations in this country for three centuries, and the official attitude of the church with respect to Negro participation in the priesthood, brings about a situation in which active church members will very often be found to have feelings of marked superiority toward Blacks and a desire not to be too closely associated with them. Indeed it has been suggested by Brewer (1966: 146) that, because of the combination of religious and secular bias against Negroes, the "dread of intermarriage, already strong in American culture, is intensified in Mormon society."

With respect to the various Spanish-speaking groups so significant in the Southwest, the Mormon orientation in many cases exhibits ambiguity. But here there is nothing in the formal teaching of the church to confirm and sacralize bias from other sources. There would be on the part of the typical active church member a desire to convert them, and the church organization makes efforts in this respect. (It may be noted here that the Mormon missionary effort has been quite vigorous and successful in parts of Latin America.) But at the same time the average church member would also participate in the usual attitudes of the Anglo milieu. In Mexico, the Mormons have been said to have gotten along well with their Mexican neighbors. Moreover, a mission was established in Mexico City around the end of the 1870's. Yet in looking over the record of residence, land ownership and school attendance for the Mormon settlement of Colonia Juárez over the years, one finds very few Mexican names. When I lived in a Mormon village in New Mexico in 1950-51, the relationships between Mormons and Spanish-Americans who owned adjoining property were positive and friendly but by no means close. But the Mormons thought of the Spanish-Americans as "good neighbors."

It has already been noted how the Mormons in their history came to develop both a missionary and a pioneer attitude toward the Indian, how they were oriented to their conversion but at the same time tended to hold a competitive, condescending attitude toward them. It is suggested that in contemporary relations with Indians Mormons will tend to exhibit this same ambiguity.

Mormons and Jews

One aspect of Mormon ethnic policies and attitudes deserves special mention. Attitudes toward the Jews have on the whole been very positive, although Jewish converts to Mormonism have been extremely few. The Mormons sent a mission to Palestine in 1841 and evidently saw their efforts related to the ingathering of Jews in the Holy Land. Early approaches to the Jews had two aspects: one the usual efforts at conversion, the second the formation of a friendly relationship, the Mormons as a chosen group feeling an affinity with another chosen group. A Jewish scholar, Glanz (1963: 78), has commented:

> Indeed, it is noteworthy that, wherever the early Mormon mission to the Jews was based on conversionist goals, it proved to be entirely futile. On the other hand, wherever it strengthened and confirmed belief in the in-gathering of the Jews into Palestine and offered the spectacle of representatives dispatched to the Jews in Palestine and throughout the world, it set a record in expanding the faith. . . . In time, an enduring atmosphere was created in which

the Mormon people continued to live even after the Mormon mission to the Jews had obviously lost any importance.

There was disappointment among Mormons in the failure to convert Jews, but there was also the belief that part of the millennium which they anticipated would be the return of the Jews into their old homeland. And to this day there is a kind of Mormon interest in the Jew as somehow like himself. Jews came to Utah in the 1860's, and as businessmen they were involved in the various conflicts of the Mormons with "Gentile" business. Yet this situation did not seem to affect attitudes to the Jews as far as their religion was concerned (Glanz 1963: 245): "The Jews in Utah had to work only for economic freedom because their existence as a separate religious group was never questioned and there was no religious battle-ground between Jew and Mormon."

Finally, Glanz (1963: 331-332) concluded: "It is also remarkable that, in addition to the historic Jewish-Christian struggle finding only weak reverberations in the new religion, the Biblical period of the Jewish people was regarded as meaningful. ... In all this Mormonism appears as the conqueror of old Christian-European inhibitions vis-a-vis Judaism and as the creator of a new relationship to the old Bible people and its religious world."

Mormons in the Southwest

The Mormons had early been interested in expansion to the south and at one time contemplated a "Mormon corridor" to the sea from Salt Lake City to San Diego, California, and at another an outlet to the sea through the Colorado River. Moreover, the armed forces which took Arizona and New Mexico from the Mexican Republic, included the Mormon Battalion, a force of 500 men recruited with Brigham Young's permission at Winter Quarters before the Mormons began their westward trek, despite the unfriendly feeling which prevailed among Mormons towards the United States at the time. Brigham Young had considered settlement in Arizona as early as the 1870's and in 1873 declared in a letter to the *New York Herald*, "We intend to establish settlements in Arizona in the country of the Apaches." Accord-

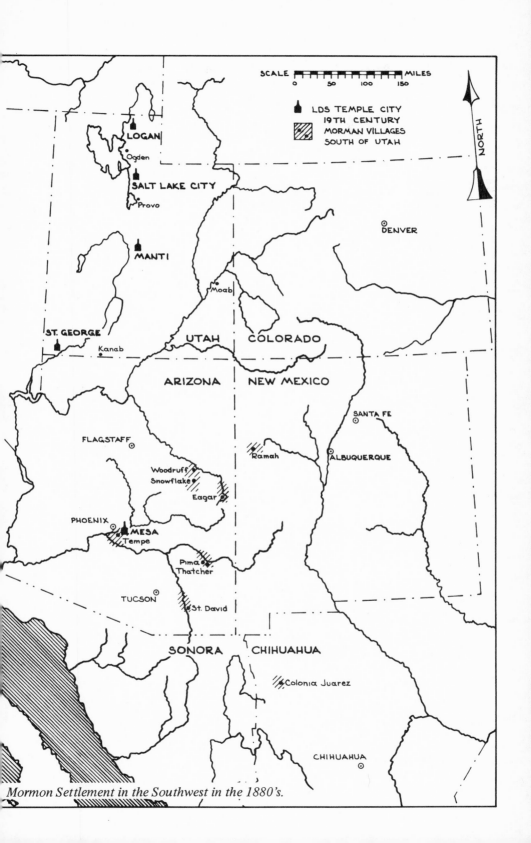

■ LDS TEMPLE CITY
▨ 19TH CENTURY
   MORMAN VILLAGES
   SOUTH OF UTAH

■ LOGAN
• Ogden

■ SALT LAKE CITY
• Provo

■ MANTI

• Moab

⊙ DENVER

■ ST. GEORGE
• Kanab

UTAH   COLORADO

ARIZONA   NEW MEXICO

SANTA FE ⊙

FLAGSTAFF ⊙

Ramah

ALBUQUERQUE ⊙

Woodruff •
Snowflake •

Eagar ▨

PHOENIX ⊙   ■ MESA
            • Tempe

Pima ▨
Thatcher •

TUCSON ⊙

St. David

SONORA   CHIHUAHUA

Colonia Juarez

CHIHUAHUA ⊙

Mormon Settlement in the Southwest in the 1880's.

ing to the official historian of the state of Arizona (McClintock 1921: 195), the leaders in each of the migrations into the Southwest were appointed by the church president, and the greater number of the settlers came by direct church "call." Settlements were established on the Little Colorado River at Sunset and Brigham City, but these first attempts were unsuccessful.

Although well-acquainted with hardship, the first Mormons to come into Arizona were frightened by the barrenness and lack of water. One group even returned disheartened to Kanab, Utah. But Brigham Young was determined and the effort went forward. At the end of the 1870's two settlements were founded across the line in New Mexico not far from Zuni Pueblo, but they were abandoned in 1880 and the settlers withdrew, presumably because of illness. In 1882, Mormons from Sunset and Brigham City, which were being abandoned, came to this New Mexican area and established Ramah, still a Mormon village today. One motivation for southern expansion at this time was to get people away from federal prosecutions against plural marriages, although there was also a real concern with missionary work among the Indians. In this early period converts were made among the Hopis, and some initial success was reported at Zuni.

Settlements in Mexico

In the mid-1880's the idea of settling in Mexico appeared an authentic possibility and negotiations were begun with Mexican authorities to that end. In January, 1885, a conference was held at St. David, Arizona, in which members of the church considered what was to be done to face the difficult situation of federal prosecution and the hunting down of polygamous husbands (Hatch 1954: 1):

> The relentless zeal of United States marshals in seeking out violators of the Edmunds-Tucker Law had put nearly all of them in danger of prison sentences. Something had to be done. The president of the Church had comfortingly promised that a place of refuge would be prepared and in fulfillment of this promise Alexander F. MacDonald, president of the Maricopa stake of Zion in Arizona, and other official scouts, had already made several exploration trips

into northern Sonora, Mexico. MacDonald was now appointed to continue exploring in northern Chihuahua where, through negotiation by Elder Thatcher, valid prospects had been opened to them.

The meeting dispersed and the word was passed to all who were in need of its comforting tidings. By mail or by messenger, it was grapevined to remotest hamlets in the Rocky Mountain region. In St. Johns, Snowflake, Sunset, Luna, Smithville in Arizona, in Savoy, Socorro and other localities in New Mexico and even in many towns in southern Utah troubled men heard the message and were moved to go in search of the promised place. A migration began that was to last for many years and as a result of which eight colonies were established in Mexico.

The Mormons established several colonies in Mexico on tracts of land purchased from the Mexican government. In 1885, Colonia Juárez, Colonia Pacheco, and Colonia Díaz were established in the state of Chihuahua. These were followed by Cave Valley in 1887 and by Colonia Dublan in 1888. The former however was soon given up. In 1892, Oaxaca was established in Sonora; in 1894, Colonia García and Colonia Chuichupa were set up in Chihuahua. In 1899, Colonia Morelos was founded in Chihuahua. After the turn of the century, in 1908, San José was established in Sonora. This was in a sense a replacement for Oaxaca, which had been destroyed by a flood a few years before. Thus some ten settlements were attempted, but Cave Valley did not really get started and Oaxaca did not last two decades, leaving a total of eight (Hatch 1954: 261).

The establishment of these colonies was difficult, but their record was for some time one of success. Their history falls into three periods. First, there was the time of settlement with its hardships and vicissitudes; second, the period of prosperity which followed successful foundation; and third, the time of troubles— the period of revolution and its attendant difficulties between 1910 and 1920 which was followed by the exodus of the Mormons. The period just before the exodus was a very difficult one for the settlers. Yet people did return to Colonia Juárez, and it was once again brought to a prosperous condition. It appears that

Colonia Dublan was also restored. In World War II, 31 young men and two young women from Colonia Juárez served in the armed forces of the United States; two men were killed. Despite their success for a time and despite the fact that President Porfirio Diaz once declared that he wished Mexico had more industrious citizens like the Mormons, they did not become integrated into Mexican life. It is striking evidence of such lack of integration that so many Mormons from Mexico became important in the church and in the United States (George Romney, for example), but none rose similarly in the Republic of Mexico. In 1954 Colonia Juárez was described in the following statement (Hatch 1954: 258): "Though the town population is but half of its pre-Exodus number, and blocks that then had a house on every lot now contain but one or two, the town in general has regained its former prosperous appearance."

Summary

What has been attempted here is the presentation of those aspects of the history and beliefs of the Latter-day Saints which are most important for understanding them as one subgroup, possessing its own subculture, in the Southwest. At the beginning the particular significance of religious and ethnic groups in the United States as identity and interest groups was noted, stressing the interrelationship of religion, ethnicity, and social stratification in American social structure. It was also observed that the history of ethnicity in this country reveals a double process, involving both a high degree of assimilation and acculturation and a considerable survival of ethnic characteristics. However, it was emphasized that the Southwest was in significant respects different from the country generally. In the Southwest there are numerous indigenous peoples who did not arrive there as part of the general thrust of the Anglo-American westward movement. Indeed the westward expansion of the United States in many respects may be said to have "jumped over" much of the region. Moreover, Spanish-speaking peoples were there before the Anglo-Americans, because of a northward movement from Mexico and earlier from New Spain. The Mormons came to the area first as part of the westward expansion, but Mormon settlement in

Arizona and New Mexico came as the consequence of the southern thrust of Mormon colonization from Utah. Hence the Mormons have their own unique place and unique identity in the region.

Mormonism founded its own "homeland" in the intermountain West and spread out from that center. It developed in a remarkably short time a character of "peoplehood," so that it became, in terms of its own self-conception, a peculiar people with a special religious mission and a particular homeland. I have characterized such a development as an indigenously evolved quasi-ethnicity which took Mormonism from sectarianism to the very threshold of national identity. At times such quasi-nationality tends to result in separatist aspirations. Yet such tendencies came to naught, and the Mormons became patriotic advocates of integration into the general American society. I use the term "quasi-ethnicity" to indicate that although all the potential elements of ethnic identity were in fact evolved in Mormon history, there did not emerge a fully conscious self-definition giving full recognition to those ethnic characteristics. Incipient nationality remained in potency; it stopped short of full realization.

Yet the Mormons do see themselves as a "peculiar people," after the model of biblical Israel. As such they feel that they have their own homeland in the intermountain West. The center of that Mormon country is Salt Lake City and the state of Utah, but it extends to adjoining states, where Mormons settled early as part of their original migration and settlement efforts. Today Mormons are rapidly becoming urbanized and a large, prosperous middle class has come into existence. Moreover, Mormonism now has its own diaspora as large numbers of church members live outside the area of the gathered.

The Mormon church experiences in its own way, in terms of its own particular beliefs and its own unique history, the religious crisis of our time. It experiences this crisis in the setting of the great transition which America as a nation, the West as a region, and the church as a religious organization are all undergoing. In that setting the church continues its confrontation with modernity and attempts to adapt itself with as little change as possible to the new conditions of the modern world. Urbanization, the rise of a middle class, the development of scientifically-based technology, and the communications revolution introduce into the position of the church today new and unprecedented elements, making adaptation difficult if not impossible and calling for profound change. With its activist leadership and its neglect of intellectual modes and methods for meeting the challenge of change, the church is ill-prepared in its present situation.

All the deep, often inchoate, and little understood elements of Mormon consciousness, the precipitates of the history and conflicts of the past century and a half, have come to be focused upon an ethnic symbol. The question of the Negro and the Mormon priesthood is the focal point of crisis for the Mormon church today. Around this issue are crystallized the positions of those who aspire to reform and those who desire no change. At the moment the dominant reaction is a defensiveness which uncritically reasserts old positions and old formulations. But there is also some evidence of a creative response. The Mormon middle class is producing in this generation many educated youth, and from these it now appears that authentic efforts at a genuine updating will sooner or later develop. It is in the growth of that response that the real future of the church will lie. This inner-church situation becomes a part of the ethnic composition of the Southwest, and developments within the church will continue to have their impact upon the region.

The Rise of the Navajo Tribe

Robert W. Young

In the concluding chapter of her scholarly work on Navajo
tribal government, Shepardson (1963: 114) observes that "a new
political system may be considered as 'fully institutionalized'
when it has developed to the point that it could not conceivably
be withdrawn from a society without effecting a fundamental
change in that society's way of life." Navajo culture has indeed,
in less than a half century, so closely woven the concept of
governmental organization into its fabric, tribal in scope, that it
could not today be removed without seriously and adversely
affecting the life of the Navajo people throughout the far-flung
reservation area.

The same general observation could be made with regard to
other institutions borrowed historically from Puebloan, Spanish,
and Anglo sources modified in form to fit Navajo patterns, and
incorporated as part of the fabric of a distinctive Navajo culture,
including the ceremonial system, agriculture, stock raising, and
formal education, to mention a few of the more significant.

The development of tribal government, however, occupies a
position of fundamental importance because it provided the
stimulus and the framework within which the Navajo Tribe has
emerged as a political entity. The 74-member Tribal Council,
elected by popular vote every four years, today governs the
expenditure of millions of dollars of tribal funds appropriated for
the support of tribal programs. In addition, the council, as the
tribal legislative body, makes tribal law and policy. The programs
and policies are carried out, and the laws are enforced by the
executive branch of government, under the direction of the
chairman of the Tribal Council. Tribal justice is administered in
conformity with Navajo values and tribal custom through the

medium of a system of tribal courts presided over by judges who are themselves Navajos.

The Navajo people have not always been organized in this manner. In fact, tribal existence, in a political sense, goes back only 47 years in time; and most of the growth of tribalism and self-government has taken place since the end of World War II— especially during the period following the discovery of major oil fields on the reservation in 1956.

Beginning as a superimposition, outside the limiting framework imposed by a family-centered, traditional form of socio-political organization, present-day tribal government has evolved along the devious corridors of historic federal Indian policy, responding to a variety of external and internal stimuli, to assume its present form and function as an integral institution of Navajo culture.

Initially, the Council was organized to deal, not with internal tribal issues, but with issues raised by the dominant society: leasing, trading, polygamy, missions. Subsequently, it became a focal point for popular opposition to the unpopular stock reduction program introduced by the federal government. In more recent times it has become an organization which is concerned primarily with internal tribal matters. It is interesting to trace the course of its development across the years against the background of crises, events, cultural constraints, federal policies, public attitudes, and other factors which have played a determining or limiting role in shaping the Navajo Tribe as a political entity, and to speculate regarding the part tribal government may play in the lives of the Navajo people in future years.

Major limiting factors in the developmental process have been the narrow political horizons inherent in traditional Navajo social organization, and the restrictions imposed by federal Indian policy, federal statutes and federal regulations relating to Indian affairs. Major events, many of them critical, which acted as stimuli in directing the development of tribal government—and, in fact, the concept of the *Tribe* as a political entity—were the discovery of oil in the northern portion of the treaty reservation in 1921; the revolution in Indian administration that took form in the 1930's, culminating in the passage of the Indian Reorganization Act of 1934; the introduction of a livestock reduction program by a conservation-minded federal administration in 1933; the socioeconomic crisis that reached emergency proportions after the close of World War II; the Navajo-Hopi Rehabilitation Act of 1950; the hiring of a tribal attorney in 1948 with the ensuing development of a tribal legal department during the 1950's, coupled with a federal termination policy; and the discovery of the Four Corners oil field in 1956, which led to a large tribal income with a concomitant need to use the newly acquired wealth for the benefit of the entire tribal membership. Consideration of each of the major constraints and events that formed the background against which tribal government developed is essential as a basis upon which to understand the form in which it has evolved to the present time.

Traditional Sociopolitical Organization

Although in historic times there was a group of people, interrelated by kinship and clan, who shared a common Navajo language and culture, thus comprising a "Navajo Tribe" from one point of view, the emergence of that Tribe as a cooperating political unit is recent. How the Navajo people were organized at the time of their arrival in the Southwest 500-600 years ago is conjectural, but their heavy dependency on hunting implies a form of organization based on family groups and loosely knit bands. Had the Spanish not entered the New Mexican scene in the 16th century it is not inconceivable that the Navajo might have adopted a village-based, agricultural way of life similar to that of the Puebloan people with whom they established early contact. However, the advent of the Spanish, with the introduction of sheep, horses, and other domesticated animals led to the acquisition of livestock by the Navajo, perhaps at some period well before the beginning of the 18th century; and to the subsequent adoption of a pastoral way of life combined with agriculture, hunting, and raiding (Hill 1936, Aberle 1961). The need for range to support the livestock discouraged any previous trend toward a village-based, Puebloan way of life, and the old social organization which had met Navajo needs as a hunting people was easily adapted to accommodate the new institution of stock raising.

At one period a small group of settlers in what is now the Gobernador-Largo Canyon-Navajo Reservoir district of northern New Mexico—a definable area known to this day in Navajo folk-history and legend as *Dinétah*—the early Navajos were gradually obliged to move southward and westward after the opening of the 18th century, yielding to the increasing pressure of raiding Utes. By mid-century *Dinétah* was abandoned, and Spanish accounts described the Navajo Tribe as one composed of groups of people living in five *cantones*, or regionally separate districts. These clusters were identified geographically as the San Mateo (the northern slopes of Mt. Taylor, New Mexico), the Cebolleta (northeast of present Laguna Pueblo, New Mexico), the Chuska (north of present Gallup, New Mexico), the Bear Spring (around present Fort Wingate, New Mexico), and the Chelley (Canyon de Chelley, Arizona). Early Spanish accounts often refer to the Canyon de Chelley as the "Navajo capital," and it was believed that the tribe maintained a presidio, or fort, somewhere in the canyon fastness.

The traditional structure of Navajo society has been described in more recent times by a number of trained students and observers, including Kimball and Provinse (1942), Hill (1940b), Kluckhohn and Leighton (1946), and Aberle (1961). It is depicted as a system of intercooperating groups, each with its own functional limits, but each merging into the level immediately above and below—that is to say, a system composed of the biological family, the extended family or family group, the land use community, "the greater community," and finally, in recent times, the Tribe in a political sense. The stratum below the biological family is occupied, of course, by the individual, and that beyond the Tribe is the state and the nation—the non-Navajo world with which the people have a more or less vague sense of belonging.

The Household

The biological family, or household, normally comprises all persons living in one hogan—in fact, a common translation into Navajo of the English term "family" is *t'áálá'í hooghanigíí* (one-hogan group). Clusters of related households commonly live as close neighbors in a well-defined locale, each usually comprising a

man and his wife, their married daughters, sons-in-law, and sometimes married sons, as well as perhaps grandparents and other
close relatives. The biological family represents the first and basic
level of cooperation in the everyday requirements of living. It is
normally headed by the father and primarily concerned with the
feeding, sheltering, and protection of its members.

The Extended Family

Beyond the biological family, in a second cooperating level is
the extended family, composed of neighboring households, usually interrelated by blood or marriage. In traditional times, and
extending into the present to no small extent, the extended
family, as a broader cooperating entity, was headed by the
father-in-law, or by some older person who controlled the agricultural and grazing lands. Farming operations, hogan construction, the planning and conduct of ceremonies, and other undertakings requiring more manpower than the biological family, or
single household, could muster, fell within the province of the
extended family.

Kimball and Provinse (1942: 22) described the extended
family as "a group of families possessing common close ties by
blood or marriage, resident in one locality, under one leadership,
whose operation is most marked in the cooperative sharing and
common meeting of crises of a greater magnitude than those
facing the family."

The Land Use Community

Beyond the extended family as an organizational entity is the
land use community which Kimball and Provinse described
(1942: 22) as "the social and economic unit [which] is numer-
ically larger and geographically more extensive than the family
group [extended family]," and as one in which "the occupants
lay claim to the country as their own on the basis of ancestral
settlement and present use."

Basing their statements on a survey of Land Management
District 4 in the late 1930's, these investigators reported that the
smallest land use community comprised an area of 15,000 acres,
while most such communities occupied about 25,000 acres; one
covered 80,000 acres of land.

Within the land use community they found several levels of leadership, including not only the father as nominal head of the family, and the father-in-law or other recognized elder in a position of authority in the extended family group, but also those individuals who, because of natural leadership ability, wealth, knowledge of ceremonies, oratorical ability or other factors, were chosen and recognized as headmen. In this role they functioned as judges, advisers, arbiters and as rallying points for such broad community projects as major ceremonials, construction projects serving the interests of many family groups and other regional matters transcending the private concern of local families or family groups.

Headmen, once chosen by the people of an area, usually remained "in office" for life, or at least so long as they commanded the respect of the people they served. They were (and are) known in Navajo as *naat'áanii* (the nominalized form of a verb meaning "to orate"); as the name implies, their leadership ability hinged closely on their powers of persuasion. They had no powers of coercion. Oratorical ability, with ceremonial knowledge, rank high in the system of Navajo values, and children were often taken by their parents to gatherings where they could listen to and learn from great orators.

Those leaders whose concern it was to lead people in the interest of peace and harmony were also known as *hozhǫ́ǫjí naat'ááh* (peace chiefs or champions of order). According to legend, some such leaders went about the country lecturing people on right living and the value of harmony. They would berate and counsel with wrong-doers whose behavior created disharmony until the miscreants broke down and cried. Then they would wipe the slate clean, as the story goes, by taking an ember from the fire, having the culprit spit upon it, and throw it out the smokehole. Peace chiefs were usually medicine men who knew the *Hozhǫ́ǫjí* (Blessing Way), and were men of great influence.

In olden times, before 1868, there were also war chiefs, men who possessed the ritual knowledge necessary for hunting and war, and who had a reputation for success in these pursuits (Hill 1936, 1938).

The Natural Community

Hill (1940a: 23) describes the fundamental political entity of the Navajo, the natural community, as follows:

This unit is an economic one, geographically determined and distinct. The Navaho territory is one in which the location of natural resources necessary for subsistence occur at scattered locations and usually sharply defined by natural barriers. As their basis, such units had land fit for agriculture, which was located with reference to surface or sub-soil irrigation, readily available timber for building and household use, water for domestic purposes, and, after 1870, pasturage for sheep. The population of these units varied in relation to the natural resources.

Hill looked upon these natural communities as groups that were largely interdependent, on a regional basis, primarily concerned with their own local problems and, so far as leadership was concerned in pretreaty times, groups oriented either toward domestic affairs or toward warfare.

In the area of warfare, leaders emerged from time to time whose reputation for success spread far and wide, and whose influence and following went beyond the locale in which they resided. Narbona was no doubt such a man, as implied by Meredith T. Moore, a member of the Doniphan expedition, in his graphic account of the first encounter between American troops and the old war chief in October 1846. According to Connelley (1907: 294-295) Moore wrote him that "as soon as an interview could be had with Narbona he sent runners in every direction to summon the Chiefs and warriors to council. These responded at once and began to assemble in large numbers, and by the third day *thousands* were on the plateau."

Sporadic warfare and raiding characterized Navajo relationships with the Spanish and New Mexicans for centuries, and no doubt one factor involved in keeping this relationship alive was the fact that Navajo raiding parties usually represented one or another local community; the Spaniards, to even the score after a raid, attacked the first Navajo camp they came upon, thus inviting reprisal from a group that had not been involved but which, following the attack, had its own score to settle. Near the end of the 18th century, the Spanish governor hit upon the happy plan of buying peace by commissioning carefully chosen Navajo headmen as "captains" or even as "generals" in the Spanish Army, and giving them regular gifts in exchange for assistance in keeping the peace. However, apart from raids of reprisal, warfare waged against the settlements was an avenue through which poor but ambitious young men could acquire wealth and prestige; bribing a few headmen, or even a few of the war leaders, had little beneficial effect. Lack of a central Navajo tribal government, with coercive power to control its subjects, closed such avenues to peace as might otherwise have been afforded by treaty-making or bribery.

The defeat of the Navajos by Kit Carson in the mid-1860's broke the war-making power of the tribe and introduced a new framework within which Navajo development unfolded in subsequent years.

Federal Indian Policy

It will not be long before the United States celebrates its second century as a nation. Over the course of that long span of years, each succeeding generation of American people has been concerned, in one manner or another, with the fate of the Indian tribes that were living on the land before the arrival of the first European colonists. The official policies of the federal government, which took exclusive jurisdiction over Indian affairs, have shifted with public opinion and popular demand across the years. At times official policy has stood in sharp contrast with popular sentiment; at other times the posture of the government has reflected the popular pressures brought to bear upon it.

A certain ambivalence has surrounded Indian relationships from the earliest days of the Republic. The Congress, in August 1789, reenacted the benevolent language of the Northwest Ordinance of 1787, vowing to observe "the utmost good faith" in national dealings with the Indians, to protect them in their rights and property; and to preserve peace and friendship with them.

But Weld (1968 Vol. 2: 218), writing in the 1790's, after

extensive travels among the settlers, was appalled by the attitudes expressed by them regarding their Indian neighbors:

An Indian is considered by them as nothing more than a destructive ravenous wild beast, without reason, without a soul; . . . Even amongst the bettermost sort of the inhabitants of the western country, the most illiberal notions are entertained respecting these unfortunate people, and arguments for their banishment, or rather extirpation, are adopted, equally contrary to justice and to humanity.

Not only was the public attitude toward the Indian people something less than generous at the close of the 18th century, but Weld (1968 Vol. 2: 218-219) reflected too the popular conviction, already prevalent in the 1790's, that the Indians, controlled land areas far excessive to their needs: "The Indian, say they, who has no idea, or at least is unwilling to apply himself to agriculture, requires a thousand acres of land for the support of his family; an hundred acres will be enough for one of us and our children; why then should these heathens, who have no notion of arts and manufactures, who never have made any improvement in science, and have never been the inventors of anything new or useful to the human species, be suffered to encumber the soil?" Weld (1968 Vol. 2: 219) quoted a Mr. Imlay whose prediction was that "our people . . . will continue to *encroach* upon them on three sides, and *compel* them to live more domestic lives, and assimilate them to our mode of living, or cross to the western side of the Mississippi."

Congress, yielding to popular demand in the face of growing competition for resources between the tribes and the settlers was often hard put to apply the principles it had adopted in the Northwest Ordinance, and after 1817 the nation was actively committed to the removal of tribes from the country east of the Mississippi, by military force when necessary. Mr. Imlay's prediction became a reality.

By the mid-19th century Indians were being confined to reservations to reduce their land holdings, and already the allotment of Indian lands in severalty was being promoted. Sometime after the return of the captive Navajos from Fort Sumner in

1868, the General Allotment Act of 1887 became law and the process of allotting Indian lands became a national policy.

The Demand for Cultural Conformity

Immigration from Europe swelled the national population during the 19th century, and the nation came to look proudly upon itself as a cultural "melting pot." Peoples from many parts of Europe, speaking many languages and representing many diverse cultural systems ran the gauntlet of assimilation after their arrival in America and emerged as members of the growing American society. Cultural and linguistic conformity, the price of "belonging," became a national value; cultural pluralism was unthinkable.

The same principles of cultural conformity that the initiated members of American society demanded of immigrants were extended to include the members of Indian societies as well. Official federal Indian policy soon became one expressed in terms of "civilizing" the Indian—that is, leading or obliging him to abandon his own language for English, his own religion for Christianity, and his traditional way of life for that of a farmer. Commissioner Lea (Commissioner's Report, 1851: 12-13) posed the question: "How shall the Indian be civilized?" He then proceeded to answer the query by observing that "their concentration, their domestication and their ultimate incorporation into the great body politic of our citizen population should be a major objective of their civilization."

Their *concentration* meant a reduction in the Indian land base to require more efficient use of agricultural resources on the part of the Indians and to open the way to such use by non-Indians. Their *domestication*, of course, implied their complete assimilation to the national culture. The establishment of the reservations and, near the close of the past century, the national policy of allotting Indian lands in severalty, opened the way for concentration; at the same time, the thrust of Indian education was toward assimilation of the Indian people. Some individuals emerged from the ordeal to become leaders—successful men by non-Indian standards—but many were not so fortunate.

Letherman (1855: 288), was somewhat less than flattering when he described the Navajos as a people, "the tout ensemble (of which gives) the idea of a man far inferior to the Caucasian and approaching in appearance the brute creation, with which they have much in common." Apart from their physical characteristics this "observer" depicted the Navajo as anarchists, thieves, beggars and heathens. "The general impression of those who have had means of knowing them is that, in this regard (religion) they are steeped in the deepest degradation," Letherman (1855: 294) wrote.

It seemed obvious to most Americans, even the most benevolent, during the 19th century and well into the 20th, that Indian problems would vanish only if the Indian gave up the "inferior" tools and institutions of his own culture and joined the great American society as a fully initiated, participating member. It was frustrating, if not infuriating, to his mentors when the Indian steadfastly declined to foresake his identity and his own cultural values, but the effort continued across the years—especially during the period between 1870 and 1930. Cohen (1942: 28) describes this period as one characterized by an autocratic federal Indian policy, one during which "the guiding concepts . . . were the destruction of all Indian tribal bonds, the effacing of Indian languages and cultural heritages, the forcing of the Indian as an individual to become identified with and lost in white life, and the breaking of tribal, communal and family land holdings into individual allotments of farm, timber and grazing lands."

This longstanding policy and statement of national objectives with regard to the Indian was still echoing in official and in public circles as late as 1923, when Commissioner of Indian Affairs Charles H. Burke issued his directive entitled *Supplement to Circular No. 1665—Indian Dancing*. In this document he lent his official support to a set of recommendations forwarded to him from a missionary conference held during the preceding year. The recommendations included official action to limit Indian dances to "one each month in the day-light hours of one day in mid-week," and a prohibition to the effect that "none take part in the dances or be present who are under 50 years of age."

The commissioner requested the support of all government employees and superintendents, expressing the opinion that "the instinct of individual enterprise and devotion to the prosperity and elevation of family life should in some way be made paramount in every Indian household to the exclusion of idleness, waste of time at frequent gatherings of whatever nature, and the neglect of physical resources upon which depend food, clothing, shelter and the very beginnings of progress."

The directive was followed ten days later by a "Message to all Indians" (quoted in Spicer 1969a: 241-242), in which the Commissioner advised them that sentiment against Indian dances was strong on the part of missionaries and superintendents, and in which he warned them to the effect that he "could issue an order against these useless and harmful performances, but I would much rather have you give them up of your own free will, . . . If at the end of one year the reports which I receive show that you are doing as requested, I shall be very glad for I will know that you are making progress in other and more important ways; but if the reports show that you reject this plea, then some other course will have to be taken."

No formal effort was apparently made to outlaw Navajo ceremonies, although in their reports, a year later, the superintendents deplored the hold the medicine men had over the people, but because distances were so great and supervision practically impossible, no action was recommended.

Commissioner Burke's futile attempt to outlaw Indian ceremonial practices has little importance in itself, except to the extent that it reflects the public attitudes and official policies in the closing years of the autocratic phase in Indian administration, and, for the Navajo, at a period contemporary with the formation of the first Navajo Tribal Council.

New Directions in Indian Affairs

A few years later, in 1928, the Meriam Committee completed an on-the-ground survey of Indian reservations and published a monumental report entitled *The Problem of Indian Administration*, a report whose recommendations became pivotal in the ensuing revolution that took place in Indian affairs (Meriam 1928).

The Meriam Report, as it is commonly known, recommended a reversal in the direction of federal policy as it related to the destruction of Indian cultures, to provide maximum liberty and freedom for self-determination on the part of Indian communities within the framework of federal guardianship, and continuing trusteeship over Indian property. In addition, the recommendations of the Meriam Committee contemplated the strengthening of Indian community life by shifting emphasis away from boarding schools toward day-school operations; the longstanding policy that called for the allotment of Indian lands was also repudiated. The committee pointed to the urgent need for more generous appropriations by Congress to support reservation development, health and educational programs. Most important of all, perhaps, was the repudiation of the previous concept of a uniform Indian policy, program, and pattern of administration that had been accepted for so many years before, with a recommendation that these elements be closely adapted to the peculiar requirements of each reservation, and that the Indian communities themselves be involved in the planning and execution of projects designed for social and economic improvement.

Many of the recommendations stressed by the Meriam Committee found their way into the policies and programs of the Bureau of Indian Affairs, and into federal legislation, during the 1930's, setting in motion a revolution aimed at righting past wrongs and paving the way toward the development of viable reservation societies. Implicit in the recommendation that Indian communities play a role in the planning and execution of reservation programs was the formation of some type of tribal governmental organization.

In 1933, Commissioner John Collier set forth the salient features of the new direction in Indian affairs, as part of his first report. His recommendations called for a halt to the allotment process, with a concurrent effort to increase the tribal land base on Indian reservations; a new approach to Indian education based on day schools, fostering continuing contact between children and their parents, in lieu of boarding schools designed to disassociate parents from their children; increased employment of Indians in the Indian Service; and reorganization of the Bureau of Indian Affairs to more effectively coordinate its many special functions with one another and with Indian life and needs on each reservation.

Many of Collier's recommendations, reflecting to no small degree those of the Meriam Committee, found their way into the new Indian legislation of the 1930's—especially the Indian Reorganization Act of June 18, 1934—and into the revolutionary policies that were generated by the new administration. Public attitudes toward Indians and Indian cultures did not undergo instant change, but across the span of the 1930's the concerted effort made by the Bureau to achieve greater popular understanding of the Indian people and greater sympathy for their problems made significant headway, both inside and outside of government.

The Stock Reduction Program on the Navajo Reservation

One statement of purpose in the Commissioner's 1933 report under the heading "Indian Lands" was destined to have a far-reaching effect on Navajo culture, touching the lives of the people in the most remote sectors of the Navajo country as no aspect of the former policy had touched them since Fort Sumner. The sentence read simply that the "wastage of Indian lands through erosion must be checked," and the conservation-minded federal administration of the 1930's immediately set out to check the continuing deterioration of Navajo range resources, which had commenced years before as a result of overgrazing. The objective was well-intentioned and quite patently justified from the point of view of halting the serious effects of soil erosion so evident throughout Navajoland, but implementation of the conservation program required reduction of livestock numbers on the Navajo rangeland; stock raising was a major feature of the traditional Navajo economy and an important cornerstone in the foundation upon which Navajo culture rested.

In the face of an increasing tribal population, threatened reduction of the customary resources for livelihood took on the dimensions of genocide in the minds of the Navajo people. As a result, the new and enlightened federal Indian policy of the 1930's met with distrust and bitter resistance on the Navajo Reservation; as it proceeded, the controversy centering around soil conservation overshadowed, for the Navajo, all other features of the national effort to right old wrongs and open the way for Indian self-determination. Ironically, a policy which embodied

180

the principle of respect for Indian culture carried a greater threat of destruction for the Navajo, than its predecessor, which was overtly aimed at destroying Indian institutions and ways of life. The controversy revolving around stock reduction and range management quickly became, and remained, a major force in conditioning and directing Navajo development for more than two decades after 1933 (Aberle 1966).

Vacillation in Government Goals

By 1940, the Bureau of Indian Affairs was looking forward to divesting itself of the monopolistic control over Indian affairs that it had exercised for so many years. Many tribes had reorganized their tribal governments under the authority of the Indian Reorganization Act of 1934; they were making excellent progress, and the Bureau was looking to those organizations for eventual management of tribal affairs. At the same time, the Bureau was looking to other federal agencies and to the states and counties as sources of necessary services to Indian people. Assistant Commissioner Joseph C. McCaskill (1940: 76) outlined these objectives in a paper, entitled "The Cessation of Monopolistic Control of Indians by the Indian Office," in which he observed that "perhaps thus, but not at once, it may be possible to cease special treatment, special protective and beneficial legislation for the Indians, and they shall become self-supporting, self-managing and self-directing communities within our national citizenry."

The long-term aim in Indian affairs outlined by McCaskill contrasts sharply with the statement of purpose made in connection with the 35th Lake Mohonk Conference of 1929, at which time the conference host stated: "It is probable that most here have in mind the general purpose of helpfulness in hastening the day when three hundred thousand partially civilized wards of the nation, living abnormally on some two hundred reservations and speaking fifty or more different languages shall, like other people living near us, become completely merged into our body politic, ceasing to be an Indian problem and known only as ordinary American citizens of Indian descent."

To some extent the two philosophical positions outlined above have been involved in a more or less continuous tug-of-war for the past forty years, but progress has generally been made along the lines proposed by McCaskill, and his views have received greater support.

During the latter part of the 1940's, following World War II, heavy pressure was generated both inside and outside the government, for the adoption of a federal policy, and the establishment of programs, designed for the early termination of federal trusteeship over Indian property and the cessation of special federal services to Indians. In 1953, this was formalized by the 83rd Congress with the passage of House Concurrent Resolution 108, declaring the policy of Congress to be "as rapidly as possible, to make the Indians within the territorial limits of the United States subject to the same laws and entitled to the same privileges and responsibilities as are applicable to other citizens of the United States, to end their status as wards of the United States, and to grant them all the rights and prerogatives pertaining to American citizenship."

Accordingly, during the 1950's, the Bureau of Indian Affairs was deeply involved in "withdrawal programming," a process involving careful study and analysis, designed to determine the readiness of various tribes throughout the nation for the cessation of federal trusteeship and services. At the same time, the Bureau embarked on an active program aimed at transferring service and managerial responsibilities to the tribes themselves wherever possible, and to states and other agencies of government where the tribes could not perform such major functions as social welfare, education, and law enforcement.

The termination policy of Congress generated fear and suspicion on the part of most Indian tribes over the country, and had a limiting effect on the success of efforts directed at the formulation of development plans keyed to the social and economic requirements of each reservation; the tribes tended to identify "program planning" with termination. At the same time, however, it stimulated the growth of tribal government. In 1958, Secretary of the Interior Fred A. Seaton attempted to reassure the Indian people that there was no intention on the part of the federal government to terminate its special relationship with Indian tribes, until such tribes were fully prepared.

In 1961, a special task force, appointed by the Secretary of the Interior, completed a detailed study of Indian problems and desires, and recommended three broad long-term goals as the basis for federal Indian policy. These were succinctly phrased in terms of: (1) maximum Indian economic self-sufficiency, (2) full participation of Indians in American life, and (3) equal citizenship privileges and responsibilities for Indians.

During the 1960's, Indian tribes generally availed themselves of a wide variety of federal programs, designed to improve housing, social and economic conditions in disadvantaged communities, under the auspices of the Office of Economic Opportunity (OEO), the Economic Development Administration (EDA), the Department of Housing and Urban Development (HUD), and others. Tribes, acting through tribal organizations, became increasingly involved in reservation development programs, including the attraction of industries, the exploitation of natural resources, the operation of schools, the management of tribal assets, and, most recently, the direction of Bureau of Indian Affairs programs themselves. At the same time, Bureau policies and programs have continued to emphasize active assistance to the tribes in developing their own governmental machinery to assume added responsibilities for the management of their own affairs. The Bureau has become a source of valuable technical services, and is now a partner, rather than the sole director, in the planning and execution of reservation programs.

The Emergence of the Tribe as a Political Entity

During the Fort Sumner period (1863-1868), plans were laid by General James H. Carleton for the establishment of a Navajo government. He proposed to divide the tribe into twelve villages, each under the control of a principal chief to be appointed by the commanding officer. The puppet government envisioned by Carleton failed to take form, and the military was obliged to rely on the former war chiefs to assist in maintaining control over the captive tribe.

A few months after the signing of the Treaty of June 1, 1868, Special Indian Agent John Ward of Santa Fe recommended the establishment of a council of headmen, appointed by the agent or military officer in charge, and representing each "district" on the reservation. From this group it was proposed that five be appointed as principal chiefs, and that these officials meet on a quarterly schedule for the transaction of business with federal authorities. The headmen, in turn, would meet twice each year at the agency headquarters to keep the agent or officer in charge informed about local problems.

Obviously, both Carleton and Ward conceived of "tribal government" as a tool for the control of tribal members by federal authorities; they were not primarily concerned with the development of a medium through which the tribe could manage its own affairs, although Ward (1868) in a letter to S. F. Tappan made the interesting observation that "the foregoing propositions, once firmly established, would serve as a foundation step towards forming a government for these people."

Following the return of the tribe from Fort Sumner in 1868, the agent leaned heavily upon the former war chiefs—especially those who had distinguished themselves during the period of captivity. Under the circumstances surrounding the Navajos in the years immediately following their return, the fact of recognition of these men by federal authorities further enhanced their influence and prestige, on a regional basis.

As time passed, however, the former war chiefs died off and the agents were obliged to appoint "chiefs" to take the places of the old leaders. Lacking the influence and reputation of the old war chiefs, the power and prestige of the appointed chiefs hinged upon federal support, and this support hinged, in turn, on their tractability and cooperativeness. When appointees became recalcitrant, support was withdrawn, and they quickly faded into oblivion.

Councils of headmen were called from time to time by the agents, in an effort to influence and control the tribe, but such measures had little effect on the people living in the hinterlands of the reservation area. Also, with the growth of the Navajo Reservation, as it was enlarged from time to time after 1878, the expanse of territory became so great that administrative contacts with the people were few.

Shortly after the opening of the 20th century, to cope with administrative problems, the Navajo country was divided into six separate jurisdictions or agencies (including the Hopi). This expedient, coupled with increased staff and a smaller land area, led to the abandonment of the previous system of appointive chiefs, and to an ever greater attempt by federal administrators to reach and influence the members of the tribe directly on a local basis. By 1910 the use of appointive chiefs was abandoned completely. In general, after the opening of the present century, with the division of the Navajo country into multiple jurisdictions, federal administration continued to be largely autocratic in its approach and methods, but with ever increasing efforts to reach and influence the people. Concurrently with the establishment of the six agencies, the tribe came to be viewed, not as one entity, but as six separate and distinct segments, including those members living in the Hopi jurisdiction, each with its own regional interests. This development itself placed a constraint on the evolution of government on a tribal basis.

The Beginning of Tribal Government

In 1921, the Midwest Refining Company was authorized to negotiate with the Navajos residing within the San Juan (Northern) Agency Jurisdiction for an oil and gas lease involving 4,800 acres of reservation land. The lease area was located within the boundaries of the Treaty Reservation, and the Treaty of 1868 required tribal consent under the terms of Article X, which provided that "no future treaty for the cession of any portion or part of the Reservation herein described, which may be held in common, shall be of any validity or force against said Indians unless agreed to and executed by at least three fourths of all the adult male Indians occupying or interested in the same."

Although the language of the treaty was construed as requiring tribal consent for the granting of a lease, it was initially decided that the consent of that portion of the tribe residing within the San Juan Jurisdiction, in the instance at hand, would suffice. To secure necessary approval a "general council," as it was termed, was held at which the lease was approved by those adult tribal members in attendance and subsequently by the Secretary of the Interior. The lease which Superintendent Evan W. Estep, San Juan Jurisdiction, signed on August 15, 1921, with the Midwest Refining Company provided for payment of rentals and royalties to the superintendent "for the use and benefit of the Indians *of said reservation*." The company proceeded to drill, and very high-grade oil was discovered at a shallow depth.

Three leases, each for 4,800 acres, were authorized at about the same time in the Southern Navajo Jurisdiction (Fort Defiance), again by a general council of Navajos resident in that jurisdiction.

The use of a general council composed of the Navajos resident in one or another of the agency juridictions or reservations, was based on the premise that the land area involved was the exclusive property of that portion of the tribe residing on it, not property in which the entire tribal membership shared, irrespective of the administrative subdivision within which they lived. Immediately after the discovery of oil several additional leases were negotiated in the San Juan Jurisdiction, but they were disapproved by the Department of the Interior which, after further consideration, held that the mineral resources of the Treaty Reservation were the property of the entire tribe, and that *all* Navajos were beneficiaries regardless of the agency in which they resided. This decision made the use of a general council unfeasible thereafter; it was perhaps possible to assemble a representative group of adult males at a central point in *one* agency area, but the problems inherent in trying to assemble the entire tribe at one point were obvious.

It was imperative then, in the interest of exploiting the oil and gas potential of the reservation, to find a practical avenue through which to obtain tribal consent for the leasing of land. Accordingly, in 1922, a "Business Council" was established. This entity, apparently appointed by the Secretary of the Interior, was composed of three members: Chee Dodge, Charlie Mitchell, and Dugal Chee BeKiss, who presumed to act on behalf of the entire tribe in the negotiation of oil and gas leases. At least three leases were authorized by the Business Council in a meeting held at Fort Defiance on January 26, 1922, presided over by Peter Paquette, Superintendent of the Southern Navajo Reservation. The "resolve" paragraph of the resolutions reads, in part, "that the oil and gas mining lease . . . be hereby approved and that Chee Dodge, Charlie Mitchell and Dugal Chee BeKiss, as the Business Council of this tribe, be authorized on behalf of the

Navajo Indian Tribe to sign, execute and deliver said lease, subject only to the approval of the Secretary of the Interior. . . . " The three members of the Council had, in effect, conferred upon themselves—or accepted from a nontribal source —the authority to act for the Navajo Tribe in the approval of the leases. (For an excellent discussion of oil leasing on the reservation in the 1920's, see Kelly 1968.)

For obvious reasons, the legality of the Business Council was highly questionable, with the result that, on January 27, 1923, Commissioner of Indian Affairs Charles H. Burke promulgated a document entitled *Regulations Relating to the Navajo Tribe of Indians*, approved on the same date by Assistant Secretary of the Interior F. M. Goodwin.

The Birth of the Navajo Tribal Council

Commissioner Burke's new creation was, according to the opening paragraph of the *Regulations*, designed "to promote better administration of the affairs of the Navajo Tribe of Indians in conformity to law and particularly as to matters in which the Navajo Tribe at large is concerned, such as oil, gas, coal, and other mineral deposits, tribal timber, and development of underground water supply for stock purposes."

In view of the decision that all members of the Navajo Tribe had an equal interest in tribal lands, irrespective of the administrative jurisdiction in which they resided, and in view of the fact that the six Navajo Reservation jurisdictions were administered independently of one another, there was an obvious need for interagency coordination in matters of tribal concern. To meet this requirement, the *Regulations* created the office of Commissioner of the Navajo Tribe, "who shall maintain a central or general headquarters for said tribe at a point to be designated by the Commissioner of Indian Affairs." The Commissioner of the Navajo Tribe was given general supervision over each of the superintendencies and "general supervision and administration of affairs of the Navajo Tribe."

In addition, the *Regulations* provided for the creation of "a continuing body to be known and recognized as the Navajo Tribal Council with which administrative officers of the Government may directly deal in all matters affecting the tribe."

The new Council was to be composed of one delegate and one alternate from each of the six jurisdictions, plus a chairman and vice chairman.

The elective process was simple; the *Regulations* required the Indians of the six superintendencies to meet, upon thirty days notice, "at a time and place designated and under the general direction of the Commissioner for the Navajos," at which time the assembled Indians were to "be *directed* to elect a principal delegate and an alternate delegate." In the event the Indians of any jurisdiction failed to meet at the time and place designated, the *Regulations* provided for the appointment of a delegate and an alternate by the Secretary of the Interior.

The Chairman of the Tribal Council was to be elected by the Council at its first meeting, and although the person so chosen was to be selected from the tribal membership at large, outside the Council itself, he functioned as a Council member as well as presiding officer following his election. The vice chairman was to be chosen by the Council from within its membership.

The Council was to meet at the call of the Commissioner of the Navajo Tribe or, at the request of five councilmen the Commissioner could, "in his discretion," convene the tribal "governing body." Section 19 of the *Regulations* prohibited Council meetings without the presence of the Commissioner for the Navajo Tribe. Furthermore, Section 20 provided that "the Secretary of the Interior reserves the right to remove any member of the Tribal Council, upon proper cause shown, and to require the election or appointment of some other delegate to take the place of the member so removed."

The autocratic federal administration of the period had no plan for the establishment of a governing body as an instrument for tribal self-determination, and the language of the first Council *Regulations* clearly reflects the intention to maintain tight control over reservation affairs. The document contained no statement of legislative or other substantive powers whatsoever; the Council was to be purely a consultative body, although it apparently had the authority to consent to leases.

The first *Regulations* were promulgated by Commissioner Burke in January 1923, but before they could be implemented, a new set of *Regulations* was issued. The new council rules were promulgated by Acting Commissioner E. B. Meritt a few months later in April 1923, and approved by Secretary of the Interior Hubert Work.

Whereas the *Regulations*, as issued in January, allowed only one delegate and one alternate for each of the six jurisdictions, the April version made an attempt to apportion Council representation on a relative population basis. Accordingly, the Northern Jurisdiction was allotted three delegates and three alternates; the Western Jurisdiction received two delegates and two alternates; the Southern (also known as the Navajo) Jurisdiction received four each; and the Pueblo Bonito, Leupp, and Moqui Jurisdictions each received one delegate and one alternate.

Curiously, the January version of the *Regulations* seemed to contemplate that, once elected, the chairman and vice chairman of the Tribal Council would continue to hold office indefinitely. No fixed term of years was specified, and Section 16 merely required that the offices be filled in the event of a vacancy "in the manner as provided for the original election thereof." Likewise no term of office was specified for delegates and alternate members of the council; once elected they continued indefinitely.

The April version of the *Regulations* provided, in Section 16, that "the terms of office of the chairman and vice chairman of the Tribal Council shall be four years from the date of their election," but again no term was specified for the delegates and their alternates.

These omissions may have been the result of an oversight, or they may have reflected the small importance attaching to the development of a tribal government in 1923, except as some such entity was required to legalize the leasing of tribal lands for oil and gas development.

On the same date that the Council *Regulations* were issued, April 24, 1923, Acting Commissioner E. B. Meritt directed a letter to Secretary of the Interior Work. The letter stated that the Midwest Refining Company had brought in a producing well and pointed out that applicants for leases had negotiated up to that time directly with the "Indian Council" (whether reference is to General Council or Business Committee is not clear). "In the interest of better administration of leasing affairs on the Navajo Reservation," Meritt said, "it is believed that a change should be made in that respect. It is therefore recommended that . . . on structures where there is no lease the Secretary of the Interior may, in his discretion, under such terms and conditions as he may prescribe in each particular case, grant a lease for any number of acres not exceeding 4,800, without advertisement. . . . Before any leases are granted or tract advertised for lease the matter will be presented to the Tribal Council for consideration whether they are willing to pass a resolution authorizing the Interior Department to lease the land under the plan outlined above, the leases to be signed on behalf of the tribe by the Commissioner to the Navajo Tribe." The letter and proposed leasing procedures were approved on the same date by the Secretary of the Interior.

The Navajo Tribal Council was duly constituted under the April *Regulations*, and it held its first meeting on July 7, 1923, at Toadlena, New Mexico. On that occasion, its first action was the passage of a resolution that virtually eliminated the reason for which it had been created. The resolution adopted by the Council granted to the Commissioner to the Navajo Tribe a power of attorney "to sign on behalf of the Navajo Indians all oil and gas mining leases which may be granted covering tracts on the treaty part of the Reservation" (Council Resolution of July 7, 1923). This power of attorney was not revoked until ten years later, by a resolution of October 31, 1933!

For more than a decade following its establishment the Tribal Council did little of importance at its annual meetings, if the resolutions it adopted are used as a measure of its involvement in tribal affairs.

However, it continued to exist and, on April 20, 1927, Commissioner Burke issued amendments to Sections 4, 16, and 17 of the 1923 *Regulations*. The amendments received the approval of the First Assistant Secretary of the Interior on the same day. The amendments made the term of office of the chairman, vice chairman, council delegates and alternates five years, and provided that the terms of those officers and members elected in 1923 would expire on July 7, 1928. Also, provision was made for the filling of vacancies that might occur in the Council membership, either by election or, "upon failure of the

Indians of any Jurisdiction to act," the vacancy could be filled by a tribal member appointed by the Secretary of the Interior. Even when the Indians of a jurisdiction acted to elect a candidate to fill a vacancy, Section 17 provided that "such elections to fill vacancies shall be submitted for approval to the Secretary of the Interior with the recommendation of the Commissioner to the Navajo Tribe."

Clearly the Council, as created in 1923 and modified in 1927, was an instrumentality of the Secretary of the Interior, not an organization for tribal self-government, and its status had not changed in 1927. The amendments promulgated in the latter year still made no provision for legislative or other governmental powers; it remained a consultative body only.

A few months later, in October 1928, further amendments were made in the Council *Regulations*. The position of Commissioner to the Navajo tribe was dropped, and the Commissioner of Indian Affairs assumed the responsibilities and duties formerly placed in the Commissioner of the tribe (Kelly 1968). In addition, the October 1928 amendments gave women the right to vote in Council elections; and the term of office of the chairman, vice chairman, delegates and alternates was placed at four years; again no legislative or other substantive powers were conferred upon the Council, and the body was permitted to meet only in the presence of an official of the government "designated by the Commissioner of Indian Affairs." The purpose of Council meetings, as set forth in Section 12 was "the consideration of such tribal matters as may be brought before it."

On July 8, 1933, the Chairman of the Council was authorized, by Council resolution, to appoint a six-member Executive Committee and seven additional Council committees to concern themselves, in a manner not specified, with water development and farming, natural resources and tribal lands, education and public health, industrial arts and crafts, livestock, employment, and chapter organization. On July 10, 1934, the alternate delegates to the Tribal Council were given full Council membership status. Further provision was made, by a Council Resolution of April 10, 1937, for the establishment of an Executive Committee, to be composed of one delegate from each of the land management districts established in 1936-37, and authorized to act, "with the authority of the Council," on all routine tribal matters.

Although, as we will note later, the Council acted to give what purported to be tribal consent in a number of areas during the first decade or more of its existence, none of its early actions affected the lives of the Navajo people and, as a result, they generally ignored its existence—if, in fact, they had even heard of it.

Over the course of the same decade of the 1920's, however, another institution was introduced by the federal government—the Navajo chapter organization—which, in fact, reached and involved many people, although in a nongovernmental capacity.

The Navajo Chapter System

A document entitled "The American Indian and Government Indian Administration," by Assistant Commissioner of Indian Affairs Meritt (1926: 5-6) provides historical information relating to efforts made by the Bureau of Indian Affairs to encourage Indian farmers and stock raisers during the 1920's:

> In 1922 a campaign was started for the adoption of a five-year program for each Indian reservation, for the purpose of having a definite outline of the best plan to develop the resources and utilize the many activities effectively, the chief objectives being self support for each Indian family. It was soon recognized that some form of organization was necessary to make a success of this undertaking, and this necessity led to the organization of groups of Indians, with their officers, for the purpose of stimulating effort along farming and stockraising lines. The Indians throughout the Service are taking unusual interest in Chapter work. The spirit of friendly rivalry which exists between Chapters is an incentive to put forth best efforts for increased acreage, better farms and garden products, improvement in health, better homes, etc. Chapters or farm clubs are in operation, or in process of organization on 25 reservations, and plans are being made for their inauguration on every reservation.

Superintendent John Hunter of the Leupp Agency, in 1927, was the first Navajo administrator to introduce the "farm chapter" idea in the Navajo country. It gained quick popularity and rapidly spread to other Navajo jurisdictions. The chapters, unlike the Council, were local in scope and organization and, as Williams (1970:37) observes, they "were integrated into preexisting, local sociopolitical structures which had at their core the extended family structure that functioned as the basic unit of social control among the Navajo people." In other words, the chapters fit easily into the pattern of Navajo social organization, and as a result they were quickly absorbed as a cultural institution.

Before the advent of the chapters, headmen had conducted local meetings from time to time to settle disputes, discuss local problems, or for kindred purposes. The chapters provided a center for the continuation of this type of community cooperation, differing from the previous pattern largely to the extent that chapter meetings were more formal; they were held on a regularly scheduled basis, with elected officers.

With federal subsidies and contributed labor, meeting houses were built at many locations over the Navajo country. Federal administrators and technicians benefited in many ways: the chapter meetings offered opportunities for the presentation of government policies and programs; the system of chapters acted as relay stations through which to pass information throughout the agency jurisdiction; they functioned as precincts for the election of Tribal Council delegates; and the custom soon developed to use the chapters as forums in which councilmen and other leaders could express themselves about local and tribal issues.

Unfortunately, as the controversy developed around the issue of grazing controls and stock reduction after 1933, the function of the chapters as forums for the expression of popular opinion led to decreased official recognition and use of these organizations on the part of federal administrators, who turned their attention to the Council on the premise that it represented the entire tribe. For a period of years, from the mid-1930's until the 1950's, the role of the chapters in federal-tribal relationships, and in shaping the decisions of the tribal government, was much reduced. In many locations chapter houses fell into disrepair, and in some the community ceased to elect officers or otherwise keep the organization alive; in others, the organization continued despite the fact that it received no further support from the federal government. Unfortunately, the chapter system was not utilized as the foundation upon which to reorganize the tribal government in 1938, although Commissioner Collier, testifying before the Senate Committee on Indian Affairs on July 3, 1937, stated that the tribal constitution committee "in their work did not follow out my suggestion of constructing the tribal system out of the chapters."

In effect, the tribal government was a superimposition from the top, rather than a grass-roots movement beginning with the people, capitalizing on existing cultural institutions and developing as an extension of the traditional sociopolitical organization of the tribe.

Presumably, the Commissioner's suggestion had reflected a recommendation made by Solon Kimball, based on the latter's study of Navajo social organization and control in District 4. Kimball had recommended a tribal government based on traditional Navajo social organization, one comprised of district councils made up of headmen who would elect one or more of their members to the Tribal Council. The tribal constitution, when drafted, would have then included provisions for the formal recognition of headmen, and their election for service on the Tribal Council. The Kimball proposal did not, apparently, elicit much support.

During the 1950's the chapter organization began to revive. At first the Tribal Council appropriated a modest amount of tribal funds to purchase doors and windows for the old chapter houses, and local communities donated labor for their repair. Later, after the opening of the oil fields in 1956-57, the Tribal Council established a chapter house and community center construction program designed to provide at least one chapter house for every council precinct throughout the Navajo country. Funds were budgeted for the payment of salaries and expenses of chapter officers, and the organization again gained status. In fact, it plays an important grass-roots role in the operation of tribal government today, and in several areas regional councils have been formed, drawing together the chapters of each such area for the discussion and solution of common problems, and to make recommendations to the Tribal Council. This development parallels the joint chapter meetings that took place periodically during the late 1920's and early 1930's in some of the agency jurisdictions, and it promises to lay the basis for the eventual reorganization of the tribal government along the lines recommended by Kimball more than 30 years ago.

The Movement for Council Reorganization

Not long after his appointment in April 1933, Commissioner Collier met with the Navajo Tribal Council at Fort Wingate, New Mexico. On this occasion he outlined some of the programs and policies which he planned to institute, and touched upon the need to conserve the deteriorating range resources of the Navajo Reservation. The subject of range and livestock control had been introduced five years before by Assistant Commissioner Meritt, but no action had followed, partly because the dimensions of the problem were not known, partly because no one knew what type of remedial measures were required.

A survey conducted by William H. Zeh in 1930 pointed to the heavy erosion which had resulted from serious overgrazing of the range, and in 1933 a series of grazing surveys were begun. These indicated that the rangelands in some parts of the Navajo country, were more than 100 per cent overgrazed. The early institution of better range management was imperative, and the immediate need to reduce livestock numbers was quite apparent. At the same time, the national administration was interested in resource conservation throughout the country, and the need to provide stop-gap employment during the depression years offered both manpower and financing.

A few months later, in November 1933, the Tribal Council met at Tuba City, Arizona, where a stock reduction program was introduced and the Council was asked to sanction it. The initial phase of the program involved the purchase of 100,000 head of sheep from Navajo owners, and quotas were set for all of the six agency jurisdictions. This effort was not successful, partly because its enforcement was left in the hands of the Council, a responsibility which the tribal government was equipped by neither authority nor experience to carry out. The effort was not without effect, however, for it sent a wave of apprehension through the Navajo population. People began to view the government program with suspicion, and if they had never before given a second thought to the Tribal Council they began to take notice of it now.

In March 1934, the Council met at Fort Defiance, Arizona, where the delegates were told that further reduction was necessary. They were asked to enact a resolution supporting the required measures, but they declined to do so. By March, public alarm had spread, and the Council found itself in a dilemma. The need for reduction appeared to be reasonable, but the Council members were reluctant to support a program which had become so unpopular. Coercion and active support of unpopular issues was not consonant with the principles upon which traditional Navajo leadership rested, and a functional tribal government could not be created by fiat.

Perhaps in an effort to increase its strength and spread responsibility among a greater number of men in coping with the growing problem posed by the government program, the Council, at a July 1934 meeting in Keams Canyon, Arizona, voted to amend the 1928 *Regulations* to accord full membership status to the twelve alternate Council delegates, thus increasing the voting membership of the body to twenty-four.

Turmoil continued to grow as the stock reduction program gained momentum and as a result, an atmosphere of suspicion surrounded efforts to explain and build support for the Indian Reorganization Act following its passage in June 1934. The flame of suspicion was fanned by demagogues who convinced many people that acceptance of the act by the Navajo people would lead to loss of their livestock and fencing of their rangelands. During the same period an effort was being made by the tribe and by the government to secure passage of a bill designed to define the boundaries of the Navajo Reservation in Arizona and New Mexico. The Arizona Boundary Bill did pass, but the New Mexico lands which would have been affected included those areas added to the Navajo Reservation by President Roosevelt in 1907 and subsequently restored to the public domain by Pres-

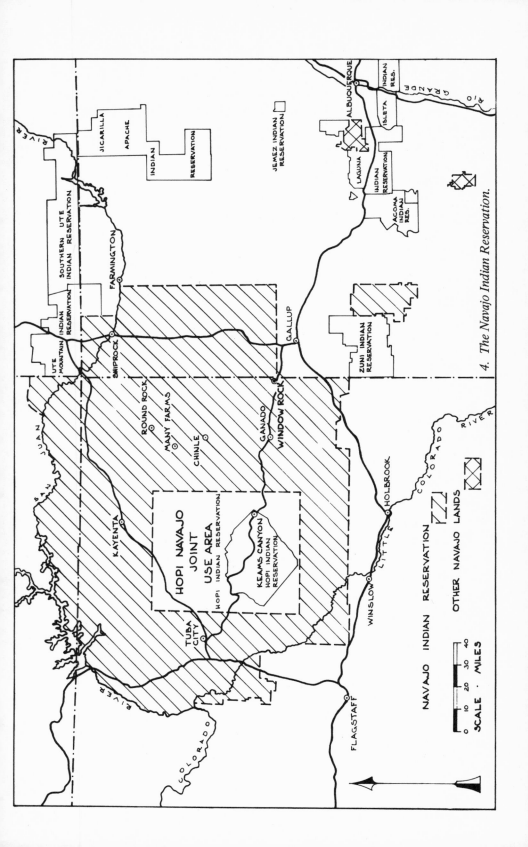

4. *The Navajo Indian Reservation.*

ident Taft in 1911, under pressure from non-Indian interests involved in a struggle for land and resources in western New Mexico. Political interests in New Mexico worked tirelessly to defeat the New Mexico Boundary Bill, and they managed to inject it as an issue in the vote for acceptance or rejection of the Indian Reorganization Act by the tribe. As a result, a "separatist" movement, begun under the leadership of Jacob Morgan, and aimed at division of the New Mexico segment of the tribe from the segment in Arizona, joined with non-Indian New Mexico interests in an attempt to exempt the tribe from the application of the Indian Reorganization Act—and, at the same time to defeat the New Mexico Boundary Bill which, if it became law, would have extended the Navajo Reservation boundaries in New Mexico and defined tham permanently!

The New Mexico Boundary Bill failed to pass, and, when the Navajo Tribe voted on the Indian Reorganization Act in June 1935, it too was rejected by a narrow margin. Sentiment within the tribe ran high, both for and against the act, as evidenced by the fact that, of an amazing 15,600 ballots cast, 7,608 favored acceptance and 7,992 voted for rejection. The election is still known as *názbąs doo alnáá'ásdzoh* ("the circle and the cross," because a circle signified rejection and a cross meant a vote for the act).

Plans for the reorganization of the tribal government along constitutional lines, including a statement of substantive powers, collapsed with rejection of the Indian Reorganization Act by the voters of the tribe. Nonetheless, plans were immediately laid for the drafting and adoption of a tribal constitution outside the Act, including special statutory recognition of the tribal government by Congress.

On July 1, 1935, the government proceeded to abolish the six separate Navajo agency jurisdictions, consolidating them into a single agency with headquarters at Window Rock, Arizona. The place had long been known, in Navajo as *Tségháhoodzání* (the perforated rock), but in an effort to symbolize the new consolidation of the Navajo Tribe—and to the glee of the Navajos—it was proposed to change the name to *Ni'Alníi'gi* (an ambiguous term translatable either as "at the center of the earth," or as "at your middle"). This move not only tended to treat the Navajos as a tribal entity, but it was also designed to foster the development of a concept of tribal government.

As time went on the old Council became more and more deeply bemired in the controversy surrounding stock reduction and grazing control, and the need for reorganization of the tribal government became increasingly urgent. As a result, the old Council finally came to a grinding halt, holding its last meeting on November 24, 1936. At that meeting a resolution, which had been proposed by Commissioner Collier on the preceding day, was introduced, calling for reorganization of the Tribal Council. In a speech to the three-man Executive Committee of the Council the day before, the Commissioner told the members that Secretary Ickes was convinced of the need for such reorganization. It was recommended that a representative committee be formed to draft a proposed constitution and bylaws for the Council. Collier made it clear that he did not have reference to a constitution of the type authorized by the Indian Reorganization Act, but that he was "talking about the Tribal Council as organized under regulations of the (Department); the Council which derives its powers from the regulations . . . should change its organization so that it will be more representative and active."

The Constitutional Assembly of 1937

On the following day the matter was presented to the full Council, which then enacted a resolution authorizing the Executive Committee to call a constitutional assembly. After careful consideration, the Executive Committee decided to visit all land use areas on the reservation for the purpose of identifying the local headmen. The committee hoped to recruit the membership of the constitutional assembly from among the natural leadership of the tribe.

By March 9, 1937, the Executive Committee had completed its canvass, having collected the names of 250 local leaders, and at a meeting on the same date it adopted a resolution to provide for the establishment of a constitutional assembly to be composed of 70 of the most influential men included among the 250 names. At the same time, in the interest of providing an instrument for the interim conduct of tribal business, the resolution authorized the constitutional assembly, once constituted, to declare itself to be the de facto Tribal Council, if it so desired. In addition, it provided for continuation of the de facto Council until a constitution could be completed and approved by the Secretary of the Interior.

Two days later the Executive Committee acted, by resolution, to call a meeting of the constitutional assembly for April 6, 1937, to adopt "an acceptable constitution for the Navajo Tribe and for any other purpose that may be necessary for the welfare of the tribe."

The Executive Committee enactments were transmitted to the Commissioner on March 12, with a recommendation for their approval. In his transmittal the Superintendent expressed the view that the 70 names chosen to constitute the constitutional assembly had already been elected, in effect, by local Navajo people, but he stated that, in the event the assembly failed to declare itself to be the de facto Council, it would be necessary to hold a general election.

These developments immediately drew the fire of the separatists, and the local administration wished to avoid the dangers inherent in a general election, if possible. The "political climate" was not right for such a move. The Commissioner concurred with the recommendations of the Superintendent, including appointment of a chairman of the de facto Council by the Secretary of the Interior, justifying his position on the premise that "the Council, existing or reorganized, is an institution created by the Secretary. Its authorities are derived from regulations."

The Secretary approved the resolutions, but he took the position that the Council should select its own chairman and vice chairman.

The first convention of the constitutional assembly was held on April 9-10, 1937. It turned out to be a stormy meeting. The separatists attended in force, and Jacob Morgan, as their spokesman, demanded that the tribe be afforded an opportunity to vote on the question of dissolving the old Council. However, a motion was made and seconded that the assembly declare itself to be the de facto Council. It carried by a vote of 66 for and 2 against.

The assembly then proceeded to nominate and elect a chairman and vice chairman, as well as a secretary, treasurer and two sergeants-at-arms.

As its first act of business the new Council proceeded to adopt a resolution authorizing the chairman to appoint a committee to draft a constitution, and by a subsequent enactment a new Executive Committee was established to "act on all routine tribal matters."

Jacob Morgan, who a few years later became Council chairman, was offered the chairmanship of the constitutional committee, but he declined and, with his followers, left the meeting after roundly denouncing the procedures and decisions which had been reached.

Under the leadership of Thomas Dodge, an attorney and son of Chee Dodge, who functioned as a legal consultant to the constitutional committee, the group proceeded swiftly to draft a constitution. The document was completed, with a set of bylaws, and transmitted to the Commissioner of Indian Affairs, on October 25, 1937, with the expressed hope that it might be recognized by a special act of Congress.

In Washington the proposed constitution came under review by the Commissioner and members of his staff, as well as by the Solicitor in the Department of the Interior. At the same time, the special Navajo grazing regulations, duly sanctioned by the newly formed Executive Committee of the Tribal Council, were placed in effect by the Secretary of the Interior, thus adding fuel to the controversy already surrounding the stock reduction issue.

The proposed constitution followed closely the format of those documents that were being drafted by tribes which had accepted the Indian Reorganization Act (IRA). It set forth the requirements for tribal membership and established a Council as the tribal legislative body, to be composed of 74 delegates apportioned at the rate of one representative for each 600 people; set their terms of office at six years and spelled out eligibility requirements for tribal office. The document provided for a president and vice president of the tribe, to hold office for terms of six years, and, most importantly, the constitution set forth the powers to be exercised by the Council as the governing body of the tribe. Again the powers paralleled those of IRA constitutions, including authority to veto the sale, disposition, encumbrance, or lease of tribal lands; authority to regulate the use and disposition of tribal property; the regulation of trading;

the hiring of legal counsel; the levy of taxes and fees on tribal members; adoption of a code of laws to govern the conduct of tribal members; and the regulation of inheritance of personal property. Provision was made for an Executive Committee, which had the effect of establishing it as a Business Committee for the tribe.

However, the constitution contained a provision transcending the restrictions embodied in IRA constitutions, to the effect that "*any* resolution or ordinance adopted by the Navajo Council or Executive Committee shall take effect as soon as approved by the Secretary of the Interior." The reorganized Council would have taken a long step in the direction of becoming, in fact and in function, a tribal governing body, under the terms of the proposed constitution, but its powers to act on behalf of the tribe would have remained totally subject to approval by the Secretary of the Interior. To no small extent it would have remained, essentially, an instrument of the Secretary of the Interior, although to a greater extent than ever before it would also have become an instrument of the tribe.

Constitutional Review and Rejection

Review of the proposed constitution by the Department of the Interior and the Bureau of Indian Affairs quickly resulted in the emergence of two opposing schools of thought. One member of the Commissioner's staff pointed out that, before the constitution could be voted upon by the Navajo electorate, it would first have to be explained and debated in local meetings with the people. He asked: "What will the effect be? Your internal and external political administrative problems are already mountain high."

This adviser went on to point out certain legal technical obstacles that would have to be overcome. He pointed out that the format taken by the proposed constitution indicated that the constitutional committee "labored under a misapprehension in its belief that it could legally obtain for the tribe and its governing authority certain powers which cannot be conferred on any tribe that has voted itself out of the Indian Reorganization Act." He pointed out that any constitution the Navajo Tribe might adopt and that might be approved by the Secretary would still remain "in its essentials, an administrative action which can be arbitrarily changed, altered, modified or cancelled by the present or succeeding Secretaries."

On the basis of these arguments the Commissioner's adviser held that it was not wise to encourage the tribe to vote on an IRA type constitution, thus creating the false impression that the document conferred irrevocable powers upon the Tribal Council. He called the Commissioner's attention to "the fact that past Tribal Councils functioned, not as a true representative governing body, but rather that these Councils were organizations created by the government because of the necessity of having some sort of tribal organization with which the Government could deal. . . . Essentially, it still is a symbol, an agency which had to be created in order to permit the Government to deal with the Navajos as a tribe instead of a collection of families and groups."

He went on to express the view that the concept of self-government, tribal in scope, had first to be built up through an educational process involving tribal leadership in the entire gamut of tribal affairs. "This cannot be accomplished, and prestige cannot be built up," he said, "by asking their consent to and active participation in any form of stock reduction. It follows logically that the enforcement of the grazing regulations, especially in the direction of stock reduction, must be assumed by the Government as its sole responsibility, while the new Tribal and District Councils might act as channels of communication, education and mediation so far as their constituents are concerned."

Other advisers took the position that "a constitution based merely on the will of the Secretary of the Interior, and therefore revocable at will, is not a constitution but a mere administrative delegation of authority." They held that, when ratified by the Navajo people, the document should be supported by an act of Congress. On the other hand, other advisers, countering the argument that the Navajo, having rejected the Indian Reorganization Act, could not legally adopt a constitution which resembled an IRA constitution and could not exercise the self-governing powers of an IRA tribe, held that "under the doctrine of inherent tribal powers (residual sovereignty) of Indian tribes, steadily enunciated by Federal Court decisions for more than a century and crystallized into law by the Indian Reorganization Act, the Navajo Tribe already possessed all the powers" contained in their proposed constitution.

The Commissioner, under the barrage of arguments and counterarguments, and faced with a perplexing set of practical problems on the reservation, concluded that it would be wise to limit the scope of tribal powers for the moment. He expressed doubt that more than three percent of the tribal members could, in fact, understand such a legalistic document as the proposed constitution, and he expressed the view that it appeared to be over-ambitious, in seeking to give the representative body a status and a set of powers appropriate to the Council of a tribe organized under the Indian Reorganization Act, which the Navajo had rejected. "I believe that any constitution submitted to the Navajo should be realistic," and "that it should consider the inchoate amorphous condition of the Navajo and that, in view of this inchoate condition, it should be short, concise, simple, limited to a few objectives and conferring initially a limited number of powers."

The de facto Tribal Council, which began its existence as the constitutional assembly and which was scheduled to terminate as soon as a constitution could be drafted, remained in office. The need to hold a general election became more pressing with each passing day as internal dissension within the tribe increased. Lack of agreement on major issues surrounding the proposed constitution within the Department and the Bureau blocked necessary approval action by the Secretary, and this combination of factors led to the conclusion that the time was not right for a referendum on the proposed document, under any circumstance.

At first, consideration was given to the promulgation of a new set of Council Regulations by the Secretary of the Interior, patterned after the set of bylaws drafted by the constitutional committee and incorporating portions of the proposed constitution, including a statement of powers to be exercised by the Council, subject to secretarial approval. The matter was referred back to the constitutional committee which, however, expressed its opposition to the inclusion, in such a set of bylaws, of any part of the proposed constitution; they held that the constitution should be placed in effect only after its approval by the Navajo people, voting in a referendum held for that purpose.

A compromise was reached in February 1938, at which time the constitutional committee approved a revised set of bylaws, patterned after those which had been drafted to accompany the proposed constitution. The title was changed from "Bylaws of the Navajo Tribal Council" to "Rules for the Navajo Reservation," and the draft was submitted for issuance by the Secretary. Section 2 of the draft stated that "these rules shall be considered regulations of the Commissioner of Indian Affairs authorized by laws of the United States and by treaties with the Navajo Tribe, and they shall be considered an agreement between the Commissioner of Indian Affairs and the Navajo people."

The draft provided for a 74-member Tribal Council, apportioned on the basis of one representative per 600 population, serving four-year terms; and for a president and vice president of the tribe, also serving four-year terms in office. Provision was made for an Executive Committee, to be composed of one of the delegates from each district, and the document included a statement of powers to be exercised by the Tribal Council. They were essentially those which had been included in the proposed constitution.

However, the proposed bylaws generated anew many of the same arguments that had surrounded the proposed constitution and, in April 1938, the Commissioner submitted an alternative document which included a statement to the effect that it was to be an interim measure for use pending the adoption of a tribal constitution. Entitled "Regulations for the Establishment of the Navajo Tribal Council," the proposal provided for a 74-member Council to be elected by the people of the several districts in elections to be conducted by the Reservation Superintendent. An Executive Committee was to be composed of one delegate chosen by and from those elected from each district, and the document included a provision taken from the old Council Regulations, to the effect that no meeting of the Council could be held without the presence of the Superintendent and the Commissioner of Indian Affairs or his representative.

This document was reviewed by the Superintendent who, in May 1938, sent to the Commissioner a substitute draft of the proposed regulations, entitled "Rules for the Navajo Tribal Council and Reservation." In this version, the statement of substantive powers of the Council was omitted, and little remained aside from the structural framework of the Council and a set of rules governing the conduct of tribal elections.

The Reorganized Navajo Tribal Council of 1938

With a few subsequent changes the bylaws were promulgated, on July 26, 1938, by the Secretary of the Interior, entitled *Rules for the Navajo Tribal Council*. The Council membership remained 74 delegates, plus a chairman and vice chairman, all elected by popular vote and by secret ballot. The terms of office were set at four years, and elections were to be conducted by the Superintendent of the Navajo Reservation. To facilitate the nomination of candidates for the office of chairman the reservation was divided into four "election provinces," and provision was made for the holding of nominating conventions at a location, in each province, designated by the Superintendent. At the conventions, the voters from each province assembled, made nominations, and voted for one or another of the persons nominated, for the chairmanship. Following the nominating conventions, the names of the candidates chosen by the voters in each province were certified to the Superintendent by the members of the existing Council and the several candidates then drew the colors that were to represent them on election day. The voter selected a ballot of the color corresponding to the candidate of his choice and deposited it in the ballot box. To be elected, a candidate had to receive a majority of the votes cast, with the result that a run-off election was often required. The candidate receiving the greatest number of votes cast in the run-off election became the chairman of the Tribal Council, and the person receiving the second highest number of votes cast became the vice chairman.

An Executive Committee was provided, to be composed of the chief delegates from each district. The chief delegates were to be chosen by the delegates elected from each district, from among their number.

The Council, as reorganized in 1938, almost attained the status of a constitutional government, but a complex of circumstances intervened, including rejection of the Indian Reorganization Act, which resulted in continuation of the governing body on the basis of secretarial regulations. Aside from secret balloting and increased membership, the reorganized Council had gained little over its predecessors. Its elections were still conducted by the Superintendent, who occupied a position beside the chairman in the conduct of Council meetings, and there was still no statement of substantive legislative powers. The Council could voice its views on matters affecting the tribe, and it could do anything that the Secretary of the Interior was willing to approve; nothing more.

The first election of the reorganized Council took place on September 24, 1938, and it held its first meeting on November 28 of the same year. It met, in conformity with the regulations, at the call of the Commissioner of Indian Affairs, although the prohibition against meetings without the presence of federal representatives had been eliminated from the final draft of the 1938 *Rules*.

When it convened, in 1938, the Council declined to activate the Executive Committee, insisting that all decisions be made by the full Council. The previous Executive Committee had sanctioned the "Grazing Regulations."

Discussion continued, in the Department and in the Bureau, regarding the need to reactivate consideration of a tribal constitution, but nothing was done until after the close of World War II.

Tribal Government from 1947 to the Present

The events of the 1930's, and of the war years that followed, set the scene for a series of far-reaching changes in the life of the people. In the historic past there had been other periods of revolutionary change, as Navajo culture literally swallowed and digested alien institutions of formidable proportions, successfully recasting them to fit Navajo patterns and, at the same time, readjusting Navajo patterns to accommodate the borrowed innovations. Centuries ago Navajo culture accepted a complex religious-ceremonial system from Puebloan sources, but in a form distinctively Navajo; agriculture and stock raising followed a similar course of readjustment to the peculiar requirements of Navajo life, taking their place with the ceremonial system as cornerstones in the foundation of traditional Navajo society. Now, in the 1930's a new wave of change was taking shape, one which would sweep the people toward tribalism in a political sense on the crest of the alien institution of representative government.

By the end of the 1930's a wage-based economy had already begun to compete with the traditional agricultural-pastoral system in many parts of the Navajo country and the innovation grew rapidly following the outbreak of the war; the institution of formal education, tolerated previously as a foreign intrusion, began to gain stature as a necessary tool for survival; and modern medicine established a niche for itself in the tribal scheme of things.

For the Navajo people the close of World War II was followed by a critical period of readjustment. People returned from military service or from off-reservation employment to the scant and neglected resources of the reservation, where work opportunities were virtually nonexistent. To meet the resultant economic crisis a number of temporary relief measures were taken by the government, including a program aimed at finding off-reservation work opportunities. Work was also begun on the development of a rehabilitation program for the tribe, looking toward its presentation to Congress and enactment into law. The plight of the people received wide publicity from a sympathetic public and from the Congress.

At the same time a demand grew for the "emancipation" of Indian tribes from federal control, with the elimination of special federal services. Further, in August 1946, Congress enacted legislation to establish the Indian Claims Commission and to authorize suits by Indian tribes against the federal government, for losses they had sustained and for wrongs they had suffered in the long period of years prior to the date of the act. Tribes were authorized to hire claims attorneys to represent them, and they were given a five-year period in which to present their claims to the Commission.

Proposals for Rehabilitation

After 1946, the Tribal Council became an active participant in the planning of the then proposed rehabilitation program, and the scope of its concern with internal tribal issues began to take on new dimensions. Tribal participation was especially active after August 1947, when the Council entered into a contract with an attorney for both claims and general counsel services.

Among other proposals to be included in the rehabilitation bill was statutory authorization for the adoption of a tribal constitution. With the growing demand for "emancipation" of Indian tribes from federal control during the period the rehabilitation program was being planned, including a demand that the tribe assume greater responsibility and a greater voice in the management of its own affairs, it followed that the Tribal Council, at long last, might secure broad powers of self-government.

Accordingly, in reviewing the draft of the proposed rehabilitation program at a Council meeting in March 1948, the newly retained tribal attorney made reference to the section providing for the adoption of a tribal constitution and to proposed language to the effect that the constitution could give to the tribe "any powers vested in the tribe or any organ thereof by existing law, together with such additional powers, not in excess of the powers possessed by other organized or incorporated Indian tribes."

The attorney pointed out that the proposed language would confine the Navajo Tribe to the powers given to tribes organized under the Indian Reorganization Act, which the Navajo Tribe had rejected, and said (Navajo Tribal Council Minutes, March 18-23, 1948, p. 85):

> You are the largest single group of Indians in the United States. You are almost like a small country or state in yourselves. You should not be limited, in my opinion, by the Wheeler-Howard Act (IRA), which you voted down, but should have the fullest possible powers that you are able to administer, and those powers will become more and greater as your people become better educated. Furthermore I think the constitution should actually be adopted—this is my suggestion submitted to you—should actually be adopted *by the Council rather than by vote of the people* although given plenty of time for carrying it back to the people and discussing it for as many months as you want to discuss it before you act. I say that because you are the men who will be working

constantly with any constitution adopted and if it should be necessary to amend it to increase your powers in any way then it could be amended in the same way whereas to have a general vote throughout the reservation is an exceedingly difficult thing.

He then read proposed language which would permit formulation of a constitution by the Tribal Council and its adoption by the same body by a two-thirds vote. Subsequently, at a June 1948 Council meeting, the tribal attorney, reviewing proposals to be incorporated into the proposed rehabilitation program, and with reference to a provision authorizing adoption of the tribal constitution, stated (Navajo Tribal Council Minutes, June 26-29, 1948, p. 66):

That was the section I think you will remember we drafted at the last meeting to provide for the adoption of a constitution and to provide for the Secretary to give you very strong powers and to advance and increase those powers as time went on. In other words, if you wait until the Act is passed and Section 5 becomes law you have much broader powers and more extended powers than you could probably get approved now.

The Council requested that their attorney proceed to draft a proposed constitution. He did so, and a few months later, at a Council meeting held in December 1948, he reported on the draft, advising the Council that (Navajo Tribal Council Minutes, December 6-9, 1948, p. 9) "this constitution has been drafted to give you, the Navajo Tribal Council and the Navajo people, all the power I could get into that constitution under the law."

The Act of April 19, 1950, commonly known as the Navajo-Hopi Long Range Rehabilitation Act, authorized the appropriation of $88,570,000 for a wide range of programs designed for the social and economic betterment of the two tribes, and included a provision for adoption of a Navajo constitution. However, the Congress did not leave approval of the document to the Tribal Council, but required its ratification by the Navajo electorate. Section 6 of the act as passed provided as follows:

In order to facilitate the fullest possible participation by the Navajo Tribe in the program authorized by this Act, the members of the tribe shall have the right to adopt a tribal constitution in the manner herein prescribed. Such constitution may provide for the exercise by the Navajo Tribe of any powers vested in the tribe or any organ thereof by existing law, together with such additional powers as the members of the tribe may, with the approval of the Secretary of the Interior, deem proper to include therein. Such constitution shall be formulated by the Navajo Tribal Council at any regular meeting, distributed in printed form to the Navajo people for consideration, and adopted by secret ballot of the adult members of the Navajo Tribe in an election held under such regulations as the Secretary may prescribe, at which a majority of the qualified votes cast favor such adoption. The constitution shall authorize the fullest possible participation of the Navajos in the administration of their affairs as approved by the Secretary of the Interior and shall become effective when approved by the Secretary. The constitution may be amended from time to time in the same manner as herein provided for its adoption, and the Secretary of the Interior shall approve any amendment which, in the opinion of the Secretary of the Interior, advances the development of the Navajo people toward the fullest realization and exercise of the rights, privileges, duties and responsibilities of American citizenship.

The Rehabilitation Act thus provided a statutory base upon which to reorganize Navajo tribal government. The arguments advanced in the 1930's casting doubts about the authority of the tribe to exercise the constitutional powers accorded to tribes that accepted the Indian Reorganization Act were of questionable validity at that time. By 1950, they were baseless. Therefore, the way was now clear for the adoption of a constitution that could neither be cancelled arbitrarily nor modified by the Secretary of the Interior.

The Rapid Growth of Council Activities

As the Tribal Council became involved in the planning of the rehabilitation program during the closing years of the 1940's, tribal government underwent rapid growth. The subject of grazing regulations again became an issue, but the Secretary of the Interior sent a representative to the reservation in 1947 to gather information and make recommendations regarding future policy and procedure. The report submitted by Lee Muck, Assistant to the Secretary, "Land Utilization," recommended the issuance of a "freeze order," placing in abeyance the punitive provisions of the special *Grazing Regulations*, with certain exceptions, in order to permit the Navajo Tribe itself to develop grazing controls in consultation with the Navajo people (Muck 1948). In subsequent years, local grazing committees were established and, after many postponements of deadlines for completion of new tribal grazing regulations, a set was finally submitted by the tribe and approved by the Secretary in April 1956.

Although in effect the long-standing controversy surrounding grazing controls and stock reduction came to an end in 1956, in the face of serious reservation economic problems the tribal regulations have never been adequately enforced to reduce livestock numbers to the range-carrying capacity and the problem posed by overgrazing continues unabated. Benefits derived from the issue have been largely in the form of the stimulus it provided in the development of tribal government, including grass-roots participation.

The increased demands of tribal business, after 1946, led to the establishment of a permanent residence at tribal headquarters on the part of the Tribal Council chairman, and, after 1950, to a rapid expansion of the tribal executive department. To facilitate the conduct of tribal business the Council acted, in November 1947, to reestablish the Executive Committee. However, because of the infamy attaching to the title "Executive Committee," stemming from the fact that a predecessor of the same name had sanctioned the special grazing regulations in 1937, the Council required that the new group be known as "Advisory Committee." This group, acting under a wide variety of authorities delegated to it by the Tribal Council, became a key organ of tribal government during the 1950's. It came to be, in every sense, an executive arm of the Council.

The Tribal Council received formal recognition in the Rehabilitation Act of 1950 as the official instrument of the tribe, authorized to plan tribal programs and request the advance of tribal funds from the U.S. Treasury with which to finance them. In fact, the act provided that such tribal funds would thereafter be available "for such purposes as may be designated by the Navajo Tribal Council and approved by the Secretary of the Interior." This new authority led to the institution of an annual tribal budget, formulated by the tribe, approved by the Council, and submitted for secretarial approval as required by Congress. By the latter part of the decade, following the discovery of major reservation oil and gas deposits, the tribe became a multimillion-dollar business organization, as reflected in the fact that the 1959 fiscal year budget provided for the expenditure of more than $22.8 million of tribal funds.

The Modernization of Election Procedures

Looking toward the formulation of a tribal constitution as authorized by the rehabilitation program, Bureau representatives began work, in 1949, toward early improvement of tribal election procedures. The election process was still that provided in the 1938 *Rules* for the Tribal Council. Before this, in 1948, the right of Indians to vote in state and national elections in Arizona and New Mexico was established by a three-judge District Court in New Mexico, which held unconstitutional those provisions of the state constitution that prevented such participation on the part of reservation Indians (*Trujillo* v. *Garley*), and by the Arizona Supreme Court (*Harrison* v. *Laveen*). There was not only a need to modernize and make tribal election procedures more democratic, but there was a parallel need to bring tribal procedures into closer conformity with those of the state and nation as a training opportunity for future Indian voting in "outside" elections.

The people of the western part of the Navajo Reservation were especially interested in amendment of the tribal election procedures and in the formulation of a tribal constitution. Numerous meetings, attended by hundreds of people, were held during 1949 at Tuba City, at which the Bureau and the western Navajo leadership developed a set of amended election procedures in an atmosphere of complete harmony and unity of purpose. When the proposed amendments were completed they were presented to the Tribal Council, which endorsed them tentatively, pending determination of their acceptability in other sectors of the reservation. To meet this requirement, a Bureau official met during the summer of 1950 with virtually every community in the Navajo country. In each location the people voted their support of the proposal and instructed their Council delegate to vote in favor of the new procedure when it was presented for Council action. As a result, on September 15, 1950, the Council gave its unanimous endorsement to the amendments.

The new procedure replaced the colored ballots, previously used to identify candidates, by a paper ballot containing photographs of the candidates for tribal office, an innovation required by the widespread illiteracy of the Navajo people at that period; provided for the selection of one delegate to the province nominating conventions by each of the 74 election communities, instead of nominations for the chairmanship by the voters themselves, a circumstance that previously had resulted in the choice of candidates for the chairmanship largely by the people who lived within a few miles' radius of each election province headquarters. It also provided for the popular election of judges for the Navajo Courts of Indian Offenses, in lieu of their appointment by the Commissioner of Indian Affairs, with confirmation by the Tribal Council as required by secretarial regulation. This latter innovation opened the way for the development of the Navajo Tribal Court system which took place after 1950.

In addition, the new election procedure permitted the candidates for chairman and vice chairman to run as a team on a single ticket, replacing the previous system which required that the runner-up in a tribal election be named vice-chairman. Further, it provided for voter registration, and provision was made for absentee voting—an innovation that was unnecessary in 1938, when nearly all members of the tribe lived in the Navajo country—but one which was essential a decade later at which time large numbers of Navajo people were employed outside the reservation area.

For practical reasons, it was necessary to provide for conduct of the first election under the direction of Bureau officials, but with the active assistance of tribal members employed by the tribe. The first election under the new procedure was held in March 1951, and it was entirely successful. Subsequently between 1951 and the end of the first four-year Council term, by an ordinance enacted in October 1954 the election procedure was again revised to place total responsibility for the conduct of tribal elections on the tribe. The revised procedure provided for the establishment of a tribal election board to carry out tribal elections, beginning with that of March 1955. Again, the election was successfully carried out, and the tribe has conducted its own elections independently since that time.

The election procedure was again revised by the Tribal Council in May 1966. At this time, in view of improved road systems and transportation in the Navajo country, the election provinces were abolished, and provision was made for a central nominating convention to select two candidates for the office of chairman of the Tribal Council. Under the previous system the four election province conventions could nominate as many as four candidates for the office, or, as happened in 1959, they could all nominate the same candidate, with the result that he could run unopposed on the ballot in the general election. Many Navajo voters were disappointed, on that occasion, by the lack of competing candidates, maintaining that "you can't have a horse race with only one horse!"

The new procedure, as amended in 1966, requires candidates for the chairmanship to name their running mate for the vice-chairmanship within five days following the close of the central nominating convention. The election date was moved from the first Monday and Tuesday in March of election years to the second Tuesday and Wednesday after the first Monday in November.

In addition, incorporated in the new Election Law of 1966, are provisions that are usually found in constitutions. These include a procedure for the removal of elected officials and the filling of vacancies. Removal of tribal officers and Council delegates can be initiated by the Council or by a delegate's constituents through the submittal of a petition for removal signed by "more than fifty (50) percent of registered voters from his precinct." However, there is no provision for a recall election; removal can be effected only by the vote of at least a two-thirds majority of the Tribal Council. The ordinance is in the nature of a further amendment of the 1938 *Rules*, and became effective upon its approval by the Secretary of the Interior.

The Draft Constitution of 1953

Work on the proposed constitution continued sporadically after the passage of the Rehabilitation Act of 1950 and finally, in October 1953, a draft was completed and transmitted to the Commissioner of Indian Affairs for review. A few months previously, in August, the 83rd Congress had passed House Concurrent Resolution 108, expressing the intent of Congress, as rapidly as possible, "to make the Indians within the territorial limits of the United States subject to the same laws and entitled to the same privileges and responsibilities as are applicable to other citizens of the United States, to end their status as wards of the United States, and to grant them all the rights and prerogatives pertaining to American citizenship." Although Indians were assured that every effort would be made to bring them to a position of social and economic parity with their fellow citizens, and that recommendations for termination would not be sent forward to Congress without first consulting the tribe concerned, the Commissioner, in 1953, indicated that efforts would continue to transfer responsibility for services to the tribes themselves or to appropriate agencies of Government that normally provide such services to non-Indians.

The Navajo Tribe had already begun to assume the financial burden for many services formerly provided by the federal government, and as the tribe's financial ability expanded, it assumed an increasing share of costs, other than construction and operation of the schools, road construction and maintenance, Social Security payments and allied major programs.

By the mid-1950's, however, the position to be occupied by tribal government in the future scheme of things was somewhat vague. The federal government was placing upon the tribe as many responsibilities as possible, and the tribe was enjoying the widest possible latitude, within the framework of federal law, to permit it to accept and discharge new responsibilities.

The tribal constitution, as proposed by the Council in October of 1953, was comparable in its scope and format to the constitutions other tribes had adopted under the Indian Reorganization Act. It included a statement of powers to be exercised by the Tribal Council, but the statement was prefaced by a provision to the effect that "in addition to the general governing

217

powers vested in the Navajo Tribal Council and without limiting such powers, it shall have the following powers, subject to any limitations embodied in the law or the Constitution of the United States." It differed from the usual IRA constitutions in that it did not identify and include a procedure for the review or approval of those types of Council enactments which, pursuant to federal law, are normally submitted to the Secretary or to an official of the Bureau of Indian Affairs holding the necessary delegation of authority.

As drafted, the constitution left undefined and unidentified the powers which the Council might exercise unilaterally in contrast with those which, under federal statutes, it could exercise only with the approval of the Secretary of the Interior. Within the context of the times, the possibility of rescission of restrictive federal laws encouraged the tribal legal advisers to draft the constitution in such fashion that amendment would not be necessary in the event controlling statutes were repealed, or in the event that the Secretary of the Interior might conclude that he could declare them inapplicable to the Navajo Tribe by appropriate interpretation of Section 6 of the Navajo-Hopi Rehabilitation Act. Of course, the same purpose could have been attained and conflict averted by the simple expedient of making certain Council actions subject to secretarial review or approval *as long as required by federal law*. Speaking about the proposed constitution before the Council in January 1953, the tribal attorney explained the advantages of constitutional government for the tribe (Navajo Tribal Council Minutes, January 5-23, 1953, p. 173):

> Now listen, you already have a Council; you already have a Judiciary; you already have your Executive officers, including the business organization, don't you? But, they are not on paper, or rather, they are scattered pieces of paper, one over here and one over there, in resolutions and regulations. The constitution merely puts this all together and says, in an orderly way, what is the Council, what is the Judiciary, and what is the Executive and what are their duties. This document is for the protection of the people, to bring order out of confusion, because

nobody knows exactly what your power of the Council, nor the Judiciary nor the Executive really is. You are all guessing about those things. In addition, it has a Bill of Rights which protects every individual Navajo against you, because you are restrained under the Bill of Rights from any moment of false enthusiasm when you might pass a law infringing on their freedom of religion, or freedom of speech or their right to petition either the chairman or President of the United States for the redress of grievances. . . . As far as the tribal organization is concerned, it protects the rights of the people against the encroaching power of either the Council or the Judiciary.

Obstacles to Federal Approval

The proposed constitution was sent to Washington in October 1953, and came under review in the Bureau and in the Department. During the June, 1954, Council meeting the attorney for the tribe reported briefly on its status, stating without elaboration that there were certain points "in conflict with statutes" that needed reconciliation in the draft, and that it was then in the office of the Solicitor for the Department.

A year later, in October 1955, the attorney stated the constitution was still under review; it had cleared the Department, but he relayed to the Council information to the effect that the Bureau wished to modify the document to permit certain state officials to enter the reservation in the discharge of their duties, and this proposal generated new problems.

The delaying tactic apparently hinged on the chance that Congress might act to repeal some of the statutes that stood in the way of tribal autonomy. As withdrawal programming picked up momentum within the framework of congressional policy, the role of federal officials in the administration of tribal affairs declined, and that of the tribe, under the leadership of the tribal attorney, expanded. Shepardson (1963: 88) observed:

There are charges that the lawyers influence the Council in too many areas; that they embroil the tribe in unnecessary and unwise lawsuits; . . . and are delaying the hearings on the Indian Claims Case, the

219

basis of their hold on the Council. They are accused of painting an unrealistic picture of Navajo "sovereignty," of dabbling in "empire-building," of fostering a "socialistic dictatorship". . . . The response to the criticism depends on how one assesses the direction in which the lawyers are impelling the tribe. Certainly, if the wisest course is toward the greatest possible development of a nearly autonomous state within a state, then the Council's lawyers are advising their clients consistently and well. If, on the other hand, this is an unrealistic picture of the Navajo situation, which includes, I believe, both the need to develop the Reservation and to integrate some members of the tribe in the surrounding society, then the strictly legal definition of Navajo authority takes a short-sighted view of the needs of the People.

In 1955 the tribe began to look into the procedures governing the leasing of its lands for oil and gas development. With authorization from the tribe, the attorneys hired two geologists as consultants to make a study of the matter. The two made the study and, reporting to the Council a short time later, recommended that the existing procedures governing oil and gas leasing be abandoned and replaced by a partnership arrangement between the tribe and outside interests financially able to develop. oil and gas. Following this presentation, the Council acted to declare a "moratorium" on oil and gas leasing until the procedures could be more carefully examined. With regard to the proposed partnership arrangement, the tribal attorney addressed the Council to explain that the proposed new approach was "legal pioneering" since, under longstanding federal laws and regulations, no similar approach had ever been taken by the Secretary in his capacity as trustee over Indian tribal lands.

A short time later, a proposal from an oil company was read to the Council, under which the tribe and the company would become partners in the exploration and development of oil and gas on 5,100,000 acres of reservation land. The tribe would provide the land; the company would provide the initial development capital. The partners, under the proposal, would each retain 25 percent of the profits, and each would leave 25 percent of the profits in a special account to amortize costs of exploration, drilling, and production. In the event of a rich discovery the tribe stood to gain; in the event drilling produced marginal or non-productive wells, the tribe stood to lose any bonus and rental payments it might otherwise receive from conventional leasing. It was a gamble and a knotty decision for the Council to make.

After considerable discussion the Council approved the proposal and authorized the Advisory Committee to negotiate and execute a contract with the Delhi-Taylor Oil Corporation covering the proposed partnership. This was a major responsibility which the Council placed upon its Advisory Committee, involving, as it did, millions of acres of tribal land.

Obstacles to Tribal Approval

The proposed tribal constitution had lain quiescent since its transmittal to Washington in the fall of 1953, with occasional vague reports by the attorney. On January 20, 1956, the attorney told the Council that during the period 1953 to 1956 his concern for a well-ordered tribal government had become secondary to his concern for development of a tribal government whose operations would be untrammeled by constitutional requirements or by statutes of Congress which limited tribal power (Navajo Tribal Council Minutes, January 17-27, 1956, pp. 103-104):

> In the legal department we were responsible for deferring the consideration of your proposed constitution in this Council meeting for reasons which have become apparent on further study and discussion with the Bureau. Attorneys in the Bureau have taken the position, and I am at last compelled to agree with them, that under the language of the Navajo-Hopi Rehabilitation Act, if the constitution is adopted, it would strengthen the veto power of the Secretary rather than weaken it, over decisions of this Council in matters where we consider you have the free and untrammeled right to make decisions.

Notwithstanding the fact that the powers of the Secretary of the Interior over Indian property represent responsibilities placed upon him by Congress—responsibilities that can be eliminated only by Congress—the attorney explained to the Council that the intent of Section 6 of the Navajo-Hopi Rehabilitation Act was that "you assume all the powers you are capable of exercising according to experience and management of tribal affairs."

Since the Secretary could not merely abdicate the responsibilities placed on him by law, the tribal attorney proposed that the Council enact a resolution to authorize the chairman, by and with the aid of the tribal attorney, and with the consent of the Advisory Committee, to prepare appropriate amendments to Section 6 of the Rehabilitation Act to broaden the authority of the Tribal Council. Again, the Advisory Committee was authorized to make a major tribal decision.

The proposed amendment was, in fact, drafted by the attorney and approved by the Advisory Committee. In effect, it was a request for piecemeal termination of federal trust responsibility in the leasing of tribal lands for mineral development purposes, and it was introduced as S-1781 in the U.S. Senate, during the 85th Congress. Had the amendment become law the tribe could have proceeded to place in effect the partnership arrangement proposed during the previous year, and also authorization would have been given for the leasing of tribal land for periods up to 99 years. The proposed legislation was never enacted, however. Much later, speaking at the inaugural meeting of the newly elected Tribal Council in April 1959, the attorney explained the delay in action on the constitution (Navajo Tribal Council Minutes, April 14, 1959, p. 19): "Postponement has been largely due to the emergent pressure of Council business which steadily increased in volume, and partially because we have expectation of amending section 6 of the Navajo-Hopi Rehabilitation Act of 1948 [sic] in respect to the adoption of a constitution. When this amendment is adopted, we should go forward with this project."

A day later, April 15, 1959, the attorney made further reference to the language of the Rehabilitation Act authorizing adoption of a tribal constitution (Navajo Tribal Council Minutes, April 15, 1959, p. 71):

> We also think that section 6 of the Navajo-Hopi
> Act which gives you the power to adopt a constitu-
> tion was too restrictive, *and it gives veto power to the*

Secretary which he did not have before [emphasis supplied]. As a matter of general law, and we think particularly in the light of *Lee* v. *Williams* Decision [*sic, Williams* v. *Lee*] which is a thorough and fundamental statement of the law brought up-to-date from an early conflict in the State of Georgia against the Cherokees, and just as your conflict between the State of Arizona and the Navajos that provision which we drafted before, can now be much simplified; and I hope by the next Council meeting to read that to you. Although many of these things will have to be left to us, I am afraid, because they involved such conflicting legal opinions of construction.

Not long thereafter, in November 1959, a congressional committee held a hearing before the Tribal Council at Window Rock, and one of the Council delegates inquired about the status of the proposed amendment to the Rehabilitation Act. In reply, a senator told the Council (Navajo Tribal Council Minutes, November 3, 1959):

I think the principal difficulty was we tried to get more than a 99-year lease. The attorneys for the tribe had told us there were other things they would like to obtain, such as adopting a constitution which would give the tribe the right to anything under the sun without the approval of the Secretary of the Interior. The Department of the Interior had strong opinions on that, and various groups in Congress thought we were trying to railroad something through. It took a long time to gather reports on all parts of it. If it had been only the 99-year lease part, it would have been much simpler and we could have done it much earlier.

Nearly a year later, on January 14, 1960, the attorney reported to the Council that a recommendation had gone forward from the tribe to the congressional committee concerned, asking that two controversial features be dropped from the proposed amendment to the Rehabilitation Act. These included, as the attorney phrased it (Navajo Tribal Council Minutes, January 14, 1960, p. 105): "An amendment to the Rehabilitation Act strengthening the powers of the tribe to have its own constitution, in respect to which we are at great odds with the Bureau on language."

Fear that adoption of a tribal constitution under the terms of the Rehabilitation Act of 1950 would indeed strengthen the role of the Secretary of the Interior in the administration of tribal affairs has continued, to this day, as a major obstacle in the way of adoption of such a document as the foundation upon which tribal government rests, despite the fact that the Council continues to rest upon secretarial regulations, exercising only those powers that the Secretary of the Interior is willing to approve— powers and authorities which, needless to say, the Secretary could conceivably rescind. A wide range of such authorities has been assumed by the Tribal Council through the enactment of enabling resolutions subject to secretarial approval, and, in 1962, these were codified by a professional firm in the form of a tribal code patterned after the federal codes. In a sense, the tribal code is the Navajo Constitution, although it has never been ratified by the voters of the tribe.

Progress and Controversies

In 1959, to meet the needs of the burgeoning tribal organization, the Council adopted an organization chart and functional statement entitled "Organization of the Executive Branch." Divided into several divisions and departments, the tribal scheme of organization was patterned closely after that of the Bureau of Indian Affairs, and designed to meet the practical requirements of carrying out a multimillion-dollar tribal development and service program financed by oil and gas revenues. An ultramodern tribal sawmill, an electrical distribution system (Navajo Tribal Utility Authority), a modern police and court system, a water development program, a community development effort—including the construction of chapter houses and community centers— and a wide range of other improvements took place throughout the reservation during the period immediately following the opening of the oil fields in 1956-57. It was something of a golden age for many of the Navajo people, who came to look as never before to Window Rock, the seat of tribal government, as the source of all bounty. Tribal government indeed had become a reality.

However, an effort by the tribal legal department to establish clearly Navajo title to an area of the reservation claimed by both the Navajo and the Hopi Tribes (*Healing* v. *Jones*) had something less than a completely successful outcome for the Navajo. This, and other controversial issues surrounding the aggressive leadership of the tribal attorneys, became involved in tribal political campaigns as early as 1959, and, by 1963, the tribal legal department was a major campaign issue in the tribal election. The Tribal Council was split, some supporting, and some declaring themselves against, the attorneys. There followed a series of court actions involving the Secretary of the Interior, accompanied by a long period of internal strife on the reservation. The turmoil did not begin to subside until after the mid-1960's, and during those unsettled times few constructive developments could be initiated. A new tribal administration, elected to office partly on a platform of opposition to the attorneys, had as one of its goals the adoption of a tribal constitution, but once again, as in 1938, the "political climate" on the reservation was not favorable for such an undertaking.

The decade of the 1950's was a period characterized by the rapid development of tribalism for the Navajo. The Tribal Council moved from its previous status as a consultative body to become a positive force in the planning and execution of reservation-wide programs, an elaborate tribal executive department took shape, and a wide range of constructive programs benefiting the Navajo people were carried out. The institution of tribal government had become firmly incorporated into Navajo culture.

An Emerging Modern Navajo Culture

Not only did tribal government become firmly established as an integral part of the Navajo cultural fabric during the 1950's, but at long last the digestive process began to turn to the school as well, an institution that had existed for many years as an intrusive element, tolerated but not a part of Navajo culture. It had always been, primarily, a tool pertaining to an alien way of life, one that was used initially to attack the foundations of Navajo culture. For many years following its introduction it met with opposition, sometimes violent and verging on bloodshed

(Left-Handed Mexican Clansman 1952). Not until the 1930's, with the shift to reservation day and boarding schools, did the institution begin to gain popular support, and not until the 1940's and the post-war period did tribal support become general.

For many years following the introduction of the first schools the English language remained the only language of instruction and the curriculum was composed exclusively of subject matter drawn from Anglo-American culture. The cultural-linguistic barrier that stood between Anglo-American and Navajo society was formidable, and the use of extemporaneous interpretation as a means with which to bridge the gap was largely ineffective. The events of the 1930's and 1940's brought the communication problem into sharp relief and led to an effort to make better use of the tool already at hand, the Navajo language itself. Accordingly, in the late 1930's the Bureau introduced the use of written Navajo in conjunction with an effort to teach adult Navajos to read and write their own language.

Primers and other teaching materials were developed and, shortly after the beginning of World War II a book entitled *Díí K'ad Anaa'ígíí Baa Hane'* (The Story of the Present War) was published in Navajo, recounting the events and circumstances that had led to the conflict. In addition, a monthly Navajo language newspaper called *Ádahooníłígíí* (Current Events) followed the course of the war for the benefit of those tribal members who could not read English. The effort continued after the end of the conflict, with widespread use of written translations of difficult subject matter into Navajo—for example, grazing regulations, the Navajo-Hopi Rehabilitation Act, tribal election laws—as a medium through which to generate public understanding of issues affecting the lives of the reservation people.

Language, in written form, however, was a foreign introduction to Navajo culture and facilities were not available for a broad approach to the promotion of adult literacy. In addition, during the 1950's, major emphasis in the Navajo education program was placed once again on the learning of English and the study of conventional subjects. As a result, literacy in Navajo remained a limited skill among the adult population, and it did not find its way into Navajo culture.

The 1950's were a period of great cultural change for the people. The Bureau, the states, and the tribal leadership collaborated in an effort to provide school opportunities for all Navajo children, with the result that enrollment more than doubled between 1950 and 1960. Parents assumed the herding duties formerly borne by children in traditional society, and dependency on wage work increased. The school curriculum was aimed at cultural and linguistic assimilation as a basis upon which to build economic parity for the younger generation of Navajos with the non-Indian population. The home training of children in Navajo tradition and culture became limited or impossible, since the children were often absent from their homes during the entire school year.

By the end of the decade significant progress had been made toward the attainment of the educational objectives of the schools and a growing stream of Navajo young people began to flow into colleges and universities, financed by grants of tribal money. The Tribal Council had acted to establish a $10 million scholarship grant fund, beginning with a small appropriation in the mid-1950's.

As the program progressed, however, the gap widened between the generations. By the end of the decade a growing concern began to make itself heard, voiced by young people participating in the annual tribal youth conferences. The knowledge, the values and the skills associated with tribal culture, and even the Navajo language itself, were slipping away from them They were shocked to find that they were losing the very basis of their identity as Navajos. Their parents, as well, became concerned over the widening gap between the way of life in which they had been reared and that toward which their children were moving.

As a result of the growing awareness of change, something akin to a counterrevolution began to take shape by the early 1960's. A demand grew that the educational process and content be recast and broadened as the basis upon which to transform the school into an institution for the training of Navajo young people in the tribal as well as in the national culture. Accordingly, the educational system began to undergo a process of remodeling, and in modified form it began to move, as other borrowed institutions had before, toward incorporation into Navajo culture. The Navajo language, Navajo history, medicine, religion, and traditional values began to enter the reservation school curriculum. Navajo leaders began to demand that teacher training be broadened to include a fundamental understanding of the Navajo way of life and some modicum of familiarity with the Navajo language; more recently interest has grown in bilingual education. Not only are the effects of the counterrevolution apparent in the reservation schools, but in colleges and universities in the area surrounding the Navajo country as well. The Navajo language is now taught as a subject, on a par with other modern languages, at Northern Arizona University, the University of New Mexico and its Branches, and at the Tribe's own Navajo Community College. The educational system serving Navajo children is rapidly taking on a distinctively Navajo garb.

The strength of Navajo culture lies in its ability to make adaptive changes without destroying or discarding the fabric of its identity. Many institutions and cultural elements have been borrowed and incorporated by the tribe in past centuries, usually in a form peculiarly Navajo, and they have found their place as Navajo institutions, not only in the culture, but in the language as well. This process continues today, and the school is now in the process of incorporation.

As new concepts have entered Navajo culture to become an integral part of the system, the language has always developed the lexicon with which to communicate related ideas. Words are rarely borrowed along with the borrowed institutions or other elements. In part, the preference for internal vocabulary development may be a result of the radical morphological disparity between Navajo and the Indo-European or Puebloan languages involved; a disparity so great that the incorporation of foreign verbal elements into Navajo is impractical, if not impossible.

Long years of association with Spanish-speaking people has left a mere handful of loan words, all of them nouns, in the lexicon of Navajo: for example, *míil* (thousand, from *mil*), *míiltsoh* (million, literally "big thousand"), *béeso* (money, from *peso*), *golchóón* (quilt, from *colchón*), *gohwééh* (coffee, from *café*), *géeso* (cheese, from *queso*), *béégashii* (cow, from *vaca*).

From English, Navajo has borrowed such terms as *nóomba* (number), *máazo* (marbles), *kááboleita* (carburetor), *késhmish* (Christmas) and *gídí* (kitty). In some instances, the meaning of old terms has been extended to embrace new ideas, as *dáádílkał* (door), originally the flap that hung down over the entry way to a hogan; *tł'aakał* (skirt), literally a "rump-flap"; *adee'* (spoon), literally "horn," the material of which a spoon-like utensil was once made; *hashk'aan* (banana or date), originally yucca fruit; and *łeetsoii* (uranium oxide, sulfur), but originally "yellow earth" or "sulfur."

The horse was acquired by the Navajo at a very early period, but the Spanish term *caballo* was not borrowed to describe it. Rather, the Navajo applied the term *łį́į'* (pet), to the new acquisition. *Łį́į'* is still used in the sense of pet or "domesticated animal," and if it is necessary to distinguish between "pet" and "horse" the latter is referred to as *łii' łi'ígíí*, a reduplication that carries the connotation of "pet that *is* a pet." With the introduction of stock raising the need for a term with which to express the concept "to herd" was met by the use of a verbal stem meaning literally "to move in a spreading manner." Thus, *na'nishkaad* (I am herding, literally "I am causing something to move about in a spreading manner"). Likewise, with the introduction of the wagon, the automobile, and other wheeled vehicles, a verbal stem relating to the rolling movement of a hoop-like object was applied to express the concept "to drive": *ni'sélbą́ą́z* (I went by wagon—or other wheeled vehicle—but literally "I caused something to make a round trip by rolling it").

Most new cultural elements and concepts are identified by coined terms which describe their function, use, or other appearance. Thus, *ch'osh doo yit'íinii* (microbe, "invisible bug"), *náhásdzo hayázhí* (acre, "small marked off area"), *tsiigha yilzhéhí* (barber, "he who cuts hair"), *tsiigha yilzhéhí bá hooghan* (barber shop, "home or place for the one who cuts hair"), *naalyéhé bá hooghan* (store, trading post, "home or place for merchandise"), *tsésǫ'* (glass, "star-stone"), *tózis* (bottle, "water-bag"), *béésh bee halne'é* (telephone, "metal with which conversation is carried on"), *bee'ótsa'í* (pliers, "that with which gripping is done"), *bihwiidoo'áligii binahat'a'* (curriculum, "the plan for that which is to be learned"), *chįįh yee adilohii* (elephant, "the one that lassoes things with its nose"), *ghąą' ask'idii* (camel, "the one with a hump-back").

In like manner, verbal concepts are expressed by extension of the meaning of existing terms or by description of the action: "to inject" is expressed as *biih yíziid* (I poured it into him) or *biih yíłt'óód* (I pumped it into him, literally, I caused it to move by suction); "to study, to read" are expressed by *íínishta'* (literally, I count); write by *ak'e'eschí* (literally, I scratch on a surface); and "to bomb" by *bik'íjį' hadah 'i'íiłne'* (literally, I dropped something roundish, heavy, and solid down on it). Even such alien concepts as "he has normal blood pressure" have found expression in Navajo as *t'áá ákohgo hadił na'ałkid* (literally, his blood fluctuates just right; "fluctuates" because of the movement of the liquid or mercury column in the apparatus).

Even non-Navajo geographic locations have acquired Navajo names, as *Yootó* (Santa Fe, literally, Bead-water), *Bee'aldííl dah sinil* (Albuquerque, literally, Where there are bells), *Hoozdo* (Phoenix, literally, Hot place), and *Ahééhéshįįh* (California, literally, Where summers follow one another in succession).

Tribal government, the *Béésh Bąąh Dah Naaznilí* (those upon whom metal [badges] sets, as the Council came to be known) and the *Táá' Naaznilí* (the group of three: president, secretary and treasurer, as the chapters are called) has generated a picturesque vocabulary, illustrated by such terms as:

Naaltsoos bee ádá nahodiit'aahígíi: resolution (literally, paper by means of which planning for oneself is done).

Bee łá adooleeł biniiyé bee hidishná: I move that it be approved (literally, For the purpose of its being approved I make a movement).

T'óó ni'ndooltsos bee hidees'na'ígíí bikéé' ninishaah: I second his motion to table it (literally, I take a position behind him in the movement he made to merely set the paper down).

T'óó ni'niiltsooz: it was tabled (literally, It was merely set down).

Naaltsoos bee ádá nahodiit'aahígíí łahgo ánályaa: The resolution has been amended (literally, The resolution was made otherwise [changed]).

Tó binda'anishji bee naaltsoos ádá nahodiit'aahígíí niiniłt-sooz: He introduced a resolution for water development (literally, He set down a resolution on the side of work on water).

*Kóhoot'éédą́ą́' tó bee bina'anish biniiyé t'ááłáhádi miil ntsaaígíí biighahgo béeso ndeet'ą́ (*or *ch'ídeet'ą́):* Last year we appropriated a million dollars for water development (literally, At this time in the past we set down [or carried out] money equal to one million dollars for the purpose of work having to do with water).

Béeso bee ádina'anish: budget (literally, money with which work is done on self).

Béeso bee ádina'anish biniiyé ninádeidi'aahígíí: budget and finance committee (literally, those who repeatedly set down money for the purpose of work done on self).

Ólta'jí biniiyé béeso siniłígíí: scholarship fund (literally, money that sets for the purpose of study).

Hastóí béésh bąąh dah naazniłígíí: Council members (literally, elders upon whom metal objects set, that is, badges of office).

Béésh bąąh dah si'ání: Councilman (literally, he upon whom a metal object [badge] sets).

Béésh bąąh dah naazniłí yá sidáhígíí: Council chairman (literally, he who sits for the councilmen), or:

Á dah nánídaahii: Council chairman (literally, he who repeatedly sits down at an elevation for someone).

Béésh bąąh dah naaz'ání biniiyé ńdiishwod: I ran for the office of Council delegate; I ran for the Council (literally, I started up running for the purpose of the Council).

Shikéé' yííziįhígíí éí Joe wolyé: My running mate is Joe (literally, Joe is the name of the one who stands behind me).

James éiyá béésh ąąh doot'ááłji atah ńdiilyeed: James is a Council candidate (literally, James is among those who start up running for Council membership, that is, for or on the side of a metal object being placed alongside).

Háíshą' Naat'áanii Néezdi béésh bąąh dah naaz'ání yá dah nánídaahgo biniiyé bee ha'oodzíí'? Who won the nomination for the chairmanship at Shiprock? (literally, Who was spoken out with [named] for the purpose of repeatedly sitting down up at an elevation for the councilmen, at Shiprock?).

Bee lá̜ adooleeł biniiyé hidees'náá': A motion for approval has been made (literally, A movement has taken place for the purpose of approving it).

Ła' yee akéé' niniyá: It has been seconded (literally, someone took a position behind with it).

T'áa doo yee akéé' niniyáhi da: It hasn't been seconded (literally, no one has taken a position behind with it).

Náhást'éigi oolkiłgo béésh ba̜a̜h dah naaz'áni yah íijéé'— ashdla'ági oolkiłgo ch'éénijéé': The Council convened at 9:00 o'clock and adjourned at 5:00 (literally, At 9:00 o'clock the councilmen ran in; at 5:00 they went running back out).

Táagi oolkiłgo neeznáá dah alzhinji̜' ch'izhnijéé': At 3:00 o'clock they had a ten-minute recess (literally, At 3:00 they ran out for ten minutes).

Béésh ba̜a̜h dah naaznili áłah danłi̜: The Council is in session (literally, The Councilmen are together).

Bee lá̜ adooleeł danohsinígíi daohsi̜i̜h: Those in favor of approval, stand up! (literally, Those of you who want it to be approved, stand up!).

Dooda danohsinígíi: Those against (literally, Those of you who want no).

Náhást'éi Siniligíi: Advisory Committee (literally, Group of nine).

Navajo humor is reflected in the application of the term *na'adlo* (deception by trickery) to describe the concept "politics." "Politician" is sometimes referred to as *bina'adlo'ii* (deceiver), and "to engage in politics" as *na'adlo' neiłt'i'* (he weaves a line of deception by trickery).

Unlike some Indian languages that have not grown to express concepts lying outside the traditional culture to which they pertain, Navajo remains a living, growing language. It can be expected that new elements and concepts that find their way into Navajo culture generally, will also find their way into the tribal language. Language is one of the badges of identity as a Navajo as well as a conveyor of Navajo culture; it is a basic element of the expanding tribal society of today—a society whose fabric remains distinctively Navajo, despite the fact that many of its major institutions have come from alien cultures.

The Years Ahead

The availability of tribal income since 1957, heavy federal expenditures, and industrial development have prevented collapse of the reservation economy and laid the basis upon which tribal growth has taken place. However, tribal income is limited and the level of future job-producing federal expenditures is uncertain. At the same time, the support potential of reservation range resources continues to decline and the tribal population continues to increase. Looking toward the years that lie ahead, the tribal government is faced with an extremely complex set of problems, most of them essentially economic in nature, upon which its very future may well depend. If it is successful in accelerating the development of new sources of livelihood on the reservation to permit an orderly transition from traditional resources to a modern wage economy for the large segment of the tribe which prefers to remain in Navajoland, its future is bright. On the other hand, if it is not successful in creating a viable reservation economy, its future is uncertain.

Nearly ten years ago, Shepardson (1963: 111) looked toward the future, from the vantage point of several years of careful study of Navajo political institutions and trends, and interpreted the objective of the Tribal Council, under the leadership of the tribal attorneys during the late 1950's and early 1960's, to be the "development of the Reservation as a quasi-autonomous state" rather than "the integration of Navajos into off-Reservation life." She saw both the Bureau and the tribal leadership as forces impelling the tribe in the direction of a tribally based, tribally controlled economy. However, she expressed doubt that the reservation would ever become a separate state, county, or other such political subdivision, in the absence of concomitant economic independence, and there seemed to be little promise of such independence.

With universal education in sight in the Navajo country, Shepardson (1963: 113) predicted a trend away from isolation and toward greater participation by Navajos in the political affairs of the state and nation, as well as in those of the tribe:

Lacking an economic base for self-sufficiency, Navajos will be forced into a compromise with outside interests. . . . I predict that they will eventually organize as an economic corporation. Such a move will preserve their tribal identity and their "Indianness," regardless of what happens to the Bureau of Indian Affairs, for years to come.

Shepardson (1963: 112) also drew an interesting parallel between the Navajo Tribe and the emerging African nations in their past efforts to attain self-government under indirect rule: "Like the Africans, Navajos enjoy an illusory sovereignty under a Governor-General (the General Superintendent), and a colonial administrative staff (the Bureau of Indian Affairs)."

Again, in a very interesting and timely paper, recently published as part of a compendium of papers submitted to the Joint Economic Committee of Congress, Subcommittee on Economy in Government, Aberle (1969), a longtime student of Navajo culture, also drew a parallel between the Navajo Reservation and areas of colonial domination. Drawing a picture of the historic exploitation of the natural resources of the reservation, Aberle (1969: 249-250) wrote:

... below ground, we would see oil, helium, coal, uranium and vanadium draining off into the surrounding economy; we would see rents and royalties flowing into the tribal treasury, but of course, major profits accruing to the corporations exploiting the reservation. We would see the slow development of roads, water for stock and drinking, government facilities and so forth, and a flow of welfare funds coming in, to go out again via the trader. The net flow of many physical resources would be outward; the flow of profits would be outward; and the only major increase to be seen would be population, with a minor increment in physical facilities and consumer goods.

Aberle (1969: 250) also drew a parallel between the reservation and a colony. "This is the picture of a colony," he said. "It can be duplicated time after time, place after place."

Pointing to the fact that the United States Governemnt subsidizes national farm programs, research and developments of military value, and other industrial operations, Aberle questions the soundness and rationale underlying the conventional procedure governing mineral development on Indian reservations—a procedure based on competitive bidding with the offer of bonuses, plus the payment of lease rentals, and royalties on production, if any—and suggests the possibility of mineral development by the tribe itself.

Hindsight indicates that, had the Navajo Tribe been ready for such an undertaking, and had the federal government subsidized it in the 1950's to carry out the expensive exploration, drilling, and developmental work that preceded the opening of the Four Corners Oil Field, the profits from oil and gas production would have been more than sufficient to finance the reservation programs funded subsequently by federal appropriations, and to provide capital for development of a reservation economy sufficient to meet the needs of the tribe for many years to come. At the same time, hindsight reflects the fact that had the government subsidized the tribe, or had the tribe entered into the partnership development arrangement involving 5,100,000 acres of reservation land, as proposed in 1955, the capital investment would not have been amortized by production and the tribe would have lost the bonus and rental income received under the lease procedure. Such appears to be the case, at least, on the basis of experience up to the present time with reference to that area of land.

It is no doubt true that the exploitation of mineral resources on the Navajo Reservation, under lease, has resulted in a huge income to the companies that financed the developments, and that the flow of these profits has been outward. It is also true that this outflow has been offset to a significant extent, not only by the more than $200 million the tribe has received in lease bonuses, rentals, and royalties, largely in the past 20 years, but also by the large amounts of federally appropriated monies that have been returned to the reservation for the construction of highways, schools, and hospitals, and for the operation of a wide range of federal programs across the same span of years.

Again, on the other side of the coin, natural resources *are* available on the reservation for development. Timber, oil, gas, uranium, vanadium, and other minerals offer opportunities for productive development by the tribe. In addition, on the basis of experience gained in the past 15 years, the tribe is in a much better position to consider local development projects than it was a few short years ago. The tribal Forest Products Industry is a successful operation, utilizing reservation raw materials, producing goods that result in a flow of money to the reservation, and creating jobs for tribal members; and it has a continuing expansion potential. It and the Navajo Tribal Utility Authority, which also provides employment and income for Navajo workers, are operated independently of the political governing body of the tribe, after the fashion of tribally owned corporations, and under the direction of competent management.

It is interesting to speculate about the possibilities for expanding local development of reservation resources through the medium of additional tribally owned corporations capitalizing on *known* raw materials, with measurable profit potentials. The tribe *might*, after careful study by experts in the field, find it feasible to take part of its oil royalties in the form of crude oil, establishing tribally owned refineries with which to process it; the tribe *might* similarly find that it would be more profitable to take natural gas from leased lands in kind rather than accept royalty payments in cash; it *might* find it feasible to diversify its Forest Products Industry still further; and it *might* find it profitable to invest in the movie industry to capitalize on reservation locations and scenery in the production of commercial movies, either as a tribal undertaking or in partnership with reputable movie companies. The tribe *might* also, after careful study and analysis, find it profitable to finance its own electronic assembly plants or other industries capable of utilizing the human resources of the reservation.

Perhaps a tribal development corporation financed at least in part by the tribe, in part perhaps by federal loan and grant funds, could build upon past experience to accomplish at least to a greater extent than at present, some of the recommendations made by Aberle (1969: 271): (1) to allow Navajos to utilize their own resources to improve their livelihood, (2) to give Navajos control over the utilization of their own resources, (3) to increase the level of income by increasing the number of jobs on the reservation and by improving the range, and (4) to permit individuals to specialize occupationally in the interests of greater efficiency. It is doubtful that the tribe can control *totally* the exploitation of its reservation resources, but it conceivably has the potential to greatly expand such local development.

Aberle (1969: 250) stresses the fact that the planning and execution of reservation development programs must be a function of the tribe itself. "The solution," he points out "is for Navajos to plan for themselves, drawing on such advice as they wish. . . . Navajos may make mistakes, [but] only Navajos are primarily concerned for Navajos." He points to the existence of a Tribal Council, as well as the chapters and regional or agency councils, representing three levels: the tribe as a whole, the regional subdivisions comprising the five agencies, and the local communities.

The framework already exists with which to create the "responsive, responsible, and flexible system for Navajo planning" to which Aberle alludes. In the absence of a tribal constitution, some of the branches of the tribal government are somewhat loosely organized—the important advisory committee of the Tribal Council has been modified periodically in structure and manner of selection of its membership to meet the demands of political expediency and the role of the chapters and regional councils needs to be defined as their functions relate to tribal government and planning—but the task of formalizing and stabilizing the government on a constitutional base is no longer the formidable undertaking it was a few years ago.

With the successful incorporation of such major institutions of non-Indian culture as tribal government, education, modern medicine, and modern business methods, modified and adapted to the peculiar needs of Navajo society, the creation of a viable reservation economy is not beyond the limits of possibility. With the establishment of a basis for livelihood, the continuation of a reservation society, sharing many of the features and institutions of the outside world but at the same time distinctively Navajo, is virtually assured for many years to come.

Preserving the Good Things of Hopi Life

Emory Sekaquaptewa

The organization of the tribal council form of government under the congressional plan of 1934, more commonly known as the Indian Reorganization Act, has had little effect on the traditional system of social and political control among the Hopi Indians of northeastern Arizona. This paper briefly sketches some highlights of history, events, and attitudes that demonstrate the nature of the dichotomy between the formalized structure of council government and the indigenous structure made up of tradition, custom, and religious influences.

Ever since the adoption of the Tribal Constitution, the government which it authorized has struggled just to maintain its superficial structure, much less gain substantive support from the Hopi people. There continues to be some opposition; and to a greater extent indifference, to the tribal government by the Hopis as individuals, as members of a factional group, or as a village community. Undoubtedly, one significant reason is that most Hopi people do not understand, and have no means by which to understand, the bases for the organization, purpose, and necessity of a formal governmental structure. On the other hand, the efforts of the Bureau of Indian Affairs and other governmental agencies to provide services and help in the development of tribal resources call for a fairly sophisticated local governmental structure; therefore, these efforts create a demand on the tribal government for responses beyond its capabilities. Thus, more often than not, the action of the council is to respond to the resources which become available rather than having the resources respond to council action.

In a secular sense, the traditional Hopi political system does not exist as a separate structure, although it nevertheless has real existence in its effects on the Hopi community as an inseparable part of the religious structure. The long history of the development of the Hopi cultural system and the fact that this development took place within the confines of fixed communities and places have so embedded the customs and traditions that a new system of government under a constitution founded under alien auspices cannot expect to win effective governmental control without something more than formal organization.

The Traditional Social System

Traditionally each Hopi village has always enjoyed complete autonomy. The leadership resides in the hierarchy of clans or extended family unit in each village. Each village has determined the organization and functions of its social, political, and religious systems, according to its own interpretation of clan migration legends. Yet, there are substantial uniformities among the several villages in the general structure of their traditional systems. Second and Third Mesa villages follow the legendary theory which recognizes the Bear Clan as the clan through which the office of chief or *kikmongwi* is exercised. There is some variation on First Mesa, which seems to place the Snake Clan on an equal basis with the Bear Clan. Briefly stated, these clans rule by virtue of having founded the villages, either aboriginally or by transplantation from a "mother" village. In a sense, these founders are said to "own" the village.

The Founding of Oraibi

Oraibi, a village on Third Mesa, reputed to be the oldest continuously inhabited town in North America, was founded by Matcito of the Bear Clan. Legend tells that Matcito exiled himself from his original village of Shungopavy as a result of a conflict with his brother Yahoya, who claimed the office of chief, or *kikmongwi*. Matcito's wife was said to have been seduced by Yahoya, which caused great shame to fall on Matcito, who resorted to self-imposed exile to protect his self-respect. Perhaps this is the origin of the practice of self-imposed exile by Hopi men when they are jilted. (Many such exiles go to the pueblos of New Mexico, particularly Zuni, where they have sometimes gained a good reputation by contributing Hopi cultural arts to the Zuni community.)

No one knew where Matcito had gone until a party of hunters discovered him living in a cave on the mesa where Oraibi now stands. Upon discovery, Matcito refused to return but did reclaim his wife, who came to live with him in the cave. Later, Matcito's sympathizers followed him and eventually helped him build up a system which would rival the society of Shungopavy. Matcito and Yahoya are said to have stood on the mesa midway between Shungopavy and Oraibi, and entered into a covenant which stipulated that the one who increased "his children" (society) over the other should prevail. The prevailing chief would claim all the land between them, the boundary running through the middle of the loser's village. Thus, this covenant is said to be a superimposition on the ruling progeny of these chiefs, even upon those who rule in later-established villages, but with authority originating from them.

The Clan and its Functions

Under the Hopi system, the female is the progenitor of the clan, and all offspring belong to the mother's clan. Clan leadership and offices are inherited by men, although female members do have important ceremonial functions. Since the transfer of clan office is restricted to the clan membership, the line of transfer is from brother to brother, or from a maternal uncle to his nephew. This relationship also exists outside of the natural family, because the kinship terms "brother" and "sister" are extended to persons who are, by the rule, members of the clan. For instance, "brothers" include male offspring of female members of the clan who are in Anglo terms cousins to each other by one or more degrees, with a loose requirement that such offspring be of the same generation. This extension means, further, that a man's "nephews" include not only his natural sister's (or sisters') sons, but also the male children of all of his clan sisters.

Each clan recognizes a female head or matriarch, who is usually the eldest woman—but not necessarily so, since a younger woman may be designated as head by virtue of the exercise of clan discretion—and her home becomes the clan home. In the case of the ruling clan, this home is referred to as *kii-kyam*, which means "their home" and suggests literal possession of the village. The female head of this home who, in Hopi terms, is either a sister or "niece" to the *kikmongwi*, takes her place beside him as *goh-aya* (keeper of the fire). In other words, she maintains the spiritual home fires, and it is this house which serves a great many of the kikmongwi's functions of office, as well as the place where his ceremonial paraphernalia is kept. This is the house that the kikmongwi calls "home," rather than the house where he, his wife and children live. Ceremonially, the kikmongwi, as is true of other married men, is a stranger in the house of his wife and children, since he is not a member of their clan. Furthermore, his teaching of clan knowledge and practices takes place in his clan home, and in the homes of his female clan relatives, where members gather from time to time. It should be noted that these gatherings are generally informal and casual, hardly ever of a formal nature except when a ceremony is conducted.

Land Assignment and Use

The kikmongwi, in Hopi terms, literally "owns" the village, but his control is not confined to it. Traditionally, he assigned lands to all the clans upon their admittance and acceptance into the village, thus exercising the power of an owner over as much land extending beyond the village as became necessary. In this role, he is said to be acting as a father to his son in providing a means for living. Logically, the kikmongwi characterizes all the village people as *ii tim*, or "my children," in his ceremonial functions. The lands assigned by the kikmongwi were originally marked by boundary monuments, and each clan within its own assignment determined how and by whom it would be used. The site of the assignments and the ceremonial references to the clan lands indicate that the intended use of these lands is cultivation for crops. The Tribal Constitution, adopted under the Indian Reorganization Act, describes these lands as traditional "clan holdings" or "established village holdings" and also recognizes the power in each village to control their use according to established custom. Other lands that are not under this mode of village control are, by the terms of the Constitution, subject to the supervision of the Tribal Council. Many ceremonial shrines, ruins, and other monuments that have historic significance to one or more of the clans lie out of village-controlled lands, and some even lie outside of the Hopi Reservation. These places are considered as "belonging" to the group which has a historic claim to them, and these claims are renewed through rituals which commemorate the historic events which gave basis to the claim. Prayer feathers used in the rituals are deposited at these places as evidence of the claim. In some instances, the place names of these monuments or ruins are given to places nearer the village for a more convenient performance of commemorative rituals.

Since Hopi tradition emphasizes tilling of the soil as a means of life, other means introduced later have had to reckon with it. When livestock production came to be accepted by some Hopis, first the federal government, and later the Council, assumed supervision through the regulation of grazing land use, but this expanded use of land also encouraged farming beyond traditional farming areas, so that questions of priority between farming and livestock uses soon became important issues. Livestock trespass on cultivated fields raised the issue of whether farmers had the duty to fence their fields, or whether livestock men had the duty to keep their stock away from unfenced fields. Even though the land use policies of the federal government and its successor, the Tribal Council, indicate that grazing lands outside of village control are open lands for roaming livestock, and that the farmer may till the soil in the area only at his peril, these policies have never been strictly enforced. In some cases of conflict, a vehement farmer or group of farmers may actually create such pressures as to cause the livestock man to put up a fence around the cultivated fields and maintain it out of a desire to avoid constant friction.

The Hopis and the Federal Government

Other examples of traditional controls have survived in spite of the new forms of control introduced through Bureau of Indian Affairs administration and the formalized tribal government. For instance, residency and its privileges in a village are determined by the traditional views of birth and marriage. One who is not attached to a village by one of these, even though a Hopi, cannot be a resident, and this could conceivably be in opposition to Anglo notions of equal opportunity under the law. Village right of self-government is primordial, and not a delegated authority from either federal law or the Tribal Constitution. Village authority, whether based on religious tradition or on custom, has not been surrendered formally to the general or tribal government.

The Limited Support of the Tribal Council

Some villages still refuse to send representatives to the Tribal Council and deny any form of Council jurisdiction over them. The basis for this seems to be the belief that one is bound by the Council's laws and actions only when one is a member of the Tribal Council in an individual capacity, in the same sense that stockholders are members of a corporate body. This misunderstanding is undoubtedly a result of the inadequate preparation in educating the Hopis in respect to the meaning and implementation of the Indian Reorganization Act. This act provides for two different types of organization, either or both of which Indian tribes could elect to accept: (1) a constitutional government, and (2) a business organization in the form of a tribal corporation chartered under federal laws. It is quite likely that the 1934 Act was represented as requiring both organizations and that, therefore, individual members of the tribe must also possess corporate interest in the tribal organization under the law. The fact is that the Hopi tribe has not applied for, and has not been granted a corporate charter under Section 17 of the Indian Reorganization Act which provides for it.

This misunderstanding has important significance in the factional controversies over support of the Tribal Council which continue to this day. It is not uncommon to hear references made to membership of individuals in the Council as determinative of their position on issues raised in conflicts between factions. Unfortunately, many such conflicts are characterized as traditionalism versus the Tribal Council by the more radical elements on each side. This forces the overt supporters of one side or the other to identify with the issue on the side they support, rather than on the merits of the issue itself. The fact is, there are some strong traditional elements supporting the Tribal Council, just as there are strong modernistically inclined supporters of the traditional system. Out of this so-called dichotomy have come terms such as "progressive," referring to those nominally identifying with the Tribal Council, and "conservative," referring to the nominal adherents to traditionalism. But since there are progressive and conservative elements in both groups, these terms have come to be used as the political whims of individuals may require.

What then should have been the fundamental consideration in promoting acceptance of the Indian Reorganization Act? The Hopi villages should have been recognized as autonomous and given the opportunity to ratify the constitution in this capacity. Instead, the Hopi people voted on the constitution as individuals, without regard to their separate political allegiances. The result was clearly a victory for the Anglo notion of rule by majority; thus, the election recognized only those who cast their ballots, but not those who did not. In the more traditional villages there were hardly any votes cast, and those were mostly in the negative. The resulting vote of 651 for adoption and 104 against have generally been attributed by the Hopi people to the strong turn-out of voters in the two or three villages under the greatest influence of the Bureau of Indian Affairs agency. The 755 votes cast undoubtedly represented 30 percent or more of the total eligible voters at that time, when the estimated population of the reservation was around 3,500. But it is questionable whether the required 30 percent was met in every village, based on their respective eligible voter population.

The Origins of Misunderstanding

The misunderstanding and mistrust of the federally sponsored tribal government have their origins in the history of Hopi contact with the U.S. government. The Hopi villages had always dealt with each other as independent entities, and it was as such that they considered themselves in their first dealings with *Wasendo* (Washington). In the latter half of the 19th century, due to the threat of Navajo depredations, the Hopi kikmongwis, each in his own name, made formal pleas to Wasendo for protection. In the 1880's these kikmongwis were Lololma for Third Mesa (Oraibi and its only colony at the time, Moencopi), Honani for Second Mesa, and Anawita for First Mesa. Their pleas were made with the help of Hopi men who could speak a little Spanish and English and also with the help of local non-Indian traders who could speak a little Hopi. At best, the understandings reached between the kikmongwis and the Washington representatives had strong traits of an unconditional relinquishment of Hopi customary rights in return for federal aid.

Because of the communication problem resulting from lack of fluency in a common language on both sides, there could not have been a true meeting of the minds. While the Hopi chiefs apparently submitted to the formal education of Hopi children in return for protection against Navajo encroachment, they did not agree to give up any claim to lands. The government saw in its commitment to protect the Hopis the necessity to define a boundary within which to confine the Hopis in order to provide a legal basis for discouraging Navajo encroachment. Therefore, the Executive Order of 1882 was issued by President Arthur setting aside the Moqui (a term originally used for the Hopis) Indian Reservation. This boundary definition did not solve the problem of Navajo encroachment. Hopi leaders continued to press the government for protection against it. On one occasion in the summer of 1890, these leaders traveled to Washington, D.C. to talk with the Commissioner of Indian Affairs. According to the written account of this conference, the general statements of the leaders were in conciliatory tones and wonderment at what they saw. Each hoped for the government's willingness to extend them protection against Navajo encroachment. Lololma's statement, in addition, lamented that, "Some of my people seem to have hearts of stone, blind eyes, deaf ears, and don't believe what is told them."

Moreover, the consequent results of the boundary definition, which may perhaps be found to have a rational basis in Anglo concepts, never coincided with the Hopi chiefs' understanding of their agreement with the government. First, the definition of the boundaries of the Executive Order Reservation of 1882 resulted in the extinguishment of Hopi title (unrecognized in Anglo law, but referred to as Indian title, the taking of which would later become compensable as a political matter) to all lands outside of that boundary—a result certainly not contemplated by the chiefs. Second, the government reserved the power to settle other

Indians within the boundary at such times as it saw fit—a power which, if exercised, certainly required the most careful consideration of the situation that brought about the necessity for confinement in the first place. And third, the failure of the government to halt Navajo encroachment, but instead to permit it under the justification of administrative convenience (which later, under a strained court interpretation, was declared to be valid and official action to settle the Navajos within the boundary) was a result which could be nothing but insult to the agreement entered into by the Hopi chiefs!

The Consequences of the Split at Oraibi

The Oraibi split of 1906 is said to be the result of controversy between two factions in the village over this agreement. Yukeoma, the leader of the conservative faction, openly accused the faction under Lololma of betraying his trust as a Hopi chief. This agreement was considered by Yukeoma and his faction as a rejection of the Hopi way of life. On the other hand, Lololma saw himself as the last traditionally ordained chief at Oraibi, fulfilling the prophecy that all *wii wimi* (broadly interpreted by some Hopis to mean cultural practices, but more narrowly by others to mean only religious practices) would be "put to rest" at Oraibi. He saw his agreement with the government as the alternative by which the Hopi people would accept the white man's way of life. This prophecy warned against the transplanting of the *wii wimi* to any other place, with the exception of *katcina* practices.

The more sophisticated view is that the division itself was the substance of the prophecy, in that it was designed in deliberation or, in Hopi terms, *diingavi*. It held that such a division was necessary to the survival of the Hopis as a people, in that establishment of another Hopi community would secure to the Hopis the lands between it and Oraibi. It also held that the sanctity of the religious authorities had become subject to more and more abuse as Oraibi grew in size and social complexity so that ritualism began to serve personal edification more than it served communal spiritual needs. It was said that much of the ritualism in traditional practices took on the character of sorcery which "preyed" on people to the detriment of natural population growth, and it was said that a new community would encourage increase in population when it existed without these corruptive devices. The division was said to be the fulfillment of prophecy taught by a religious ceremony in which an act in finale by the participants was a declaration in unison that "this is the way we shall go to *Kawestima*." The participants would make this declaration just as they left the kiva, after having wrapped up their altars and put them over their shoulders. Presumably, this commemorates the prophecy that the Hopi people will return and reclaim the ancestral home of *Kawestima*, which name was said to belong to the kikmongwi of that ancient village. This place was said to be northeast of Oraibi and recognizable by a certain tall Douglas fir and a spring. Yukeoma and his followers were to seek and resettle Kawestima after their ejectment from Oraibi. Thus, the Lololma agreement with Wasendo was said to be merely an instrument to dramatize the conflict and to represent it as a political one. Hopi historians say that dramatization was necessary in order to generate high emotions on both sides, which would evoke greater determination and dedication to their respective causes, tending to lessen the difficulty of those who had to uproot their homes and families, and also promoting their adjustment to harsh conditions of living wherever they resettled.

The Founding of Hotevilla

The contest to determine who would leave Oraibi was not settled until late in the afternoon of September 8, 1906. (According to Harry C. James, author and friend of Tewaquaptewa, the year was 1907.) Tewaquaptewa, nephew of and successor to Lololma, led the faction which ejected the Yukeoma faction. It is generally accepted by most Hopis that the Yukeoma faction far outnumbered the Tewaquaptewa faction and could have turned the events differently if it had depended on purely physical circumstances. Instead, the decision as to who must leave was determined by a "push over" of Yukeoma across the line. This contest required the two opposing leaders to face each other across a skirmish line and, in a fashion similar to football linemen in scrimmage, they pushed against each other with the help of their respective supporters behind them. It is said that Yukeoma, the older of the two leaders, was forced up above the pushing crowd by the pressure and was apparently suffering from exhaustion.

And so in this manner, the contest was decided, and the ejected faction picked up what belongings they were permitted to take and began the trek northwestward from Oraibi. With few hours of sunlight remaining that day, Yukeoma and his people traveled only five miles by nightfall. The site of their encampment was a familiar place to the party because a spring located there had for a long time served the Oraibi people in irrigating the terraced gardens there. This site became a permanent settlement because the leadership would not go on further for reasons only Yukeoma himself must have known. And so Hotevilla was founded.

(Many writers have mistakenly assumed that the name Hotevilla refers to the spring which flowed out of a small cave at the foot of the mesa, the low ceiling of which caused a person to scratch or scrape his back as he withdrew from the cave after getting water—the derivative Hopi expression being *hoet bele* or "back-scraped." This is perhaps a minor point, but it seems important that the meaning which is accepted as the correct one by the Hopi people should be stated. The spring was important to the people of Oraibi, who were accustomed to using water from springs much farther away than Hotevilla; such springs were known by proper names based on descriptions of their surroundings. This spring was referred to by the Oraibians as *ho atvela*, or "juniper slope," because there was a thick growth of these trees on the slopes overlooking the spring.)

The first winter at Hotevilla was spent under the large junipers, which were built upon with branches from other trees to form a kind of hut. But when the first signs of spring came, the Hotevillians were eager and ready to demonstrate their independence by tilling the soil and producing all their needs, rather than to have to yield to the government's demands on them to cooperate in return for aid. In those early years, the Hotevilla farmers were successful and gained a reputation for hard work which has carried over into recent times. The government, in the meantime, dealt with them harshly, attempting to impose upon them many of the programs which were already accepted by other Hopi villages. On many occasions, a detachment of troops was called in by the superintendent of the government agency to forcibly seize and commit school-age children to the school 40 miles away at Keams Canyon. Yukeoma and many of his advisors, as well as other men with school-age children, were threatened and sometimes arrested by the soldiers for failure to cooperate in these matters. In an entry of the Hopi Agency superintendent's report for November 10, 1906, it is stated: "I visited the Hostile camp with troops yesterday, captured twenty-eight school children. Took twenty-one men who had defied the government order, to work on the roads." As prisoners, many of these men built roads for freight wagons in and around Keams Canyon. The bitterness engendered by this treatment from the government did not always result in dejection, but often found vent in greater determination and dedication to succeed independently. Their determination was further encouraged by the vexing ridicule directed at them from other Hopis who were cooperating with the government.

Continuing Factionalism at Oraibi

Meanwhile at Oraibi, Tewaquaptewa at first showed a desire to carry out Lololma's agreement with the government. To demonstrate this, he allowed himself and his wife and their adopted children to be sent away to the boarding school at Sherman Institute in Riverside, California. There he took pride in wearing a military uniform and undoubtedly enjoyed the favors extended to him by officials of the government whose motives were to polish up this man and his family, so that on return to the Hopi country they would be models of "progress" for the rest of the Hopi people. The adopted children, Myron Polequaptewa and his sister Mina (now Mina Lansa), were of the Parrot Clan and were to be raised in apprenticeship to Tewaquaptewa. The reason for the adoption was that Tewaquaptewa was the last of the Bear Clan line, and Matcito, founder of Oraibi, had covenanted that in this event the successor clan should be the Parrot Clan, to which his wife belonged.

During the absence of Tewaquaptewa from Oraibi, there was much confusion over who should exercise leadership in his stead. There were several brothers who remained, each of whom was under pressure from different elements to move in and use the influence of the position. Tewaquaptewa himself left no instructions about his temporary successor, because his understanding from Lololma was that there were no longer any devout purposes to the kikmongwi's position, and, therefore, no rituals needed to be performed while he was away. In addition, the government sought to insure that the people of Oraibi remained loyal to their commitment to cooperate. To achieve this the agency offered material and helped to build new homes for all who would come down off the mesa and live near the school at its foot. This first step toward assimilation required that the government interject, even if indirectly, its own judgment concerning who should exercise influence at Oraibi, in order to encourage the migration of the Oraibians to the new community around the school. At the same time, this migration no doubt pleased the Christian missionaries by discouraging traditional practices at Oraibi, because it created a shortage of people to perform them and because it made access for the missionaries easier to those who had left their familiar traditional surroundings and had resettled in the unfamiliar Anglo-dominated environment. These diverse motives operating in Tewaquaptewa's absence became the makings of another factional division in which he would again become the ejector—this time ejecting the people of the newly-formed community of Kikotsmovi (place of ruins), as the village at the foot of the mesa came to be called.

Upon his return from Sherman Institute, Tewaquaptewa is said to have been very disappointed at the turn of events while he was away. Thereafter, he seemed to become impervious to the demands placed on him by government officials to influence his people toward "progress." Instead, he withdrew his commitment to the government and began to reestablish the traditional system, even if only those rituals in which the kikmongwi had direct functions. To make up for the shortage of performers, Tewaquaptewa accepted the offer of allegiance from the people of lower Moencopi village, which permitted men from this village to fill functions in the Oraibi rituals left vacant by men who migrated to Kikotsmovi.

Although Lololma had chosen Tewaquaptewa as his successor "even while he was still in the womb," when the time came to pass the title by ceremony, Lololma had hesitated and finally denied Tewaquaptewa the full title. The customary way of passing the title requires the "washing of the hair" of the one who is to receive it. This ceremony is performed by religious priests known as the *qwa qwant*, (one-horned priests), and is in effect an ordination. This formality had been denied to Tewaquaptewa, but he nevertheless was allowed possession of the paraphernalia for performing the *Soyal* ceremony, which is the principal rite of the kikmongwi. He solemnized this rite each year for several years and initiated Myron and Mina into their places in the ritual as rightful heirs-apparent. During these years there had been some vacillation by Tewaquaptewa in allowing Myron to act in his own right in conducting the ritual. Myron never forced the issue with him, until finally old age and its infirmities forced the old man to yield to Myron. Under pressure from the Parrot Clan matriarch, Myron confronted Tewaquaptewa with proof of the intention behind the adoption and initiation of Myron into the *Soyal* ceremony and with the fact that Myron could perform the ceremony in his own right. The two reaffirmed the covenant anciently made by Matcito that the Parrot Clan would succeed to the Bear Clan title, and so Tewaquaptewa confirmed Myron as his successor.

Myron Polequaptewa did not have the strong personality of his predecessor and consequently sat by uncertainly as to when and how he should assert himself as the new kikmongwi. He devoted most of his time and energy to herding his flock of sheep and to his farming, but during evening hours he spent a lot of time with various men whose knowledge of history and current affairs he respected. Then, following Supreme Court affirmation of the District Court decision in *Healing* v. *Jones* in 1962, which determined the legal rights of Hopis and Navajos in the Hopi Executive Order Reservation of 1882, Myron presented himself before the Hopi Tribal Council to be recognized as the representative of Oraibi. The Council did recognize him, under provisions in the Tribal Constitution, which provided that each Hopi village was considered to be under Hopi traditional organization, with the Kikmongwi as its leader, until other arrangements were effected under provisions of the Tribal constitution. (Under the constitution each village is recognized as having the right and power to decide for itself how it shall choose its representatives.) Without sufficient education to understand the mechanisms of the Anglo-oriented democratic procedures of the Tribal Council, Myron has found it considerably confusing and, therefore, has been unable to push his own views on issues for fear of being rebuked for some infringement of protocol.

Although he has some formidable support at Oraibi for the actions he has taken, his sister Mina has taken up a cause of her own against any cooperation with the Tribal Council. Mina finds her support outside Oraibi and has publicly allied herself with factions from Hotevilla and Shungopavy who are resisting the Tribal Council and, in some instances, the government. With the help of non-Indian friends, she has expressed her views through newspapers and television, representing herself as the "chief" of Old Oraibi. A number of reputable publications, including the *Christian Science Monitor*, printed articles recognizing her as the first woman chief among the Hopi people. In reality, as *goh-aya*, she has a definite place beside the kikmongwi and in that position can undoubtedly influence him, but Hopi tradition clearly excludes women from priestly office, which the kikmongwi's office necessarily is. However, the traditional mode of passing title to this office would allow transfer from Myron to one of Mina's sons, who stand as *diio ayam* to Myron. (The term *diio ayam* designates the children of a sister, or of a clan sister in the extended sense.) Whether Mina, as the mother of Myron's *diioayamuy* ("nephews,") realizes this consequence of custom law is difficult to determine from her activities against Myron, which at times seem to deny his right to the office of kikmongwi.

Land Controversies

Among all the factions operating on the Hopi Reservation, whether they are labeled "progressive" or "traditional," the chief issue is land.

The 1882 Reservation

When the Executive Order of 1882 was issued establishing the Hopi Reservation, it stated that it was also for "such other Indians as the Secretary of the Interior may see fit to settle thereon." This Executive Order was not ratified by Congress as required by law until 1958, the ratification stating that the reservation was for the Hopi Indians and "such other Indians as the Secretary of the Interior has heretofore settled thereon." This raised the question of which Indians had acquired an interest, recognizable in Anglo law, in the reservation between 1882 and the time of its ratification by Congress in 1958. In the 1962 case of *Healing* v. *Jones*, which dealt with this question, the court found that from 1882 to the mid-1930's there was no valid action by the Secretary under the Executive Order of 1882 to settle other Indians on this reservation. However, during this period there was frequent administrative condonation of Navajos moving in and settling down. Besides administrative planning by the Bureau of Indian Affairs to divide up the reservation for both Hopi and Navajo use, it also extended customary services to the Navajos who were within the reservation without official approval. In spite of repeated complaints and appeals for help by Hopi leaders, the Bureau continued this practice, reasoning that the Navajos were the responsibility of the government no matter where they were located. The court thus found that by extending its services to Navajos coming into the 1882 Reservation and either failing or refusing to prevent their coming in, the Bureau sanctioned the settlement of Navajos, according to the authority granted to the Secretary of the Interior in the Executive Order to settle such other Indians as he saw fit. Although this situation had existed long prior to 1930, the court chose to recognize only the sanctions of the mid-1930's as being imputable to the Secretary. Furthermore, the court held that the individual Navajos thus settled not only acquired an individual right to be in the reservation, but also acquired on behalf of the Navajo tribe a tribal interest in it. On this belabored reasoning, the court held that the Navajo tribe had an equal interest with the Hopi tribe to a portion of the 1882 Reservation, which was nearly three-fourths of the original area of about two and a half million acres.

The 1934 Reservation

From about 1900 to 1934 there were several executive orders designating so-called "public" lands surrounding the Hopi Reservation for Indian uses. Then in 1934, these designations were in

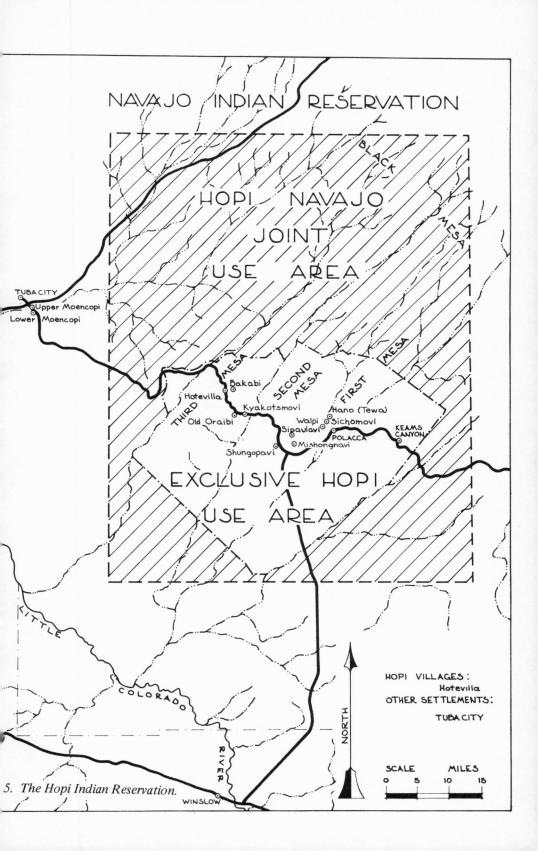

5. *The Hopi Indian Reservation.*

aggregate established by Congress as a reservation for Navajo Indians "and other Indians already located thereon." The original Hopi Reservation was specifically excluded in this action. Included in the 1934 Reservation was the Hopi village of Moencopi with all of its adjacent areas of Hopi land dating back to long before 1934. Also included were many other places of ceremonial importance to the Hopis, who maintained traditional claims to them through yearly commemorative rituals. Although Moencopi Hopi land use management is conducted by the Navajo agency of the Bureau of Indian Affairs, which at times indiscriminately applies Navajo tribal regulations, except as to certain Hopi individual allotments, the internal affairs of Moencopi village are governed by Hopi constitutional and traditional leadership.

The situation of the Navajos' claim to the 1882 reservation by virtue of being the "such other Indians" and the Hopis' claim to the 1934 Reservation as being the "other Indians already located thereon" has presented an interesting problem between the two tribes. While the Navajo claim to the 1882 Reservation has been litigated and a legal interpretation put on the conduct of the Bureau in relation to settlement of other Indians on reservation lands not expressly set aside for them, the Hopi claim to the 1934 Reservation has not been so litigated; however, it presents an almost identical situation in reverse, except perhaps the words "other Indians already located thereon" in the 1934 action are stronger than the words "other Indians heretofore settled thereon" in the congressional ratification of the 1882 Reservation. In both situations Bureau of Indian Affairs' conduct is substantially the same. If the Hopi claim based on these circumstances was given the same weight as the Navajo claim was under similar circumstances in *Healing* v. *Jones*, the Hopi Indians would have an equal interest in the 1934 Reservation with the Navajos. In the words of the Hopi tribal attorney implying that this should be so, "What's good for the goose is good for the gander."

Negotiations with the Navajos

Since the decision of *Healing* v. *Jones*, the Hopi and Navajo tribes have each appointed committees which have met several times in an attempt to negotiate the use and occupation of the area in the 1882 Reservation in which they were given joint interests. Because the Navajos have almost exclusively used and occupied this area with the help of Bureau of Indian Affairs' administrative fiat for a greater part of the period from 1882, they have been led to believe that the court decision resulted in a loss rather than a gain of an interest in land as the court reasoned and concluded. For this reason, the Navajos have preferred to reject the decision in its entirety, which makes it impossible to negotiate any of the conditions of right, title, and interest laid down. The Hopis, at least the Hopi Tribal Council, on the other hand, do not reject the decision and show a willingness to negotiate some division of the use and occupancy of the joint area in accordance with the decision. This has been extremely difficult, because the primary interest of the Hopis is to gain exclusive use of their share of the joint area, which puts a terrific burden on Navajos living on the joint land to abandon their homes. Several alternatives could be discussed, if the Navajos had not taken an uncompromising stand against the decision. This situation has rendered the negotiating committees on both sides impotent in looking after their respective interests in the joint area, so that the Bureau has taken greater control for the implementation of programs that affect both tribes. The division of the problem into surface and subsurface uses has undoubtedly changed the Navajo position on the decision itself, because the Navajo agreed to enter into a joint mining lease for coal located within the joint area on Black Mesa. But the differentiation between surface and subsurface uses for purposes of continuing economic programs did not originate from the negotiations—rather, this idea was interjected from without and never really formalized as a compromise between the Hopi and Navajo negotiating committees.

In pursuing their primary desire to expand their exclusive use and occupancy, the Hopis rely on their claim to the 1934 Reservation as a lever to bring about an exchange with the Navajos—that is, they want the Navajos to relinquish their rights to certain areas of the joint land, in exchange for the Hopis' comparable relinquishment of their claim to the 1934 Reservation, in such a way as to permit enlargement of Hopi land use.

Thus, as the matter stands today, it is up to the two tribes to resolve the land use situation. But in the meantime, pressures for economic development, interpreted in terms of non-Indian goals, have stepped up efforts on the periphery of the negotiations between the two tribes. These efforts will undoubtedly force some kind of a solution—but a solution which will perhaps be phrased in terms of the government's ideas as to what is good for the Indians in the way of economic development. Indeed, spokesmen for both tribes have stated that the land situation between them is one created by the white man and ought to be solved by the white man, but there have also been indications from each tribe that the solution had better be a satisfactory one to both Hopis and Navajos!

The Way to Self-Determination

From the standpoint of the federal government's policy of Indian self-determination, implemented through transfer of some community services to the tribal government, the Hopi Tribal Council may well lack the central administrative authority and ability to assume this responsibility. This deficiency does not lie in the individual Hopis who have dedicated their support to the constitutional form of government, but in the procedural uncertainties in the adoption of the constitution, which in turn leaves local village authorities apprehensive about entrusting the Tribal Council with the authority to administer programs affecting them. This is indicated by the preference of those villages which are not overtly supporting the Tribal Council to look directly to the Bureau agency for administration of these programs.

What appears, then, to be a dichotomy, in the sense of two mutually exclusive and opposing groups, between traditional notions of political controls and the present constitutional system is one which perhaps only exists as a myth. The broad principles stated by the Constitution cannot be said to be in conflict with Hopi *navoti*, or "philosophy," supported by the prophecy that one day the Hopis would find themselves in the midst of white men under pressure to assimilate. Thus, to preserve his identity, the Hopi must learn to deal with the white man in terms that the white man is capable of understanding. Basically, this is what the preamble to the Tribal Constitution provides for in stating it "is adopted by the self-governing Hopi and Tewa villages of Arizona to provide a way of working together for peace and agreement between the villages, and of preserving the good things of Hopi life, and to provide a way of organizing to deal with modern problems, with the United States Government and with the outside world generally."

It is now up to both the Bureau of Indian Affairs and the Hopi people to dwell less on the idea that the unwritten traditions and customary practices have no place in modern life and more on how to implement the values underlying these traditions and practices in administering the Constitution. This is the essence of self-determination.

Mexicans in the Southwest:
A Culture in Process

Ernesto Galarza

Let me say at the beginning that this is not a research report carried out for scholarly purposes. It is more a loose meditation on some 40 years of field experience in "a land full of wonder but not much information," to borrow from J.R. Tolkien. My view of the subject is perhaps slanted, by the fact that I have been in this land not as a participant-observer, but as a participant-adversary. I have not liked much of what I have seen in the intersection of cultures in the Southwest, where cultures do intersect, and I have been more prone to object than to be objective.

There is something else less personal that ought to be said. I have not been able to observe a Mexican Southwestern culture, working itself out in isolation. On the contrary, at every point I have seen an infraculture in compulsory contact with, and subordinate to, a supraculture. For this reason I am continually unsure, when I imagine I am dealing with an aspect of the Mexican culture, whether it is an *action* of that culture or a *reaction* to its containment.

It is from these points of view and with these predispositions that I shall try to follow the scheme of discussion which Spicer has given us. We were to address ourselves mainly to: (1) the content of Southwestern cultures, (2) the historical experience of each of them, and (3) what he calls the self-concept or evaluation that sets the critical boundaries between cultural types. In this framework, he asks, can we recognize the processes that produce plural societies and maintain them, or that undermine them and destroy them?

My effort to respond to these instructions divides this essay into its natural parts. First, I will attempt to explain what I mean

261

by the concepts I use. I will then try to outline how the Southwest culture of the Mexican looks to me at the present time. Within this view, I will discuss the cultural implications of the Mexican's historical experience, as well as the cultural forms that he has preserved throughout that experience. This will bring me to a Mexican community whose profile is typical and illustrative of my theme. I will then deal with what I call the cultural reactivity of the Mexican, and will try to suggest how this culture looks in action, rather than in reaction. Finally, I will make some observations on the two cultures face to face.

Concepts for the Understanding of Mexican Culture

The intellectual tools available to us in this connection are not as sharp as they might be. Terms like "minority," "acculturation," "traits," "primitive cultures," and "self-image" quite obviously derive from an anthropology that is itself a product of the culture that has overrun the world in the last 300 years—the culture of the western European white man. Is there, by chance, any bias in this of which we should be aware in observing the regional Mexican culture?

The word "minority" is a simplistic numbers test that does not explain some important matters. It does not remind us that there are minorities within minorities, which outsiders tend too often to regard as monolithic social groups. It is easier to explain them this way. Neither do numbers alert us to the fact that a Mexican can be and very often is a member of other minorities—as a trade-unionist, for example.

Further, the current terminology does not invite us to consider more carefully those select minorities, reckoned by economic influence rather than skin color, that wield enormous power over all the others. Both Learned Hand and Walter Lippman have hinted that we should not be so impressed by numbers: Hand, when he said that "we have come to think of the problem of democracy as that of its minorities," and Lippman, when he wrote that "every country is a mass of minorities which should find a voice in public affairs." And, I might add, every minority is a mass of individual human beings in more or less desperate search for security and identity.

262

We can see where the numbers method leads us. If a minority makes up ten percent of the total population, it should receive, some argue, ten percent of the available decent housing, ten percent of the jobs and so on. But why not ten percent of the civil liberties?

Acculturation

Let me next consider the term "acculturation." We are coming to the point where it means a sort of recapping process, a replacement of cultural treads. The implication seems to be that the reconditioning produces something as good as new. I do not believe that this is so. Acculturation, in my view, occurs only once in the life of any individual, during the early years when he is enfolded in the very tissues of the social group into which he is born. Later, he is conquered or he emigrates. Necessity or force compels him to learn different ways. This I would call "remedial acculturation," which I suspect is as inefficient, costly, and ultimately unsatisfactory as remedial reading.

Culture Traits

Identification of cultures by "traits" is convenient but hardly clarifying. To be sure we are able to associate individuals in groups by speech, intonation, address, and even by the way they walk. But this rule seems to be safest when the group we are talking about is small. Trait lists for Mexicans have been made and demolished. I have counted some 40 supposed traits offered as identification of the Mexican in the Southwest. As for Mexicans in Mexico, Monroy Rivera (1966) has offered just one, which I might translate as "runtism," from the title of his book, *El mexicano enano* (The Dwarf Mexican). He goes on to assign some 90 subtraits, but I must emphasize that his is a dour and sardonic list drawn with no scientific pretense.

Primitive Culture

Counting minorities by the numbers, regarding them as a *tabula rasa* for a second acculturation and reducing them to trait counts, belongs in the same category of concepts as that of "primitive culture." Primitivism is the conceptual child of contact between the overwhelming advance of the western European

263

white man and the native societies of Africa, America, and Asia waiting to be conquered by him. In the Southwest we have a residue of it. "They live like savages," I have heard white agricultural employers say of Mexican migrants who were forced to live under conditions which were, indeed, primeval. Anglos who are less outspoken in their judgments than such employers nevertheless employ a language of sympathetic condescension. The Mexican minority is described as "disadvantaged," "culturally deprived," "underdeveloped." And since poverty appears to be self-perpetuating under the current American social system, we have become reconciled to separating the "little traditions" of the poor from the "great traditions" of the elite. Matthew Arnold would have gone mad, I dare say, in the Mexican Southwest. So might we, unless we remember that it is not the contrasts between cultures, but the inward consistency of each that makes them worthy of serious study, respect, and possibly imitation. For it is only from that inward consistency that we can hope to understand the multitudinous ways in which humanity has sought, and continues to seek, the answers to its universal needs.

Let me underscore, without abusing it, this matter of inward consistency. After becoming lost in the painstaking explanations of culture handed down to us by the masters of anthropology I went back to Webster. I fingered my way down his column of definitions: *culture*, the intellectual content of civilization, a particular stage in civilization, the trait complex of a separate unit of mankind. Then I came to the biological connotation: *culture*, the cultivation of microorganisms in a nutrient medium. But why, I asked myself, should the biologists monopolize such a useful concept? Is it not as plain, on the basis of the data, that human beings, like microorganisms, cannot grow, cannot even survive without a passage into life through the nutrient medium of culture in a social group?

Here, I think, is the crucial difference between a cultural process and a cultural package. I have only a slight quarrel with those who have to deal in cultural packages for the sake of convenience—academic, ideological, or commercial—as long as we remember that it is for the sake of *their* convenience. And as long as we do not forget that the striving for an inward pattern of a culture is the projection in a social group of the strivings for security and identity of the individuals who compose it.

Self-Image

The foregoing offers, I hope, a more promising approach to the question of "self-image" or identity. I believe that both identity and security grow side-by-side in the individual life history. Both are embodied notably in the learning of language, which is only one of the vital social securities that group life offers. These social securities are inseparable from the web of a culture. To identify with them is to participate in them with a sense of security, trust, and reliance. If the original process of acculturation—and it happens only once, as I have said—provides, even as it imposes the bonds, restrictions, and prohibitions of the particular culture, a sense of enjoyment of those securities, then the foundations of identity are also laid. Thereafter the individual who is thus happily equipped is able to cope.

This is why I am not overly impressed with the cries of indignation from Mexicans, especially the younger ones, who bewail their loss of self-image. I find that they are almost always individuals with a certain ruggedness, or at least aggressiveness, of self. They are not asking "Who am I?" but "Why don't those racists like what I am?" It is those Mexicans who are *not* protesting a loss of self-image at the hands of Anglos who concern me more. These have indeed been damaged psychologically. Their self-security has crumbled step by step along with their self-identity. But I am not sure how much of this must be charged to the Anglo culture and how much to the Mexican. Physical violence to children is not unknown in the Mexican family.

Considerations on the Maintenance of Culture

As briefly as I can, I will now attempt some answers to the questions which Spicer has posed. What maintains a culture is access to an environment adequate to its survival and subsistence and shelter, and freedom from outside constraints on its own forms of value, ritual, art belief, feeling, and institutional behaviour.

The significance of cultural activities—speech, thoughts, techniques, and the like—is that they represent the individual search for security and identity in a network of human relations. It has been said that there is nothing more useless than a single telephone, and it can likewise be said that there is nothing less functional and more desolate than a single individual. Kinship groups are widening circles of relations that provide basic security and identity for the individual. Once this core is established, a person will feel aggrieved or resentful in the face of derision, mockery, or affront, but he will not feel broken.

Historical experience has been stressed by Spicer as a bond of culture. I would say that the historical experience of the social group that makes the difference in the living generation is not so much the textbook record of its victories glorified and its defeats borne with dignity. It is the fabric of those cultural forms that have survived and again make it possible, today and now, for the individual member of that group to know his identity and feel his security. History tells us the origin of those forms and the common experience that lies behind them. It helps us not to confuse culture with ethnicity, which merely insulates it; or with society, which embodies it; or with the state, which likely as not will pervert it; or with government, which polices it.

Since so much is being said about community in the Mexican Southwest, I have to touch upon this subject also. Community means to me the social group living together in ways which somehow seem self-relevant, and which somehow keep to the human scale of social behavior. It appears necessary, for community to exist, that there be a resource for survival and security accessible more or less to all of its members. Communication also is on the scale, and a satisfactory compromise between the restraints of the community and the display of the individual ego appear most possible in community.

The Mexican Southwest Today

In what follows I use the word "Mexican" as Spicer uses it, a cultural type existing in the Southwest which embraces five varieties: Hispano, Chicano, rural Norteño, urban Norteño, and Mennonite. We are talking about some five to six million persons living in five states: California, Arizona, New Mexico, Colorado, and Texas. It is a vast area in which the Mexican population has distributed itself in seven fairly discernible regional groupings: the San Francisco Bay basin, metropolitan Los Angeles, the Central Valley of California, the Salt River Valley of Arizona, the upper Rio Grande Valley of New Mexico and Colorado, a less-defined area centering in Denver, and Texas. There is an eighth which affects in its own peculiar ways all the others, and which I will call the "Border Belt."

The present demographic shape of the Mexican population of the Southwest has been developing for 100 years or more. We might say that for a century men have been fleshing out the skeleton of communication and settlement marked out during the previous 300 years. The pivots of seven of these areas are San Jose, Los Angeles, Fresno, Phoenix, Denver, Albuquerque, and San Antonio. The eighth, the Border Belt, has no center. It is a narrow stretch of desert, some 1800 miles long, between Browns-ville and Tijuana, located on both sides of an imaginary line drawn by treaty, ignored by nature, and transgressed by men.

Emigration and Immigration

We can call it a Mexican Southwest today mainly because through the Border Belt the northward migration of Mexicans has continued, recharging with population, not only the areas north of the border but those lying just south of it as well. The immigrants did not come to find virgin lands and to organize new societies in them, like the Mormons. Seeking work they scattered over the region, each man and each family in accordance with their own luck.

Since it was not propelled by kings, emperors, or presidents with national ambitions, or by designs of aggression, this immi-grant flow did not disturb the historic cultures which were already there. In these cultures, as in those of the Pueblos of New Mexico, differences in environment, resources for subsistence, and isolation made for differences in cultural forms. These sur-vive today in the styles of the Norteño, of the Hispano, of the Indian reservations, of the New Mexico villagers, and others. This is why it is necessary to allow immediately for varieties of the Mexican type and why we must concede to local pride and tradition the possibility that even the varieties may break down into variants.

This explains a problem that contemporary anthropology has created for itself in looking at the Southwestern Mexican. The anthropologist feels compelled to order, classify, arrange, and tabulate human groups in a way that will make them understandable to him. As a purely intellectual and altogether commendable procedure—a necessity if we are to be tidy in our thinking—it seems to imply also an effort to place their subjects in an order of merit or a hierarchy of importance. This feeling, universal throughout the Southwest, is an important datum for the researcher, one which Spicer would probably deal with under the heading of "ethnic boundaries."

It would not surprise me if there is a storm of indignation when it gets around that a few of us have met here and agreed that there is a cultural type called Mexican. Some years ago Landes (1965) offered a friendly suggestion that the type be called "Hispanoid." She only succeeded in annoying many people. I suggest that we try for agreement, not on a name but on a slogan. I borrow it from Mexican folk wisdom, in which there is a saying, "*juntos pero no revueltos*" (which, if you will pardon my translation, might be read as "sunny side up, not scrambled").

This suggestion is not as trivial as might appear at first. There is now emerging something called *La Raza Unida*. It is in part a desperate attempt, in the political area, to link and coordinate a number of regional styles and many local varieties of those styles. These styles, and varieties too, have gradually taken shape in accordance with the local environment and the degrees of political starvation which the Mexican has been experiencing. As a political device, the slogan, "*La Raza Unida—Juntos pero no revueltos*," could have interesting psychological effects and important practical applications.

Cores of Poverty

Going back to the Mexican culture, we find that within the eight major regions into which the Mexicans have sorted themselves we have to trace more detailed patterns. In each of these regions, not excluding the Border Belt, there are compacted cores of population in which the rural Mexican of 50 years ago is being transculturated into the urban Mexican of today. The heart of these areas are those census tracts into which Mexican poverty has been compressed. If, in looking at any culture, we must first notice its ecological setting, with the Mexican we must begin in these cores of poverty. Nearly 90 percent of the Mexicans are today living in or near them. There are variations in the pattern, but the differences are not in the quality of life. It would be hard to say who is poorer, the landworker of Tierra Amarilla or the chronically unemployed laborer of East Los Angeles.

Earlier in this essay I said that an important fact to grasp about any culture is its inward consistency. Following Benedict (1934), I now want to add that this consistency flows through a pattern or configuration which is peculiarly polarized. It is important to seek this pole because it leads us to the field of human energy around which other forms of that culture tend to arrange themselves. Victorian England gravitated around London, and London, around the culture of the City. The trade, politics, strategies, ideology, and weapons of empire gravitated around all three. We can draw concentric circles around this dynamic power, each in turn wider than the last, each embracing more marginal manifestations of the English way of life at that time, such as the slums and the coal towns. I am not trying to compare English culture and the Mexican situation here. All I am trying to point out is that the Mexican culture, too, has its polarization and its configuration; that its core is poverty and not power; and that the cultural ripples it sends out, therefore, hardly go beyond the limits of the census tract.

The massive immigration of the last 50 years, which accounts for the demographic pattern I have described, brought with it no formal institutions to perpetuate its culture. Of these the most important would have been schools. In the highly segregated barrios and colonias the Mexicans had to accept the educational agents of a different culture. And frequently these agents forbade the use of Spanish, gave unintelligible intelligence tests, adopted tracking systems by which Mexican boys and girls were switched permanently to a siding, and taught reading as ritual.

The lack of indigenous institutional anchors has been characteristic of Mexican culture in respects other than education throughout the 20th century. The church, Roman Catholic or Protestant, is still a proselyter, essentially the partner of an alien, secular power that long ago destroyed the economic and political autonomy of the original Mexican societies. In the arts and literature no peculiar institutions have emerged to train the artist and the writer in a Mexican tradition, to give him a base and a public. The Mexican has not even been able to defend and preserve his language. Altogether, the Mexican culture has been not a ship, but a raft coming apart, plank by plank, among hostile tides.

History and Culture

Let me turn now to the Mexican culture in the light of its history and later to a notation on some of its cultural survivals. The opening line of the familiar Mexican song, *El caminante del Mayab*, could be my theme for this section: *"Cuan lejos estoy del suelo donde he nacido"* (How far I am from the land where I was born). It is the song of a wanderer, a personal lament such as we can hear in many other cultures. In the Southwest today a loud note of cultural nostalgia is being sounded, not sentimentally but militantly. It comes mainly from those who were born on the northern side of the border, but who are ignored in the history of the land of their birth, and who now seek to find one in which they feel they belong. We have to examine the roots of this feeling from the angle of the two political systems which have divided that history between them.

The Two Conquests

For some 300 years what the indigenous social groups in Mexico had to contend with was the Spanish version of the eruption of western Europe throughout the world. Contrary to what happened elsewhere, the native Mexican tribes were not annihilated. They were, rather, kept in a servitude whose economic molds are well-known, such as the encomienda, the hacienda, and the mita. The native economic systems did not totally disappear. They survived in the out-of-the way places where the Spaniards found it too expensive or too inconvenient to bother about taking over. Elsewhere, the Spaniards dominated and domineered for 300 years as a minority, if we go by the numbers. There is an estimate that during those centuries fewer than a million white men emigrated from the Iberian peninsula to New Spain.

To me the notable thing is that the indigenous Mexican survived and multiplied until he put his genetic and cultural stamp on the mixed society that emerged. But this is not altogether what the Mexican activists are emphasizing currently. Out of the period of servitude they abstract something else, the brand of bondage. "We are a conquered people," they are saying.

Less than half a century after Spanish rule was ended by revolt there came the shock of the defeat of 1848. By this time there was a Mexican Northwest, which by courtesy we can continue to refer to as the United States Southwest. Those who were living in this region came under American rule. Here was a second conquest reinforcing the first one, still remembered in bitterness.

This attempt to draw the line between the Anglo and Mexican cultures by reaching into the past is an ambivalent one. In the process the Mexican will be turning up skeletons along with precious jewels, like some digger in the ruins of Yucatan. But for now it is the jewels that count—the valor, the defiance, the gallantry, the science, literature, and art of a race that went down, and even the bronze color of the skin.

That an "inferior" culture, the white one, could have done in a "superior," the brown, was not only unjust, it was offensive. The offense and the injustice to the Mexicans continue in the domination of the white man. He owns the productive lands that once belonged to them, and he continues to appropriate the fruits of their labor. He drafts their youth and sends them abroad to be killed in the service of an ill-defined national interest. When the tourist trade or refrigeration or electronics or atomic energy make the desert increasingly possible for business, he comes back and picks up the pieces of it he had overlooked, not to make more room for the Mexican, but less. You can see what I mean if you will stand on the roof of a skyscraper in Phoenix and look around you.

The rewriting of the history of the Southwest which Mexican intellectuals are planning will not be a purely academic exercise. It will have an emotional drive as well. It will be an effort, not to live history again, which is not possible, but to feel it again, which is. Maybe this has advantages and disadvantages. The advantage may be that the Mexicans thereby are tempering their wills for still another test they do not clearly foresee. The disadvantage may be that, in fixing on the past, they fail to notice that the engines of their historic defeats have not spent their force. The high-energy industrial civilization of the Anglo-American, which is continuing its intrusion into the agrarian societies of the world, includes Tierra Amarilla, the Central Valley of California, the Salt River Valley, and the lower Rio Grande Valley in its sweep.

I would not say that the Mexican of the Southwest is on a pointless sentimental journey in his emotional appeal to history. His revivalism is valid on certain grounds. When a social group is conquered and continues to live dominated, its history, at least, should not be appropriated by the intruder. Moreover, that history is the only way there is for him to find out why the Mexican has no land base as part of his system of identification. And having no land base where else will he find one? How, lacking it, prevent the slow erosion of the inward process of his culture—the forgetting of his history, the decline of his speech, the corruption of his manners, the starvation of his young?

How long it would have taken the Mexican emigrant peon of the 1910's to reconstruct his culture in the Southwest, is of course, idle speculation. In his numerous regional cultures he was essentially agrarian, a village man, with collectivist and communitarian traditions. The liberal political revolution of the 1860's neglected him, and then gave way to the long dictatorship of Porfirio Díaz, whose alliances with foreign capital undermined even more the material basis of the native cultures.

Encounter with Industrial Civilization

It was this Mexican who was propelled into the migrant stream of 1910-1940, headed northward, bound for an encounter with a high-octane industrial civilization. In that civilization a combination of revolutionary changes was under way. The railroads were creating an American common market. The telephone and telegraph were giving it unprecedented speed in communication. Agribusiness was laying its foundations. The legislative lobby as an instrument of politics was already demonstrating its ability to shape national policy. And the legal systems of the Anglo confirmed his title to the cream of the environment from which wealth was to be made. There was also underway a massive migration to the cities, into whose ghettos the Mexican would be driven.

I cannot stress too much that these technical revolutions offered jobs, and that mobility was the price of being hired. This was a mobility of individuals, or families at most, not of a numerous social group moving together and therefore keeping its culture more or less intact. By the 1880's, most of the former institutions of Mexican colonialism had been destroyed or reduced to mere relics by Anglo society, for example, the pueblo, the presidio, the mission, the rancho. After this, the two cultures could no longer coexist on equal terms. The California constitution of 1878 marked the end of true biculturalism, as it did of bilingualism, in the schools, courts, newspapers, and public · administration.

All this, too, became a part of the historical experience of the Mexican in the Southwest, at least of the large majority of those persons who presently make up the Mexican cultural type. We have yet to study and understand more thoroughly two important chapters of that history which between them divide the last seventy years. Up to the early 1940's, the story is principally that of the Mexican landworker, locked into an exploitative wage system by mob violence, police power, and legal process. After the 1940's, the story is mainly that of the displacement of these same people toward the cities, with still another cycle of drastic changes such as the shift from agrarian to urban vocations, the dissolution of the family as an economic unit, the loss of the communitarian sense of the rural colonia.

It is this last chapter which stands most vividly before the Mexican today, for he is experiencing it himself. I will merely catalogue some of those experiences. As a worker, he is finding that the economic ladder to the better-paying jobs is becoming more like a greased pole as industrial processes are automated and skills are refined. The public school system presents him with a dilemma of choice between vocational training that only leads into winding, if not blind, alleys on the one hand, and the liberal arts on the other, for which the Mexican community offers limited professional opportunities. In politics, wherever the enfranchised Mexican represents a critical swing vote, the two

273

major parties have contrived to permit him to do just that—swing. His extended family is becoming more and more the extenuated family, with the wife-mother working, the young dissenting or revolting, and unemployment finally driving it into dependency on public assistance.

These are broad generalizations, of course. Nevertheless, I think the Mexican experience falls within them, and I now want to comment on some of the implications of this statement.

A Culture in Transition

León-Portilla has said that the reality of the Norteño culture emerged in the Northwest basically through the establishment of the villages, the mining towns, the presidios, the ranches, the haciendas, and the missions. As he takes the historic process at the flood, I take it at the ebb. The cultural reality of which I am speaking has submerged with the disappearance of these structures. Without them there were no alternatives to acculturation and assimilation by the Anglo. If it is true that it is the characteristic institutions of a society which most deeply affect human behaviour, then we are prepared to agree that the Mexican's behaviour in the Southwest has been most deeply affected by the disappearance of his own traditional institutions.

I want to look now at those cultural forms which have kept their vitality in spite of the disappearance of traditional institutions, and to indicate how and why that vitality has diminished.

The Endurance of Spanish

The first and most important of these is language. Spanish is spoken throughout the Southwest, in the family and on the streets. It is the language in which public meetings are conducted and in which a good deal of business is transacted. The closer to the Border Belt one moves the more Spanish one hears, the spontaneous kind that expresses promptly the spirit of the speaker. One can walk for blocks in Albuquerque, San Antonio, Los Angeles, San Francisco, or Denver and hear the continuous flow of Spanish conversation. Here and in innumerable smaller communities from Corpus Christi to Sacramento menus in Mexican restaurants are printed in two languages as a convenience for their Anglo, not their Mexican, customers. The work talk on the job and the gossip of the town is Spanish.

We can attribute this endurance to a number of factors. One is the family in which the older members are native Spanish-speaking. Another is the continuous replenishment of adult newcomers who can speak nothing but their native Mexican tongue and who remain firmly attached to it all their lives. Their family ties across the border are likewise durable for at least one generation. Family visits to and fro are another strand of this familistic bond.

In ways which anthropologists and sociologists have not up to now observed too closely, Spanish serves more subtly to maintain the cultural network. It continues to be the medium, for hundreds of thousands of persons, by which important information gets through. This communications system operates through informal conversation groups which convey the names, locations and other sufficient data for finding work, obtaining social services, avoiding unwelcome contact with authorities, finding help in distress, or companionship in leisure. Insofar as the urban barrios have survived, they remain the centers of this interchange.

If we were to attempt to locate the area in which the Spanish language in the Southwest is most likely to keep its roots deep and vigorous, it would be in this non-Anglo world. As we move away from it the depth lessens and the vigor declines progressively, and both can be measured by generation as well as by area. By stages Spanish becomes a second language and finally a decorative fringe of the stepmother tongue, English, which takes over inexorably.

It is in the fringe area that we find the academic bilingual programs. They are an attempt to reconnect the speech with its cultural medium by Anglo institutional programs and educational devices. They face many obstacles. School administrators who are culturally monolithic and therefore monolingual make room for bilingual programs with reluctance or skepticism. Those who are more enthusiastic or sympathetic are obliged to filter Spanish instruction through curricula dictated by Anglos and not by the Mexicans. In spite of these initial difficulties, it seems possible, at least in districts where Spanish is the natural spoken tongue, to develop institutional support for a return to the bilingualism of the mid-19th century. The important question is whether the Anglo state is willing to settle down to an effort which will have to last for generations to accomplish that end. It is my estimate that the past five years and the next ten will be no more than an experimental stage, during which the Anglo intention will be tested and the technical problems worked out.

Changes in Family Life

When we look at the family we see again the importance of time in the formation of cultural forms. Complete family units are constantly being transplanted from Mexico to the Southwest and with these there come not only the original language but also the values, the rules of deference, the etiquette, the hierarchies, and customs.

Two or three generations after migration these break down. I think it is inevitable that they do. In the Anglo manner Mexican mothers go to work for wages outside the home. Where the educational opportunities have been better and the economic status is higher, the Mexican housewife begins to take part in public affairs, until a kind of separate *and* equal competence shatters the classic image of the dominant Mexican male, the *macho*. In this process first the children, then the grandchildren, have also slipped from the old molds and the generation gap is further widened by the cultural gap. So today the Mexican family in the Southwest presents a very wide range of familistic cohesion. One can hear Mexican youth refer to the father either as *el jefe* or as "the old man."

There is another variation in the family patterns. Where agricultural migrancy still exists, as in California and Texas, the Mexican family continues to transmit occupational skills to the young. That they are low-wage skills, and that they are accompanied by serious educational penalties, has long been known. I raise the point here only to make it clearer that the urban family has totally relinquished this role with regard to its young.

As the Mexican family acquired its cultural retreads in successive generations, an interesting situation came about that we can observe around us today. The family is no longer the most resistant barrier to Anglo assimilation. The resistance is now coming from the young, often the very young. It takes the form of public denouncement, not of private devotions to a traditional way of life. The young, in their passionate criticisms of the *gabacho*, every *gabacho*, accuse him of a plot, only a part of which has been deliberate and malevolent. The rest of it is the way of societies in interaction. The truth is that bars are let down as well as forced down, and it is important to be able to tell the difference. Not to be able to do so can lead to ethnic paranoia.

By forcing down of bars, I mean such acts of Anglo barbarism as the punishment of children in school because they spoke in their mother tongue, often the only one they knew. By the letting down of bars, I mean the substitution by the family of English-speaking television programs for Spanish ones, or the disuse among the younger adults of the relationships and the terms *mi comadre* and *mi compadre*. Nor have I heard in 30 years a Mexican bride defy her older brother for the first time in her life shielded by the possessiveness of her brand-new husband: "*Ya tengo otro que me mande*" (Now I have another who commands me).

Residence: Colonia and Barrio

It has been around the family and through the medium of living Spanish that the Mexicans more recently settled in the Southwest have improvised their patterns of residential togetherness. Some of these residential patterns have been ephemeral, like the farm labor and railway construction camps, which, for all that they may have remained in one place for 15 or 20 years, were nevertheless merely stopping places. Much more lasting were the *colonias* and the *barrios*, terms which have not always been mutually exclusive. The colonia once meant the settlement on the fringes of a city or large town, accessible to farm, railway, and industrial jobs. It also meant the whole of the Mexican community in a given district, usually urban, whether scattered or concentrated in one neighborhood. In the larger cities, such concentration easily adopted the original Mexican descriptive name of barrio.

It was in the colonias and the barrios that Mexican culture transferred itself more or less intact. In them the language kept its strength and its flavor. The food, the manners, the music, and the religion were original Mexican. The cooperative inclinations, as well as the belligerent individualism, were at home. Twice a year the colonia and the barrio celebrated *Cinco de Mayo* and *Dieciseis de Septiembre* as they still do, with queens and *gritos* of nostalgic defiance against invaders long since dead.

The out-of-the-way places where the agricultural colonias were formed early in this century remained safe from Anglo intrusion for several decades. They were built on useless or marginal land. As labor pools which filled or emptied with the harvest cycles, they distributed agricultural manpower conveniently at no cost to the industry. Of these communities many have disappeared. The economic development of the Southwest and the urban spread of the last three decades have obliterated them. Only on the fringes of this advance do they cling, diminished and parched.

The urban barrios like the colonias of the countryside, started as cultural enclaves in the Anglo world. It cannot be said that the Mexican culture which they replicated on so small a scale flourished, but it did survive, replenished by continuing immigration. With little or no institutional life, the barrios stabilized a population of low-income wage workers from which the surrounding city drew manpower. In the barrios ethnic identity was strongly provided. The familiar words by which friends and kin expressed secure relationships came straight from working-class Mexico: *compadre, paisa* (for *paisano*), *vale, cuate, tocayo, carnal, raza*. Likewise the words that set the ethnic boundaries between the Chicano and the Anglo: *gabacho, gringo, bolillo,* and *guero*. In the barrio the instruction of the young was, of course, turned over to the American English-speaking public schools, but their education, Mexican acculturation in manners, continued in the homes—at least as long as there was enough of the barrio to enlarge and reinforce the forms of behaviour demanded by the family.

It cannot be too strongly emphasized that the cultural vitality of the barrio depended upon the numbers of Mexicans living in close contact and the stability of its location. It also depended upon the retention of the successive generations within the cultural mold, and the resistance of Spanish speech and Mexican manners and customs, to alien example. In other respects the barrio was always a dependency of the host society.

The barrio has begun to break down. In many cities it has been wiped out by urban reconstruction. From a distributor of manpower it is becoming increasingly a reservoir of unemployment. Its young are more and more anglicized in speech and in manners. Demolition, economic deterioration, and cultural dilution threaten the barrio at this point. How it can resist all three, if the Mexican is to retain it simply as the haven that it has always been, is the vital cultural question he must answer.

Wetbacks

It would seem, as something to speculate about, that the cultural mode to which Anglo society would like the barrio to conform is that of the wetback. This variety of the Mexican way of life in the Southwest is a direct product of public policy on the part of the two national governments. The border, more or less open to provide an escape hatch for millions of utterly poor Mexicans, is like a cunningly designed filter that separates the economic utility of the Mexican illegal entrant cleanly from the rest of his cultural makeup. Never a participating member of the community or society, as Samora (1971) describes him, the wetback lives anthropologically in a no-man's-land. Wetbacks hide throughout the Southwest by the hundreds of thousands, contributing only their labor power and receiving only their bargain basement wages. Yet as a group they represent the most authentic transplant of Mexican working-class culture in the United States. And as a person this particular Mexican shows how culture, the original acculturation, provides the real identity, rather than the labels that society invents for it. The wetback may have been a bracero, a border commuter, a "green carder," and he may and does become a resident alien, or finally a naturalized citizen. This, at any rate, is the ladder every wetback hopes to climb, and in the Mexican barrio he finds the first rungs among people who give him a little of their own cramped space.

Alviso: A Case in Point

At this point I am going to bring what I have been talking about into focus by an illustration. For this I have chosen Alviso, a town of some 1800 people located at the southern tip of San Francisco Bay. Its boundaries enclose 14 square miles of marshland, settling ponds that produce salt, orchards, and building sites that over the years have been filled with rubble. When the winter rains are heavy, the bay backs up to meet the floods of Coyote Creek and Guadalupe Slough, the waterways that meander by.

Alviso's population in 1966 was 68 percent Mexican and 31 percent Anglo. It has been a way station in the wetback underground, a bracero pool, a summer campground for harvest hands, and a dump. The Mexican families presently living there settled out of the migrant stream or moved from surrounding communities attracted by the inexpensive lots and the lower rents. Until recently the area has been isolated, marginal geographically and economically—one of those places where a typical colonia could take root, unmolested because of its dismal appearance.

In the late 1960's the community resembled a partially deserted, rundown boomtown of the 1930's, with poorly paved streets and rubble-filled vacant lots. The houses were dilapidated and overcrowded, and many did not have adequate plumbing. The one elementary school was the only educational and recreational facility in the city, with the exception of a park which was nothing more than a vacant, muddy lot without any grass or trees. A converted motel building housed a medical clinic, and a half-century-old building was used for the police and fire departments, as well as the city council chambers, a day-care center, and a community meeting hall. Roughly 70 percent of the families had incomes of less than $5,000 a year, and many were on public assistance. At the same time the entire city had an assessed valuation of less than $3,450,000, of which approximately $250,000 represented the assessed value of the homes of residents. The average level of educational attainment was the eighth grade.

In Alviso, Mexican culture did not flourish but it did survive. The predominant language was Spanish. The ways in which people were congenial or quarrelsome were Mexican. Here the minority was the majority, and English was the second language of the neighborhood. Its religion was Roman Catholic. Individuals and families made trips to Mexico as often as their savings would permit, and visiting relatives from home found Alviso comfortable, because of the familiar tone of life. Characteristically it was a talking and not a reading community. Town politics pivoted around kinship; cliques and factions were more significant than party lines. There were fewer than 400 registered voters in the town.

Such a culture could hardly have been the envy of outsiders concerned with power politics and progress. And so it was, until progress had soaked up all the available real estate in Santa Clara County, which includes Alviso. During the past two decades, down both sides of San Francisco Bay, a new megalopolis has been forming. Along the Nimitz and Bayshore Freeways, which between them embrace the bay, suburbs, electronic plants, an airport, light industry, and automobile assembly plants have closed in. Land values skyrocketed until prune orchards could be priced at $30,000 an acre for residential tracts.

The tide of investment polarized around the city of San Jose, the county seat. Under a shrewd, engrossing city manager, it annexed and consolidated wherever it could. The heart of San Jose itself was chopped up to make way for a grid of freeways, and in the process the barrio of central San Jose, an old Mexican community, was wiped out. The city boundaries touched those of Alviso to the north, and evidently the time had come for something to be done about so much unused land—14 square miles of it—occupied by so few Mexicans.

The strategy to annex Alviso to San Jose was launched some ten years ago. Annexation was rejected by the Alviso voters in 1962. The little town, unincorporated and at the end of its bonding powers, waited for the next annexationist attempt, which came in 1968. Previous to the election a private development association was organized by some wealthy property owners of Alviso, with which the city council of San Jose negotiated a contract guaranteeing the residents of Alviso civic improvements of various kinds. Copies of this contract, in English and Spanish, were distributed to every householder.

Exploiting the propaganda value of the contract, San Jose city hall agents and local partisans of annexation waged an intense campaign. Petitions were circulated, jobs were offered, modest payolas were tendered, confidential negotiations were conducted and the voters were courted as they never had been before. On election day residents who had moved away years before showed up at the polls, and other techniques of winning an election were applied. The annexationists won, 189 to 180.

On appeal, the validity of the election was upheld by the Superior Court of Santa Clara County. However, in September, 1970, the California Supreme Court reversed the decision and invalidated the election on the ground that 11 voters were ineligible. (Jesus Canales *et al.* v. City of Alviso and City of San Jose). While the election has been overturned, it has left the Mexican colonia divided by the issue of annexation. If it had been upheld, Alviso as a name would have disappeared from the political map of Santa Clara County, and the deteriorated houses in which the Mexicans live would have been marked for destruction by real estate developers. The residents would have had to move to San Jose and pay two or three times their present rent, or to "south county," a pocket of poverty resulting from the demolition of other colonias. As there is no guarantee that the proponents of annexation will cease their efforts, the residents of Alviso may yet suffer this fate.

As it is with Alviso so it is with Union City, Guadalupe, and many other colonias throughout the Southwest caught in the tide of progress. Anthropologists may well ask, as the barrios and the colonias go down: where will Mexican culture in the United States find a land base in the next 50 years?

The Past 70 Years: A Recapitulation

Here, I will stop for a flashback, to sharpen the outline of Mexican cultural evolution in the Southwest since 1900.

It has been, and largely continues to be, a culture of immigrant poor people coming from a society in convulsion and radical transition. The civil war that lasted more than 20 years obscured the other revolutions that were taking place in Mexico—

in transportation, in the agricultural economy, in the process of industrialization, and in class structure. Except as its victims, those who fled into exile had had no part in the old regime; except as its casualties, they had none in the new.

Propelled across the border, again they found a society in the midst of radical change—a revolution of transportation fully under way, a massive drift from country to city picking up momentum, vertical and horizontal integrations of the economy (including agriculture), mobility of residence to match mobility of jobs. In a half century the Mexican immigration spread itself well beyond the Southwest, into the Northwest and Middle West. Scattered and thinned out, its efforts to drop anchors have failed. What were some of these?

The Failure to Gain a Land Base

As a small farmer, as a husbandman, as a yeoman, the Mexican failed. Even though he was unquestionably a dedicated and industrious worker of the land, he acquired none of it for his own in the United States. And this was not because of a prejudice in American society working notoriously and exclusively against him. It was because even small-family farming—the only kind accessible to the landworking Mexican—was beyond his means, and because family farming was proving no competitor for agribusiness. Because he came, typically, from rural Mexico he fitted appropriately into rural America in the role of an agrarian proletarian, not in that of a brown yeoman on the Jeffersonian model.

The colonias became the residential base of this proletariat and remained such for many years. In the way in which a people have of dealing with their fate, the colonias were a rough shaping of the Mexican culture in exile. But their livelihood depended upon their being used, their survival upon not being noticed. But their usefulness declined; the bracero and the wetback competed even with their miserable living levels, and machines took over many jobs as well. The lands on which they squatted became noticeably more valuable to the Anglo entrepreneur. The colonia was condemned. Alviso and Pascua Village in Tucson both illustrate the process.

The Fate of the Labor Contractor and the Work Crew

Let us now see what took place in the process of agricultural production itself. I want to mention two things: the labor contractor system and the crew system.

The Mexican farm labor contractor early became something of a polarizer among the Mexican farm migrants. Aside from unusual abilities and initiative, his assets were a system of contacts with Anglo employers of seasonal labor, transportation facilities, a camp, a store where food could be bought on credit, and often a bar where job leads could be obtained free and hiring deals closed. These were the more respectable functions of the labor contractor as a cultural agent. He had others, such as wine, women, song, and marihuana.

But the contractor had a brittle lease on his role among rural Mexicans. That role was a parasitic one, transparently dependent on the Anglo's economic dispositions, and in the 1940's those dispositions called for the bracero program, a system of managed migratory labor and administered wages into which the contractor did not fit. As an anthropological situation it was intriguing; the farm labor contractor was displaced as a cultural agent by the Anglo's farm labor associations, if by any stretch of the sociological imagination it can be said that such an association has been or could ever be a cultural agent. Many contractors survived, but on condition that they assume the more menial tasks of managing the brown manpower for agribusiness.

The same fate overtook a form of organization around which Mexican rural life, dimly and gropingly, tried to arrange itself, namely, the crew system. The work crews were teams of seasonal laborers that put themselves together spontaneously in the colonias. They were based upon neighborhood acquaintance, kinship, and a common experience that sorted out the industrious workers from the lazy. Crew leaders emerged; they were not appointed. Crews tended to develop ties of confidence over the years. They became incipient bargaining units operating on a rough democratic basis. Their membership was voluntary.

It is possible to imagine how, in the long run, the rural work crews could have themselves become polarizing agents in the Mexican society. But there was to be no long run. The crew system was destroyed. How this was done I have described in *Merchants of Labor* (1964), where you can read how the farm labor association combined forces with the U.S. Department of Labor to bring about that destruction. Considering how short-lived the crew system was, and how small the number of workers it reached, in proportion to the farm labor force, one can appreciate how feeble, how incipient, this Mexican cultural process was when it was crushed.

The Impact of Urbanization

With no roots in rural America of their own, the Mexicans were ready to join the exodus to the cities. Beginning in the 1940's, Mexican society again experienced a severe wrench. Its demographic location moved drastically.

From a predominantly agrarian subculture, it became a predominantly urban infraculture. By 1970 close to 90 percent of the Mexicans in California were city dwellers and workers. I have indicated above how they have distributed themselves regionally and compacted themselves in the tracts of city poverty..

In the cities the cracking of the social fabric has continued. The family no longer works together, as it did picking and harvesting. The cohesion that the authority of the male head imposed, however arbitrary, is gone. Fathers and mothers both work to make ends meet in moonlighting families and consequently their young are out of sight and out of hand.

Does the barrio offer a last resort for the culture of the Southwest Mexican? I do not think so, the way matters stand and the way they are moving. The barrios are physically marked for destruction. From one end of the Southwest to the other they, like the colonias, stand in the path of Anglo progress, political requirements, suburbanism, planning, and primitivism in sociological perception. I have cited the case of Alviso. Multiply the Alvisos many times as to land area and population, and you will understand how Mexican neighborhoods in San Jose, Oakland, San Antonio, Albuquerque, Phoenix, or El Paso, have been abolished.

I am not speaking here of points of friction between two cultures, but of points of attrition, at which the destructive power of the dominant society is at work. If contemporary social science were inclined to study these effects it would meet with two difficulties. First, the evidence is quickly removed from the site; the Mexican residents scatter as a kind of human débris that is as quickly removed as that of the smashed and splintered homes. Second, federal programs of various sorts are already busy with remedial acculturation. The list of their lenitives is long: subsidized housing, cross-town busing, urban remodeling, brown minicapitalism, perpetual training, occupational prosthesis, a modicum of community participation, headstarts up short alleys. After all this, what is left to the Mexican minority are its cultural residues. Where, among them, will Mexican culture find a base?

The Cultural Reactivity of Mexicans

I have called this part of my essay "cultural reactivity" to imply at once that the Mexican type and its varieties are beginning to act in response to containment by the Anglo. I will mention some of these manifestations, well aware that I am not so much looking at minority Mexican culture in isolation as I am at its interactions at many points with the contemporary society of the majority. The responses include the student movement, the news media, economic security, the search for identity and history. We can regard these as areas of cultural protest that appear at the same time to want in and to want out of the larger, encompassing society. No one individual or group or organization is planning this protest. There is not one national, coordinated Raza Unida but a hundred or more.

The Search for Identity

Basic to all the other expressions of the protest culture which I am going to try to outline is the reassertion of· a self-image worthy, as the Mexicans see it, of themselves. First of all this requires the destruction of offensive stereotypes. These have been the products of Anglo literature, of motion pictures, and of advertising. At least it has been the ads and the movies which have flaunted these caricatures on a mass scale. The effects have been highly visible. A character type that historically belonged to the Mexican because he created it—the vaquero—was rustled and retouched as a gringo hero, the "good guy" cowboy. Another character type that grew out of the Mexican's typical economic roles of farm and section hand was perverted into a picture of the peasant dozing by a cactus. Comic strips and cartoons picked up this distortion, adding to it a gallery of bandidos, comic opera generals, paunchy bar tenders, and brown-skinned lackeys. Stereotypes of a more subtle kind have pervaded novels and textbooks by Anglo authors.

All of these are under heavy fire, and no matter from what sector of the Mexican minority it comes, its object is the same: to destroy the caricature. For example, Mexican social scientists are busy taking apart certain lists of alleged ethnic traits supposedly characteristic of Mexicans. As the caricatures are demolished the goal becomes clearer, and it is simply the return of self-confidence. How firmly this self-security will stand up in those who are asserting it presently, and how soon it can spread as an experience rather than as a slogan in the mass of the Mexican population, remains to be seen.

The remaking of the image amounts to an assertion that inferior status is no longer to be accepted as a means of survival. As I have suggested it is taking place in many quarters of the Mexican culture. It can be heard loudest and seen most dramatically in the Chicano sector—that is, the young avant garde. Its stress is on Mexican Me, not on the American Me of 20 years ago. In this sector the keynote is impassioned defiance, the determination is to "show them." It is an emotional drive of reckless courage and jubilation that for the time being occupies most of the front stage. If there is a moment when passionate self-expression is the only spur that can set events in motion, the Chicanos are providing it. It is from them that new pejoratives are being flung: *Tío Tomás, vendido, coyote, placa.* Chicanos rehearse these, mixed with the traditional obscenities, with great delight. They declare that "our blood is our power," that they are the deliverers of "the land of our birth," "the destroyers of precision, profit, and conformity." All this, too, is part of the return of self-confidence, perplexing as it may seem to some.

However grandiloquent the Chicanos may sound when they identify themselves with their Indian ancestors, the Empire of Aztlán, they are in this respect moving with a significant effort at historical reinterpretation. No one writer has yet put all its pieces together, but several are beginning to try. It will be the work of scholars and therefore painstaking and slow in coming. In the meantime, the effort to achieve a sense of common history, as part of the recovery of image and self-confidence, exalts traditional heroes and forms of political address. Emiliano Zapata is now worshipped by the grandchildren of men who fought with him. The *plan*, as a form of public address, is the historic version of the manifesto, and there have been published in California a Plan de Delano and a Plan de Santa Barbara. A Mexican journal of social criticism is called *El Grito*, of which there has been only one in Mexican history—the call to revolt by the Reverend Miguel Hidalgo y Costilla a century and a half ago. And on the marches of militant farm workers, banners of the Virgin of Guadalupe are raised again.

In this great leap backward to recover the common historical identity, the Mexicans of the Southwest have unconsciously jumped over a void in their chronicles. They have practically nothing in print that tells them what happened to the immigrant La Raza after 1910. The efforts to fill this void have been mainly those of Anglos. During 40 of these 70 years, the Mexican experience was largely that of an agrarian culture in transition and in conflict. It is this most recent period of the Mexican evolution that holds important lessons that will not be learned until they are written down.

Matching this gap, there is another, namely, the lack of critical understanding, especially among the youthful Mexicans of the Southwest, of the drift of the Mexican Revolution. The young Chicanos want to go home again, but if they do, they will find that Mexico, too, is on the way to becoming a land of precision, profit, and conformity. Its model is the complex industrial civilization of the United States. Their joint product is the formless society of the Border Belt wetback, their common goal, the partition of common markets.

I must say, in the light of these comments, that the search for historical identity is still pretty much in the fiesta stage. Or, to change the metaphor, the worship of Zapata has become more the end of a pilgrimage than the beginning of a search for the historical forces that lie behind tragic symbols like his.

Language and the Schools

More immediate results can be expected in the area of bi-lingualism. There is a very broad base for this revival in the persistence of Spanish in everyday life. University courses are being designed "to develop confidence in its use, to combat negative attitudes toward it and to improve the ability to understand and speak it." If printed Spanish does not yet go much beyond the headlines of the militant press, or the occasional article translated into Spanish but written in English, all the same the Spanish language is no longer on the defensive. I have already said that the formal bilingual programs in the public schools have a long way to go, but they are going in the right direction because they, too, reflect a cultural reassertion of the Mexican community.

This suggests an additional comment or two on the educational involvement of the community. There is no level of public instruction to which the Mexican is not giving vigorous attention. The stimulus of the Headstart program, and the increasing awareness of dropouts, retardation, the miscarriage of testing, and the devious malfeasance of tracking systems have given the Mexicans new causes around which to protest, if not yet to organize. It is a zig-zag progression through issues that have not been sorted out. Characteristically, there has been more controversy over busing than over the philosophical issues of a Mexican concept of education. The closer we come to the university level, the more likely we are to find persistent pressure on the curriculum, the instructional budget, the recruiting practices, the content of courses, and the ethnic color of the instructional staff.

Confrontation with the Media

As with the schools, with the press, radio, and television media the Mexicans are showing their positive discontent. One form of it is the local Chicano publication, ephemeral but stinging. A press association of these papers has been formed and when one member vanishes another appears promptly to take its place. The point is that here, also, on the cultural spectrum the young Mexicans are determined to have their own devices for communication, since the commercial newspapers will not carry their news or their denunciations.

A more conventional approach is also being tried on the media. This consists of demanding more staff jobs for Mexican reporters, script writers, and various kinds of technicians. It is contended that this not only opens more job opportunities, but also guarantees that a Mexican interest, if not a Mexican point of view, will be reflected in the news. Already one national conference on the subject has been held, in which the Mexican participants declared that their purpose was to bring about more articulation of their minority through the mass media.

The other way of accomplishing such articulation—by creating an independent press—has not succeeded to date. The Spanish language dailies that are published in a few of the metropolitan areas do not link the mass of the Mexican population. There is no provincial press to create this network. Publication is a capitalist enterprise which has needed half a century to establish a Negro press of even a million circulation. Whatever the approaches, all pose the same question: why has the Mexican been thus far screened out of the dissemination of information and opinion in the affluent society?

The Mood in the Universities

In the universities the critique of education is under way. It is now almost entirely in the hands of students and professors who are clear about what they want and why. First of all they want larger numbers of Mexican students on the campus. They want proportionately more of the resources of the university for increased enrollments. They want, not always but often, parallel institutions controlled financially, administratively, and academically by them. Once a piece of the educational establishment is in their hands, they candidly state that they want to parlay it into a liberation movement, a cultural home for the rediscovery of self, and a means to reconquer a sense of community for all Mexicans. The Plan de Santa Barbara, through which some of these ideas run, is worth reading.

The first result of this critique has been the establishment of ethnic departments within which Mexican studies are offered. I do not have an exact count but I am sure there are nearly 100 universities and colleges in the Southwest where this is occurring. What once was supposed to take decades to develop—graduate studies, postgraduate degrees, advanced research, and full complements of ethnic staffs—is taking place in the span of a few semesters.

The upcoming Mexican scholarship is announcing its purposes with gusto. It will, it says, begin by slaughtering the sacred cows of academic scholarship in general. It intends to lay the myth of the conquering Spaniard. It will expose the Anglo as a cultural sneak thief. It will create its own scholarly journals on which Anglo editors will not sit in editorial judgment. This is iconoclasm with a program. It already has a fairly critical edge. Mexican intellectuals, activists, organizers, critics, and students compiled a volume of documented indictments for the Cabinet Committee Hearings on Mexican-American Affairs, El Paso, Texas, 1967 (1968).

Political Action

As to politics, the Mexican today is in a secessionist mood. Over the past 20 years a small segment of the minority was learning and applying the techniques of vote delivery. The meteor-like course of the Kennedy Clubs may well have been the brightest and briefest moment of the Mexican partisan apprenticeship. The Democrats had previously asked not what they could do for the Mexicans, but rather what the Mexicans could do for them the next time around. They gerrymandered no "safe" districts for barrio loyalists, who point out that there is not a state with a Mexican governor, nor a large city with a Mexican mayor.

So, if we are to cite expressions of the current mood, they would be those of one political organization that has announced it will no longer be a kept woman, or of another which has adopted the slogan, "*Huelga*" (strike), vis-a-vis both Democrats and Republicans.

Political dissent thus far has the ring of disgruntlement more often than that of social criticism. But it could move in that direction. The way is being prepared by others who do not aspire to public office, directing their talents and their energies to economic issues.

In this sector, again, there is no concert of plans or of action. The criticism comes from many angles and is aimed at many targets. In the last year or two the statistics have been gathered and published which at last document how far down the job ladder the Mexican blue- and white-collar workers really stand. Brown pressure is responsible for statistics of this kind, as it has compelled negotiations to establish at least a minimum quota system in trade-unions. It persistently asks why the barrios have rates of unemployment double or more the national rate, in good times and bad. Much talent has been coopted by federal programs, with the consequent short-run loss of brains for the critical examination of the economy. As this talent multiplies, it is not likely that such programs will absorb the whole or necessarily the best of it.

Economic Insurgence

Without any doubt the two most dramatic thrusts in the economic area during the past decade have been the insurgence of the villagers of New Mexico and the strike of farm workers of California. The New Mexican *Aliancistas* have been crushed, but their defeat has been a timely reminder to Southwestern Mexicans how far the Anglo is from returning to them even a token portion of the land base necessary for an autonomous culture and a genuine identity.

With the farm laborers the frame of reference, as the sociologists say, is somewhat different, but it is still an Anglo frame of reference. Fundamentally this is a movement which accepts dispossession from the land as final and the conversion of husbandmen into an agrarian proletariat as irreversible. The movement leans heavily on a coalition of sympathizers to protect the recognition which Mexican farm workers are gaining; the boycott, a belated stirring of organized labor's conscience; a deep sympathy for the lowest of the underdogs which has been stirred by the struggles of 30 years; the tarnishing image of agribusiness; and money in sufficient amounts, for the first time, to organize, propagandize, mobilize and publicize on an adequate scale.

I have not said anything about many matters that deserve not merely mention but attention. But I am running out of space and I can only list what I have omitted: the *Teatro Campesino*, now rapidly becoming also the *Teatro del Barrio*; the construction of urban *mercados* (markets), which could go either in the direction of a rash of Olvera Streets or in that of a community-centered life; the urban-wide coalitions and unity councils; the Southwest Council of La Raza; a potential pattern for regional direction of all the Razas Unidas now milling about; the new literature by Mexicans about themselves; the storefront reading centers and libraries; the tutorial programs through which thousands of students are sharing knowledge and companionship with younger ones who have had little of either.

I cannot say whether these fragments of culture are moving toward an inward consistency, a polarization, a configuration, or drifting past us on the surface of a tide that will sweep them into a turbulent pothole somewhere. Any of these are possible, and that is why I want to conclude with some fragments of my own concerning the minority and the majority cultures, face to face.

Anglo and Mexican: Some Final Questions

We should not overlook this fact: whatever the Mexican cultural process may be at the moment, and wherever it may be moving or drifting, the Anglo will continue to look at it through his own eyes, particularly through the eyes of his own anthropology. By "his own" I mean that discipline which has been rigorous enough in its scientific method, but which has gathered its classic materials at best by participant-observation or merely by observation. This is not, however, the relationship of Anglo to Mexican culture in the Southwest today. It is a relationship of container and contained—of two cultural processes enormously unequal in all those components which a genuine culture, integral and whole, commands, blends, and diffuses among the men it holds together.

I do not say that American anthropology, in looking at the Mexican Southwest, has allowed itself to be biased by the culture from which it springs. I just want to make sure that it is not. This anthropology began with the detailed study of primitive isolates. They were regarded as laboratories which stayed fairly fixed while being observed. It was an early conditioning to a primitivistic outlook. During this time anthropological work was principally devoted to the identification and analysis of cultural traits, rather than to the study of cultures as articulated wholes. I suspect that this infirmity continues today.

Moreover, when we look at the Mexican minority, we are not distinguishing between cultures that have at hand all the elements for autonomy and cultures that have been deprived, deliberately, of some of these elements—land, for instance. It has been said that history cannot be reconstructed from the ruins of a decaying memory. Nor can a culture be reconstructed from the fragments of a dismembered society.

For that is what happens when two social groups palpably unequal in technology or some other vital factor intersect each other. Those who are overcome, if they are not annihilated, are left with the residues of culture, those resources and institutions which are least useful or threatening to the winner—indeed, which might even be amusing to him. Thus cultural pluralism can conceal paraplegic subcultures that were not born that way. Mexican Southwestern culture has been crippled; that is the essence of its history.

But we must look further. Within the minority culture what I would call a militant penetration is constantly going on. Inflation does not stop at the edge of the barrio; if anything it causes more havoc inside of it than out. The economics of land speculation have decided the fate of colonias and barrios. The electronic teaching machine, displacing the human teacher, is making its way into classrooms of Mexican children. This militancy is not being checked by vigorous counter values armed with appropriate institutions, and there is no future for a culture in this condition.

Still more important to take into account, in case it is lurking somewhere among our assumptions, is the proposition that integral cultures can exist as plural members within a complex industrial society of the current American type. And by integral, may I say again, I mean cultures that have access to those nutrients that satisfy all of the basic biologic and social needs of men. Therefore when we say that cultural pluralism is possible—indeed, is extant in this society—we ought to discuss whether the minority plurals are not much more than residues, surviving by sufferance.

I suspect that this has not been clarified, because the Anglo culture has not talked as much about its own minorities as it has about other peoples'. Let me get at this in a roundabout way. The industrial society on the scale of the American is complex by definition. Complexity is a cultural process which is unique to industrialism on this scale. It is an arrangement of complicated working parts necessary to maintain its far-flung balance—an arrangement that tends to enlarge beyond the ability of its human attendants to cope with. With this exception: professionals do emerge who can manage the complexity by a division of labor of their own. These managers are few relative to the whole society and they tend to become fewer. They function in the locus of power, which becomes more and more remote from the many who cannot cope. Those who specialize in that power are the most important minority in America today. With regard to this power, American society is not culturally pluralistic.

This is the criterion which must guide the Mexican in the allotment of his efforts. Some of them will have to be applied to preserve of his culture what the Anglo, for whatever reasons, has allowed him to keep. Some will have to be directed to extending the pluralistic principle to those essentials which an Anglo minority has reserved for its singular possession.

But Mexican ethnic policy will not be able to hew to this line easily. Mexicans must take care that theirs does not become a culture of protest only. As such it is unified mainly from without; its strategies must depend on alien decisions; it is constantly forced to be where the reaction and not the action is; its anger is constantly liable to turn inward under frustration; it forgets that some protests can be cooled into grievances and these into settlements, while others should not be quieted by anything less than basic transformations. Protest will eventually lose its appeal for larger numbers of the minority if it continues to lament that "we are a conquered people." The Aztecs fell, but the Mexican youth that I see today are not acting like a subservient lot. Something in them will sound increasingly hollow if they make this the burden of their complaint.

Separatism is another course many Mexicans are seriously considering—separation by stages, with total separatism as the goal. The separatism of the Blacks of the early 20th century, of the Mormons, and of the Zionists are hardly needed as historical case studies by the Mexican separatist. His drive is immediate and self-fulfilling. It does not take into account two things: that separatism, if achieved by all the ethnic minorities, must cut them off from the possibilities of mutual aid; and that ultimate separatism, economic and political, lost its last battle in the western hemisphere with the American Civil War. Even if the Mexican separatists could imagine, in the distant future, their own Zion, undoubtedly it would be one that would hang on decisions made in foreign capitals.

Separatism, fashioned on strictly ethnic lines as a tactic of protest carries an insidious danger of the very racism the Mexicans are combating. For the present, separatism must continue to demand its share of the national charity fund, for which other minorities compete, principally the Blacks. To justify this demand by an appeal to skin color is a temptation to which the Mexicans, too, are exposed.

To achieve ethnic solidarity by the route of a common historical experience presents another difficult task. Such an experience, to be shared, must first be written and then widely diffused. This indispensable historiography must fill with facts and interpretation the gap in the Southwestern Mexican record between 1900 and 1970. To this end Mexican scholars must determine their own strategy.

Politically, it remains to be seen how the Mexican sums up his frustrations. He could be lured back into the party folds, or he could learn the lesson and make his own political behaviour a faithful response to the needs of brown people.

There is also the practical problem of communication between the dispersed efforts of La Raza Unida. These efforts are taking place in every corner of the Southwest, itself a vast territory. But more, they are clamoring for attention and support in a dozen other states, from Oregon to Illinois. To link these widely separated efforts is an urgent order of business for La Raza.

It is not so much a case of approaching an ideal definition of a culture (for example, Malinowski 1944)—a functioning, active, efficient, well-organized unity—as it is of compensating for the disunities that are at work. There are a dozen ideologies striving for influence, from the sayings of Netzahualcoyotl to the sayings of Chairman Mao. The Mexicans who are "making it" are doing so unevenly, and many are not making it at all. The class cleavage is beginning to show.

With all this and more to ponder, the Mexicans of the Southwest waited for the end of 1970, which has been declared somewhere to be the Year of the Chicano. The year ended as it had begun, pretty much, for the minority. Perhaps it was the beginning of the decade of the Chicano, or his century. The longer the stretch, the better the chances for his culture.

Plural Society in the Southwest:
A Historical Comment

John H. Parry

The history of the Americas is full of verbal ambiguities. Our carelessness in geographical nomenclature, derived from early 16th century guessing, has become a habit. The persistent use of the term "Indian" to describe the ancient Americans is the most obvious example. The very name "America" was invented to describe South America, in commemoration of the exploits of a Florentine explorer who never set foot in North America and did not know of its existence. It was not extended to include North America until the second half of the 16th century. The founders of the United States appropriated the name to describe their own country, without thought of the confusion, sometimes the irritation, which this might cause to people concerned with other parts of the Americas. It is impossible today to use the term "American" in any precise sense, without some additional phrase to explain which kind of American is meant.

Defining the Southwest

With this tradition of verbal confusion, it is not surprising that we, in discussing a particular area of the Americas, have been unable to find a satisfactory name for it. "Southwest" alone will not do; what is south for some, obviously, is north for others. Spicer speaks of the "Greater Southwest," but this name is even less likely to commend itself to Mexican students of the area. León-Portilla ingeniously suggests "Mexican-American West," which avoids some of these objections, but which still retains the imprecision of a relative direction. West of what? Our area is, in fact, east of most of California. Any accurately descriptive name would probably be so cumbersome as to be unusable. We must, I think, admit defeat; we cannot name our area, we can only try to define it. It is the area of close and continuous contact between Hispano-American, Anglo-American, and Amerindian. It is the only such area; nowhere else in the Americas are these three strains vigorously and continuously present. It covers the whole of New Mexico, Arizona, and Sonora, and parts of Chihuahua, Texas, Utah, Colorado, and the Californias.

The Indians: Farmers and Hunters

We seem to be agreed that this great area constitutes a region with a coherence of its own. It has common features, both in its geographical structure and in its range of human activity, strong enough and numerous enough to distinguish it from other regions. It is, characteristically, a border region, not only in the superficial sense that the present political frontier between Mexico and the United States happens to pass through it, but also in more fundamental senses. For at least 2000 years, it has been a border between the desert and the sown, between farming village-dwellers and hunting-and-gathering nomads. Neither village-dwellers nor nomads dominated the area; between them was a wide range of more numerous semisettled peoples who practised some sort of extensive agriculture in addition to hunting and gathering, and who, many of them, shifted their dwellings with the changes of season. Some of these peoples—Apache and Navajo—formed bands which ranged over considerable areas. For 300 years or so before the Spanish invasion, the bands had shown a fairly consistent tendency to migrate from north to south, some settling in the region, some passing through to press upon richer lands far to the south. Through the centuries of their existence, then, the settled Pueblos appear like rocks, literally rocks in some cases, but also metaphorically, in their social and economic permanence, their tenacity and endurance—rocks around which successive tides of wandering people ebbed and flowed. To the Pueblo peoples the Spanish friars and fortune-hunters who penetrated the area in the 16th century must have appeared as one more in a long series of incursions, one more visitation to be endured and, as far as possible, resisted or ignored.

It is a relatively unattractive border region. To say this is not to deny its agreeable climate, its gaunt and dramatic beauty, or

300

the scientific interest of its complex natural life; but it is not, for the most part, an area in which a farming people, if they had much choice, would choose to settle. Much of it is uninhabitable mountain or barely habitable semidesert. Most of it is arid for most of the year, except in the valleys of its few permanent rivers. There are some small areas of ancient irrigation, but it is only in very recent years that systematic large-scale irrigation has added hundreds of thousands of cultivable acres to the resources of California, Sonora, and Arizona, and that mass-producing industry has provided employment for urban immigrants, impairing—often avoidably, through thoughtless and wasteful location—the natural beauty of parts of the region.

Because of its harsh character, the region has always been thinly populated. It is relatively thinly populated even now; and at the time of the Spanish conquest there were probably not more than a quarter of a million people in the whole area. The village-dwelling Indian communities—contrasted, for example, with the densely populated towns of pre-Conquest central Mexico—were always small, and widely separated one from another, each with its fields and its dwellings tightly gathered near a reliable supply of water. The various Pueblo groups had—and have—many features in common, and from very early times there was some trade between them, but for most purposes they were self-sufficient and self-contained, separated not only by distance but by language and tradition. They rarely made common cause, even against invaders. The Pueblo rising against the Spaniards in the late 17th century was a very exceptional event. The Pueblos wanted only to be left alone. Against the incursions of other Indians, which took the form usually of periodic raids rather than of continuous pressure, their normal reaction was a purely local defense, and this remained true even after the Spanish conquest, when some seminomadic groups such as the Apache acquired horses and thus became—though not very numerous—more mobile and much more dangerous than they had formerly been.

The Impact of the Spaniards

The settling Spaniards in the 17th century were a very small band, a few hundred only. Their ability to coerce, proselytize, or administer was limited, but they brought with them the means of changing the whole economic life of the region: domestic ani-

301

mals. They ran large and increasing flocks of sheep, and a little. later herds of cattle, over immense areas of sparse, rough, open grazing. When in the middle decades of the 19th century English-speaking Americans began to enter the region in appreciable numbers, they in turn learned the techniques of open-range stock raising in arid country. The Greater Southwest—I use Spicer's term for the sake of convenience—thus became, and was to remain almost to this day, a predominantly pastoral borderland. The only other important occupation, apart from some small farming, was mining, but until recently prospecting was a small-scale, highly individual, characteristically frontier occupation, involving relatively few people. The impact of these changes upon the Indian groups varied greatly. The Pueblo peoples were the least affected. The cattle population, though it became very large in total numbers, was like the human population, thinly spread—necessarily so, in view of the nature of the country. It was possible for the Pueblos to retain the relatively small areas of land which they needed for their intensive farming; they were not overwhelmed by the cattle, and did not drastically alter their own way of life. They acquired some domestic animals them-selves—horses, a few sheep, rarely horned cattle—but pastoral activity was, and is, marginal in their economy. The Pueblos were affected in other ways, of course, by the Spanish impact, espe-cially by the establishment of missions in their villages, and by the pressure of proselytising, both secular and religious. To this pressure they responded usually with a patient, flexible syn-cretism, at which they showed themselves remarkably adept, adopting—at least outwardly—such Spanish rituals and devices as they could assimilate without excessive strain, retaining the essentials of their own beliefs, observances and ways of life.

The impact upon the more scattered peoples was more dras-tic. Their more extensive use of land competed more directly with open-range grazing. The Spanish authorities were usually not strong enough to compel their congregation in mission com-munities, as was done in some parts of Mexico, but missions were established in their territory, and most groups came under pres-sure. Some, especially the Yaqui and the Tarahumara, suffered over long periods from the devastation of their scattered fields and from demands for forced labour in the Parral mines. They showed considerably less skill and sophistication in dealing with Europeans than did the Pueblo peoples. Further north, some of the more mobile peoples, in whose economy hunting had always been important, transferred their attention from wild animals to domestic ones and became stock raiders. A few groups, particularly the Navajo and some Apache bands, themselves became sheep or cattle raisers, and raided in order to add to their stock, rather than directly for food, but from the point of view of the people raided, this made little difference. Raiding continued until late in the 19th century. The groups involved came into periodic conflict not only with ranchers but with regular armed forces, first Spanish, then Mexican, and finally North American; these hostilities led eventually to an attenuation of their numbers, and to their confinement on reservations inadequate to preserve their traditional way of life.

The Cattle Borderland

As for the European-stock settlers themselves—Spanish, Mexican, Anglo—they developed, through their pastoral activities, social characteristics which distinguished them sharply from their compatriots in other parts of Mexico or the United States. Not all the settlers were open-range cattle raisers; the Mormons were a major exception, the first important group of irrigating farmers in the area, apart from a few Indian groups. But in general, the pastoral economy predominated until very recently throughout the region, and in our discussions we have perhaps paid insufficient attention to this fact. It was a key characteristic; one might, indeed, suggest as a name for our region, "the cattle borderland."

León-Portilla drew our attention to the prominent part played by Norteño leaders and their following in the civil commotions of independent Mexico, down to the early decades of the present century, and attributed it to the individualism, the pugnaciously independent spirit produced by struggle against a harsh environment. This we can accept, but was it not connected also with the circumstances of a pastoral economy? Open-range cattle raising is an occupation demanding periodic bursts of great energy and skill, rather than continuous plodding application. The cowboy must be a good horseman, inured to hardship, but there are periods of the year when he has not much to do. Living in relative isolation from society, he tends to form strong attachments of loyalty, especially if his employer possesses the courage and the equestrian skill and dash which he admires. Most of the Norteño leaders did possess these qualities. They made excellent commanders and their vaquero followers made excellent recruits, for an irregular cavalry. In a country with great expanses and with little urban industry, such as Mexico was until recently, a loyal irregular cavalry was the best possible arm for winning civil wars. The pattern was not confined to Mexico; the llaneros of Venezuela and the gauchos of Buenos Aires province played a part in the civil upheavals of their respective countries similar to that played by the vaqueros of northern Mexico. In the United States major civil commotions have been rare, and temptations to employ irregular cavalry against the centers of power in the distant East rarer still. Even so the cowboy of the Southwest has exercised a powerful influence on the national imagination, and his qualities, or supposed qualities, have helped to form, in the minds of many people who have never mounted a horse, a romantic ideal of masculine behaviour.

Isolation and Neglect

The Greater Southwest has always been a remote and isolated region. To some extent it still is. Some writers, attributing to it a historical importance it did not possess, have described it as the area of intersection between two major European thrusts, the south-to-north thrust of the Spanish, the east-to-west thrust of the English-speaking Americans; but this is an exaggeration. In colonial times the principal axis of the economic and social structure of New Spain was an east-west axis, running from Seville through Vera Cruz to Mexico City. From Mexico City branches ran out: a long, attenuated but important branch to Acapulco and across the Pacific to Manila, shorter branches to Guadalajara and to the mining settlements, mostly in Nueva Galicia. The most northerly mining settlement of importance was Parral, and the discovery of silver there in 1631 produced a considerable thrust of Spanish population into Chihuahua. Beyond Chihuahua City, however, there was little except rough grazing to attract settlers, and population, as we have seen, remained very thin; there were scattered ranches, even more scattered missions, a few small townships, and a few military presidios to protect them—a precarious presence.

In the 18th century, something which might be called a thrust took place, or rather two thrusts, one northwest into Upper California, the other northeast into Texas, but these were military thrusts rather than thrusts of population. They were provoked not by the attractiveness of the region, nor primarily by Indian raiding, troublesome though this was, but by the activities of other Europeans. The California thrust was to forestall Russian or British sealing, trading, and possibly settlement on the Pacific coast. The Texas thrust was to counter the ominous interest shown by both French and English in the Mississippi Valley. The foundation of San Antonio was a conscious retort to the threat, or supposed threat, from New Orleans. The great central area of the Greater Southwest—Arizona, New Mexico, northern Sonora and Chihuahua—remained neglected. Nor, after independence, did the government of Mexico take much interest; as León-Portilla reminds us, it had more pressing matters to attend to. The vast area annexed to the United States in 1848, as the result of war, still contained relatively few people; among them, people of European stock were still probably a minority, and of that minority, few spoke English.

The English-speaking thrust into the western United States in the 19th century similarly by-passed the Southwest. The people who rushed to California in the middle of the century mostly travelled by sea. The wagon trains which, a little later, carried settlers to the coast, mostly passed north of our region, or through its northern fringe; those which passed through it did not linger. The Mormons, who settled in northern Utah, were a conspicuous exception; a self-consciously chosen people, victims of persistent persecution, they found remoteness an advantage and harsh conditions a salutary challenge which—as O'Dea so ably explains—they triumphantly surmounted. It may be noted in passing that the Mormons were exceptional in yet another way: whether because of their peculiar beliefs about Indian origins, or from enlightened self-interest, or from an inherent gentleness, they usually maintained relatively good relations with the Indians they encountered. True, the Indians of northern Utah were few and not very dangerous; how the Mormons would have dealt with, say, the Comanches, we cannot know. In any event, for most of the westward-travelling pioneers, an arid and Indian-infested Southwest had few attractions. California and, in a lesser degree, Oregon were the magnets. Today the Greater Southwest still lies off the main axis of North American activity. Lines drawn from any of the great industrial cities of the East to any of the major cities of the Pacific Coast either pass, again, through the northern fringe of the region, or miss it altogether.

Southwestern Plurality Today

All these features of the Greater Southwest—remoteness, isolation, great area, small population, general aridity, widely scattered sources of water, absence of major economic attrac-tions—help to explain the characteristic of the region which we met to discuss: its social plurality. The Indians are still there, probably not less numerous than they were 500 years ago. The little Spanish-speaking community of northern New Mexico, with its roots in 17th century settlement, is still there. Other, larger, groups have entered the region more recently: Anglo-Americans, obviously, including one subgroup, the Mormons, who have a recognizable geographical base and who maintain, in many ways, a self-conscious and effective separateness. In this century many Mexicans from other parts of Mexico have moved into the region, not only into Sonora and Chihuahua, but farther north still, into the United States. These people differ in many ways from the older Spanish-speaking population—a difference of which both communities are aware.

The larger groups, however, have not, as yet, absorbed or overwhelmed the smaller. In the Southwest, there has always been elbowroom; there have always been corners where small, highly conservative societies could live their own lives, not indeed undisturbed, but not in constant danger of expulsion or annihila-tion. There has been much conflict in the region, sometimes acute and dangerous, but it has rarely been carried *à l'outrance*. There was never much likelihood that the Navajo or the Hopi or even the much mistreated Yaqui would go the way of the Mohawks; Spicer tells us that nearly all the Indian groups in the region which were identifiable in the 16th century are present and identifiable today. Plurality survives, in the contiguous presence of many languages and many cultures. Some at least of the communities in the region are so separate as to merit consideration as distinct societies, each with a distinct historical experience, a consciousness of distinct identity, and a distinct formal structure for the maintenance of internal discipline, one might almost say internal government—with, of course, the overriding limitation that each is constrained to live in general conformity with rules laid down by one or another of two encompassing state-societies: Mexico and the United States.

Survival and Change

It is relatively easy to explain historically how this plurality of societies came about, much less easy to see whether, and on what terms, it can survive in late 20th century conditions. All the circumstances which favoured plurality in the past have changed drastically in recent decades, and continue to change. There is much less elbowroom in the region than there was in the past. Nomadism, and tribal migration from bad locations to better, are now impossible. Population has grown enormously and disproportionately. Though most groups have increased, the two largest— Anglo north of the border and Mexican on both sides of it—have increased much more than the others. Extensive stockgrazing is no longer the one characteristic occupation; it is still important, but in some parts of the region, at least, has been replaced by urban industry, intensive irrigated farming, and mechanized mining on a very large scale. Improved mechanical methods of procuring water have made these developments possible. On both sides of the border, they are the principal factors favouring population increase by immigration. North of the border they are mostly Anglo-directed, but employ large numbers of Mexican-Americans, many of them recent immigrants; thus, the two communities, though different in language, in many social conventions and habits, and to some extent in local standing, have become highly interdependent.

The Pattern of Dominance

A new pattern of dominance has emerged, a new type of relation between employer and employed, in which the employed are very numerous and, to a disquieting extent, anonymous. This change is most obvious and striking north of the border, where the Anglos are dominant, not merely because they are a majority, but because they are in general much richer than the others, because their language is the national language, and because they have more opportunities of access to, and influence upon, the national government. Class divisions, ethnic divisions, and cultural divisions largely coincide. As for governments themselves, here as in most parts of the world their physical capacity for enforcing their will has increased enormously in the past half-century. It is extremely unlikely that the Mexican government, or that of the United States, could now be effectively defied or physically resisted by local groups, as both sometimes were in the 19th century, and as the Spanish viceregal government often was in the 17th and 18th. The fortunes of all groups in the region depend, to a greater extent than ever before, upon decisions made in Mexico City or Washington, and the smaller, older groups depend chiefly upon the national governments for protection against the larger and more powerful.

Plural societies, or pluralities of societies, tend to be unstable. They depend for survival upon conventions of mutual tolerance and respect, which may break down under stress. They are always subject to forces tending to disturb their delicate internal balance. Sometimes these forces are centrifugal. A strong and cohesive minority group may feel itself inhibited or threatened by inclusion in the tightening circle of a larger society, and may try to secede before it is too late. Something of this sort happened recently in Nigeria, a plural society split by deep divisions, with little affection or respect between its component parts, but held together by administrative habit, economic necessity, and military force. Only a very strong minority group can hope, in modern conditions, to break away successfully. In a plural society where one group is clearly and confidently dominant, the tendency is usually the other way. The members of the dominant group will often try to remove differences which—to them—are anomalous and troublesome. They will seek greater uniformity, for the sake of administrative convenience, or for reasons of national security, or perhaps for the psychological satisfaction which comes from consciousness of a civilizing mission. Members, especially leading members, of the minority groups may support these endeavours, whether for the sake of economic advantage, or for fear of the possible consequences of dissent.

The Formation of Composite Societies

These forces tend to turn plural societies into composite societies; a plural society being one in which the component groups are sufficiently distinct in character and formal structure as to be separable; a composite society, one in which the groups are so closely interdependent that they could not be separated without vital damage. Plurality is sometimes said to encourage vigour and inventiveness; but this is surely more true of composite societies, whose closer organization offers more intimate opportunity for mutual borrowing and synthesis, and presents a stimulating social challenge with less danger of internecine conflict. Most of the nation-states of western Europe—vigorous, inventive, and durable over a long period—are composite societies, having developed steadily in that direction from an earlier, looser plurality.

Extermination

The processes which push plural societies into becoming more unified or more nearly composite may be roughly listed. One is crude extermination. The long record of human cruelty contains many examples of the extermination, or attempted extermination, of stubborn minorities by dominant groups. Within the lifetime of the participants in these discussions, deliberate and systematic projects of extermination have been undertaken by the governments of highly developed states. Repugnant though the notion is to a civilized mind, we cannot afford simply to dismiss it as unthinkable.

Symbiosis

At the other extreme is the process which may be called symbiosis. A subordinate group may willingly accept absorption by a dominant society, as a natural and advantageous development. This acceptance often originates within a ruling class among the minority. Wales is an example of this. In the 17th and 18th centuries, the Welsh aristocracy, with relatively few exceptions, found it agreeable and to their interest to become Anglicized. Many moved into England, and some came to play a prominent part in the conduct of English affairs. The principality was left without leadership, except in so far as chapel and trade union could supply it, and the generality of Welshman also in time became partially Anglicized, but less so than their "betters." Some still speak Welsh; most differ from Englishmen in their mode of speaking English and in many of their social conventions. Despite these differences, England and Wales form a composite society. There is an arguable case today for a greater degree of administrative devolution, but most Welshmen regard Welsh nationalism, in the sense of agitation for a separate state, as a nostalgic eccentricity.

The Welsh example, of course, is not the only pattern of symbiosis; a reverse situation can arise. Where the dominant society is highly industrialized and the subordinate group is markedly less so, an aristocracy may resist absorption as a threat to its own privileges, while the generality of people within the subordinate group welcome it, in order to find industrial employment and to obtain the attractive products of mass-producing industry. Pool has reminded us of how strong these motives can be. They do not necessarily destroy the feeling of cultural distinctiveness, nor of themselves transform plural societies into composite ones—one can drink Coca-Cola without necessarily imbibing the cultural values of those who purvey it—but they are a strong force in that direction. Confronted by them, a conservative aristocracy may be reduced merely to fighting a delaying action against the forces of change.

Assimilation

Between the extremes of extermination and symbiosis we may list assimilation: the endeavour of a dominant group in a plural society to persuade or compel other groups to become more like itself. The endeavour may be undertaken for reasons of religious conviction, or out of a desire to improve the social or economic lot of subordinate peoples, or in order to facilitate economic development and exploitation, or to tighten national unity and insure against rebellion or secession, or merely for the sake of administrative convenience. It may indicate no more than an unreflecting impatience with persistent difference.

The means of promoting assimilation are as various as the motives for it. The most obvious is the imposition of a uniform system of law and uniform obligations, such as taxation or military service. Economic or financial pressures may be applied, which weaken the economic bases of difference, as when peasants or pastoral nomads are pressed to adopt regular work habits —on the one hand by restricting their access to land, or on the other by offering them wage-earning employment. A dominant group may engage in active religious proselytizing (though this can sometimes operate in reverse); it may consistently ridicule, or even prohibit, habits, beliefs, and rituals distinctive of subordinate groups. Probably the most effective of all methods, in modern conditions, are propaganda and advertisement through the channels of mechanized entertainment and formal education. The question of whether, how far, and by what means to pursue a policy of assimilation is most acute in colonial situations, but it poses itself in all societies where significant differences of culture exist. The problem for the dominant group is always how best to close the fissures which may divide a plural society without impairing the healthy diversity of a composite one.

Assimilation has its converse. A dominant group may prefer not to attempt assimilation. Especially in dealing with relatively small and helpless subordinate groups, it may adopt a policy of conservation, encouraging the members of those groups to maintain their traditional ways of life, shielding them as far as possible from the influence of the dominant culture. The motive for such a policy may be a genuine respect, even a nostalgic affection, for the values and traditions of a subordinate group, and a fear of social disintegration should they be seriously eroded. During some periods of British imperial history, affection for primitiveness and respect for the internal discipline of simple societies, with concomitant dislike and suspicion of "educated natives," was characteristic of many colonial officials. The motive may be intellectual. A generation ago, some anthropologists maintained that a remote, primitive, and obviously vulnerable region such as New Guinea should be protected from contact with industrialized peoples—preserved, in effect, as a living anthropological museum. On a more superficial level, the uniformity of industrialized society provokes its own reaction, in a vogue for the quaint and the picturesque. This vogue has been spread and vulgarized in recent years by the growth of a mass tourist trade. Quaintness and picturesqueness have a market value, and people who are the objects of this kind of interest often find it profitable to mount an external display of "traditional" behaviour, which may be spurious, invented for the purpose. In these conditions a kind of symbiosis may emerge; a dominant society may treat subordinate groups as, in effect, domestic pets which it cherishes and maintains for the amusement of its own members, and the subordinate groups may, however reluctantly, accept this status.

The Example of the Scottish Highlanders

These various processes, each tending in its own way to produce greater uniformity in a plural society, may alternate or coexist. In the complex story of the Scottish Highlands, for example, traces of all of them can be seen. The Jacobite uprisings in the 18th century were punished by a period of brutal repression, amounting in some places to depopulation. This was followed by a crude policy of assimilation, consisting for a time chiefly in the prohibition of distinctive habits, such as the wearing of the kilt, and an active discouragement of the use of Gaelic, but also assisted by the recruitment of Highland regiments during the French wars. In the 19th century, Highland landowners, wishing to derive profit from their barren lands, discovered a common interest—a symbiosis—with Englishmen or Lowlanders who wanted to buy or rent sporting properties. There followed the pitiful episode of the evictions. Thousands of crofters moved to the Clyde shipyards, or else overseas, where a developing empire offered a market for their talents. A human population, sparse already, was largely replaced by sheep and wild deer. The few who remained, in many instances, found employment as ghillies or gamekeepers. The Highlands became a playground for the rich, and in consequence became fashionable. Tartan plaids, kilts, bagpipes and the like—once the workaday artefacts of a primitive peasantry—became modish accoutrements. It was discovered that the inhabitants—those who remained—possessed a proud and dignified reserve, much admired by visitors; Queen Victoria herself made a confidant—pet, one might say—of a particularly surly Highland gamekeeper. All this, in the circumstances, was probably the most economic use of an area which, on the whole, is unsuited to agriculture; some Highlanders accommodated themselves to the situation, encouraged the vogue, and profited by it. The drain of population, however, caused anxiety to government, which in recent years has tried to halt it by establishing industries in the Highlands to employ local labour. These attempts have not been uniformly successful, partly, perhaps, because the playground business offers a more painless way of meeting English requirements. This has boomed in recent years, in a new form: a large-scale tourist trade, the promoters of which, while busily constructing motels and ski-lifts, have an obvious interest in preserving the illusion of shaggy romantic solitude. All in all, one may say that the Highlands are assimilated to the rest of Britain in a composite society, but at the cost of losing a large part of their population.

Prospects for Assimilation in the Southwest

The plural society which formerly existed in Britain involved only three groups—four, if one counts the Lowland Scots—all of kindred stock. The Greater Southwest is much more complex. Which of these processes operate there? Not, clearly, extermination; most groups are growing in numbers and it is 100 years or more since even the most bloodthirsty pioneer could talk openly of the necessity of exterminating Indians. In Sonora, it is true, military operations against some Indian groups continued well into this century, but these were regarded as disciplinary measures, intended to enforce assimilation, certainly not as wars à l'outrance. On the other hand, there are few instances of willing symbiosis. A symbiosis of a kind may be said to exist between Mexican-Americans and Anglos north of the border, in the sense that the two groups are economically interdependent, but it is an interdependence profoundly unsatisfactory to the subordinate group. A Mexican-American has little opportunity of participating in Anglo prosperity, except as a casual labourer. Apart from their employment relation, the two groups are strangers to one another. The Mexican-American probably, of necessity, knows more about the Anglo than the Anglo knows about him; he may even find aspects of Anglo culture to admire, or at least envy. The Anglo, on the other hand, as a rule, sees little in the life of the Mexican-American to respect, certainly nothing to envy, nothing even calling for conservation as a curiosity. The Mexican-American, unlike some Indians, is not even picturesque. Only by assimilation, it seems, can he improve his lot significantly, and his assimilation presents problems of peculiar difficulty.

Assimilation then? It is important to remember in this connection that the groups or societies of the region not only differ greatly one from another; they vary greatly in their degrees of difference. The Mormons, for example, are an integral branch of the Anglo stock. They play a full and successful part in the economic life of the United States in general. They are distinguished by their religious beliefs and by certain social conventions dictated by those beliefs. The beliefs show no sign of significant weakening; their church has probably gained more members by proselytizing than it has lost by apostasy. Some Indians, it is true, regard them as a separate people, just as other Indians formerly regarded the Jesuits, but this may merely reflect their distinctive behaviour towards Indians. They have certainly a formal organization which exercises a considerable degree of discipline, but it is discipline within the framework of the law of the encompassing society. This was made clear, as O'Dea told us, by their decision to abandon polygamous marriage in 1887. The Mormons are clearly more than a sect, but they are probably less than a separate people, a separate society. To speak of assimilation in connection with the Mormons seems superfluous, almost absurd.

The Indians

The various Indian groups, on the other hand, are clearly distinct peoples, and some of them are distinct societies. It is possible to imagine the Hopi deciding to live, and being allowed to live—since they are few and harmless—in complete isolation from the encompassing society. They would lose in economic opportunity and convenience, but this they might accept; the attitude of the people of Walpi towards electricity is significant in this connection. The Hopi, no doubt, are exceptional, and even among them, there are many who do not appear to share this suspicion of the outside world. The two encompassing societies have usually assumed that Indians would be better off if they were more closely integrated into the dominant societies. The Mexican government, like its Spanish predecessor, has always pursued a policy of assimilation, though usually indirectly, through economic pressures. It has made partial exceptions in dealing with the Yaqui and the Tarahumara, but there are no Indian reservations in Mexico. The government regards Indians as Mexicans and expects them to behave as such, though in practice many of them do not. The United States government in its dealings with Indians has employed an organization resembling, on a small scale, the administration of a European colonial empire, but without the advantage of a trained and dedicated colonial administrative service. It maintains reservations; it has provided subsidies of various kinds; it has occasionally legislated separately and specially for Indians; it has permitted—indeed encouraged—the formation of elected tribal councils, some of which dispose of considerable funds, though the legal basis of these organizations is somewhat flimsy and uncertain, and the process of election itself is in many instances alien to Indian tradition. With these qualifications, however, the general drift of official policy has been strongly integrationist. To a large extent it still is.

In recent years there have been some indications of change; the official stance has tended to become less aggressive, less coercive. There is a more patient acceptance of the fact that Indian life, for as far into the future as anyone can usefully peer, is likely to be based on a mixture of Indian and Anglo—in some instances also Spanish-American—habits and assumptions. If the mixture is to be satisfactory to Indians, its proportions must, so far as possible, be left to Indian choice. An Indian is far more likely to live happily and successfully in an Anglo-dominated society if he leaves his reservation and enters that society by an act of choice; if he knows that the reservation is still there for him to retreat to, perhaps in old age, if he so desires; and if he feels himself adequately equipped to move and compete in the

315

Anglo world without denying his identity as an Indian. This is a question of education. The education provided for Indians in the United States has been designed unimaginatively, and, in the past, sometimes brutally, to eradicate Indian habits and conventions. To a large extent it has been self-defeating, not because Indians are opposed to education in itself—many welcome it—but because the education has failed to "take." Very many Indian children, confronted with instruction on unfamiliar subjects, in an unfamiliar language, and in unfamiliar surroundings, have abandoned the struggle in despair. Here, too, there are some signs of change. The idea is gaining ground that a satisfactory education for Indians—even if its ultimate purpose is to be integration—must make use of Indian languages, at least in the initial stages, and throughout must take account of Indian habits of mind, historical experience, and sense of identity. To train a body of teachers equal to this delicate and complex task would be difficult and expensive, but there is no short cut.

Three other factors in the relations between Indian and Anglo societies remain to be mentioned briefly. One is the presence on some reservations of valuable resources, chiefly mineral and timber, which Indians are sometimes accused of neglecting, and which Anglo corporations may wish to exploit. Exploitation may, under equitable agreements, enrich the tribe concerned, through the agency of its tribal council. Under inequitable agreements it may impoverish. This is probably still a field in which tribal councils cannot safely be left to themselves to negotiate as best they can; the parties to such negotiations are too unequal. This, once again, is a matter of appropriate education and experience. Until Indian communities possess a leadership sophisticated enough, and with enough legal training, to deal with such matters, the central government must reserve an ultimate control to ensure that Indians are not robbed, and must maintain a trained staff for the purpose.

The second factor is the attractiveness, already briefly noticed, of a great range of consumer goods available from Anglo sources. Some Pueblos with conservative leadership resist the introduction of such goods, on the ground that it may corrupt traditional values, but probably the tide cannot be stemmed for long, and in any event "corruption" is not the real danger.

Canned food and motor cars do not in themselves corrupt. Mormons do not, apparently, find their religious beliefs incompatible with modern business methods; a Navajo does not lose his identity by substituting a pick-up for a wagon and team. The danger is more subtle; to paraphrase Pool's felicitous phrase, it is that of mistaking the cafeteria for the culture. Anglo culture does not consist merely of a capacity to produce a range of desirable goods and services, but it is often presented, by vigorous advertisers and even by "educators," in such a way that unthinking Indians—and unthinking Anglos—might be pardoned for concluding that it did. It is all too easy to assume that if Indians are enabled—by successful exploitation of reservation resources, or by whatever means—to acquire the material conveniences of Anglo daily life, they automatically become participants with Anglos and the rest in a genuinely composite society. On the contrary, the superficial similarity of widespread gadget-owning can easily conceal more deep-seated resentment and distrust. Again, the key is probably education—an education which not only takes account of Indian experience but also conveys genuine understanding of the nature of the society in which Indians are being invited to participate.

But there is a converse to this proposition. It is all too easy to mistake the external trappings—even, sometimes, spurious trappings—of Indian culture for the culture itself. This is the danger of the vogue of the picturesque Indian, which has been produced by the recent immense growth of the tourist trade in the Southwest. The uninstructed visitor likes to see Indians—even Pueblo Indians—capering in war-bonnets and wielding tomahawks; the Indian may find it profitable to oblige, probably despising his audience and himself the while. He may be tempted, in other words, to accept a "pet" status for his culture. But pets do not really participate, and Indian culture does not consist of spurious dances for the benefit of tourists; it includes religious beliefs, social mechanisms, poetic imagery, and artistic creativeness worthy of serious respect and, it may be, of imitation. Yet again, there is here a question of education. The only answer to a cult of the spurious is respect for, and serious study of, the genuine. In this connection, probably one of the most hopeful developments in Indian life in the last 20 or 30 years has been the remarkable revival in local crafts—chiefly weaving, pottery, painting, and jewelry—producing articles of high artistic value. That these articles are chiefly sold to discriminating Anglos does not much matter; their quality and form are most emphatically not dictated by Anglo taste. What does matter is their integrity and their intrinsic merit. Here is one small but visible contribution to the cultural stock of the composite society—not, we may be sure, the only possible contribution—which only Indians could make.

The Mexican-Americans

We return, finally, to the Mexican-Americans in the Southwest of the United States—the immigrants, that is, or children or grandchildren of immigrants. (I exclude from these generalities the long-established Hispanos of New Mexico.) The Mexican-Americans, the Chicanos as they are beginning to call themselves, are the least known, probably, of all the groups in our plurality. They are ten times more numerous than all the Indians together. The government acknowledges no special responsibility for them, as it does for Indians. They have no reservations to retreat to, nor do they want them. They are far removed from the heartland of their culture, and few of them are likely ever to return there. Most of them are poor. They participate only marginally in the affairs of the dominant society which surrounds them and dictates the terms of their work. True, they have votes, but they have few acceptable candidates for election. True, they have trade unions, though only recently; one union has lately won a notable success in securing recognition, but this success was possible because enough sympathizers, mostly in the eastern states, were willing to abstain from grapes. They are utterly dependent. They are certainly not likely to accept, or to be offered, a pet relationship with the dominant society; there are too many of them, and they are not picturesque. On the other hand, if they become "militant," as the current jargon has it, they invite suspicion and perhaps repression.

How can Mexican-Americans become full participants rather than mere hangers-on in a composite society? Mexican-Americans, though they represent a distinct culture, do not form a distinct society, as many Indian groups do, and successful integration in the dominant society seems to be, for them, the only possible future. But how? Money, of course, helps. The United States lags far behind most industrialized western countries in recognizing a governmental responsibility for providing minimum standards of housing and public services; there seems to be a strong argument for making a special case, in this respect, for Mexican-American barrios. Education for Mexican-Americans, as for Indians, also presents a special case—a case for elementary education through the medium of Spanish. Many children are unable to assimilate the early teaching which they are offered; they never catch up, and become dropouts. In all situations where language difference hampers education, a solid bridge between the minority and majority languages should be constructed as early as possible in the child's career, and obviously the construction must begin in the child's own language. An extensive, and no doubt expensive, effort is required to recruit and train primary teachers whose first language is Spanish. Then, public authorities, especially education and health authorities, could do much more than they do at present, to identify respected leaders in the barrios and to seek their advice, cooperation and support. It is encouraging to find one local clinic in Tucson which is doing this vigorously, and apparently with success. But most important of all, in dealing with this most intractable of social problems, is the identification of the special skills and abilities which Mexican-Americans possess the special contributions which they can make to a wider community than their own. Of course they contribute their labour, but anyone can pick lettuce. Have Mexican-Americans any particular social talents, any forms of art or poetry or imagery which are all their own, from which Anglos and others may have something to learn? No one seems to know, and no trouble has been taken to find out. Again, a need for study.

The Need to Contribute

Social contentment comes not merely from assured material well-being, but from consciousness of making a contribution which is worth making and which is respected and appreciated. An individual feels loyalty, not merely to the society which harbours him, but to the society to which he contributes. We appear to have assumed in our discussions, without thinking much about it, that social plurality is desirable. If by plurality we mean merely a situation in which a number of widely differing societies or groups coexist, without actual fighting but with only superficial contact one with another, I do not think that the facts support the assumption. Such a situation exists in the Greater Southwest and has been admirably described in the papers presented here. We can hardly be content with it. We may agree that a single homogeneous, uniform society in the Southwest is neither possible nor desirable; but our hope surely should be for a society much more closely integrated—a composite society in which the component parts are distinguished not by their separate existence but by their distinctive contributions.

Plural Society in the Southwest: A Comparative Perspective

Ithiel de Sola Pool

To one who has heretofore known the Southwest only remotely, this conference has been an enlightening experience. The excellent papers stimulated lively discussion that reflected both scholarly knowledge and the deep involvement of the participants in the life of the various communities of the area. The intertwining of scholarship and personal experience has given a quality to this gathering which could not have been achieved had the conference consisted solely either of detached scholars or of ethnic spokesmen.

An outsider like myself can only bring to such discussion a comparative perspective. As I listened here, I kept noticing similarities to findings from studies of communication and contact between modernized and less modernized ethnic groups in which I have been engaged in such places as India and Vietnam—studies of the impact of development advisory programs and of radio and television in those areas. Also, as a political scientist I have been interested in the general theory of cohesion and in the relation of subcommunities to nation cohesion. In writing on that subject before, I have argued that subcommunities often strengthen the cohesion of the larger unit of which they are a part rather than weaken it (Pool 1967: 22-52).

The Dimensions of Cultural Pluralism

At the outset it seems to be necessary to distinguish at least three dimensions of cultural pluralism. A society may be characterized as more pluricultural than another either because of: (1) the number of different cultures within it, or (2) the degree of difference between them, or (3) the strength of the people's identification with the ethnic subcultures.

Consider first the number of cultures. In discussing Spicer's paper, we attempted to identify the distinctive character of the Southwest, or Mexican-American West. One conclusion was that it is distinctive in having three different on-going cultures: Anglo, Indian, and Mexican. There are other areas of the United States with problems of contact between two contiguous cultures, but the outstanding feature of the Southwest is the presence of three or more quite distinct cultures side by side. There are places in the world that are equally or even more pluricultural: for example, Malaysia with Malays, Chinese, Indians, and Europeans; or Israel with Western Jews, Oriental Jews, East European Orthodox Jews, Arabs, and Christians. Clearly, one dimension by which we can call a society more or less pluricultural is the number of cultures within it.

A quite different dimension is the degree of difference in the content of the contiguous cultures. A point made in O'Dea's paper was that the Mormons were only marginally different from their Gentile Protestant neighbors. To be more accurate, he characterized Mormonism as quite "Methodist" in perspective, and as involving an intensification of many of the salient features of American culture by theologizing them. That is certainly true of their optimism, achievement orientation, and their work and health ethic. But suppose the Mormons had persisted in polygamy. If they had successfully gotten away with it, that would have been a basic deviation from American cultural values and would have made Utah a much more pluricultural society than it is today.

Because of complexity, we have no good way of measuring degrees of similarity or difference between cultures. Anthropologists would differ as to the rank order of similarity and difference between Anglo culture and that of each of the Indian tribes of the Southwest. However, at the extremes there is no problem distinguishing degree of difference between cultures. Hopis and Anglos are clearly more different than are Blacks and Whites, or Irish and Italians in the cities of the Northeast. Thus the large differences among the cultures present in the Southwest provide another dimension along which we can characterize it as a pluricultural society.

Strength of identification is a third dimension. Two major population groups exist in Northern Ireland today. To me, a stranger, they look not very different. They dress, eat, and talk the same way. Yet, clearly, they feel very strongly about their differences. This third dimension is the one which Spicer chose to stress. His starting point is that people recognize distinctions among themselves and apply names for identifying the various "we-groups." The basis for applying such names, he notes, is always a recognition of some differences—sometimes large, sometimes small—in cultural content, a sense of distinctive historical experience, and an image of the group vis-a-vis other groups. It is on the basis of this dimension of pluralism, namely self-conscious identification of ethnic group membership, that Spicer reaches the very important conclusion that the disappearance of ethnic groups is a relatively rare event and that the trend in the Southwest is not toward homogenization, as the dominant Anglo often believes, but if anything toward increasing pluriculturalism.

On this particular dimension of self-identification which Spicer has stressed, I believe that he is right. Ethnic identifications are hardy things indeed. In the cities of the Northeast people continue to think of themselves as Irish, Jewish, Polish, Italian, or WASP, long after significant differences in their cultures have largely disappeared. The persistence of the sense of identity of these groups despite the American tradition of assimilation is what gave point to *Beyond the Melting Pot* by Glazer and Moynihan (1963).

I have introduced a distinction among dimensions of pluriculturalism because the picture might look differently depending upon which dimension one chooses to stress. Specifically, I believe that, in respect to degree of difference among cultures living side by side, there is most likely to be a process of cultural homogenization despite continuing differences in identity. It is clearly not necessary that these two things go together.

Degree of *consciousness* of difference is not necessarily correlated with degree of *real* cultural difference. The American Negro has had his original culture largely taken from him and has

323

been forced to become in effect a black white, yet he has been harshly denied the recognition of his assimilation. German Jews were the most assimilated of all Jews, but that did not stop Hitler from putting yellow stars on them and exterminating them. On the other hand, despite obvious physical differences which compel continued separate identification, as well as enormous differences in their original culture from that of the host society, Chinese in American cities assimilate remarkable freely and rapidly (Chin 1969, 1970).

The Future of Diversity in the Southwest

What are the implications for the Southwest? Let me sharply separate predictions from normative statements. First, for predictions: One prediction, also made by Galarza, is that there will be a gradual weakening of cultural diversity and a gradual assimilation of the content of the dominant culture, without this necessarily causing the disappearance of ethnic identities for generations to come. This has been described as the usual Anglo assumption. But that does not make it necessarily wrong.

The reasons why the content of the dominant culture is likely to be increasingly accepted by the other cultural groups are many and obvious. One reason which applies on both sides of the border is the population balance in the area. In 1960, on the Mexican side, those people officially counted as Indians numbered about 120,000 among some two million people in Sonora and Chihuahua. In the same year, on the U.S. side, the Indians of Arizona and New Mexico numbered perhaps 150,000, and the Mexican-Americans some 600,000, out of nearly two and a half million. On both sides of the border, migration from the majority culture areas of the country continues to pour in. In Arizona, for example, Maricopa County already includes one-half of the population of the state, growing by 45 percent from 1960 to 1970, primarily from immigration.

But numbers are only part of the story. Wealth is an even more important factor. Whatever intellectuals may think, cars, television, Coca-Cola, medicines, and canned goods are enormously appealing to people everywhere. The genie of industrial civilization is going to be had wherever people can have it. In our discussions some references were made to the findings of Inkeles (1969) concerning the striking similarities in values produced by the experience of industrial work in all societies. Reference was also made to the experience of Japan. Certainly the content of Japanese culture 100 years ago was vastly different from the content of American or European culture. Equally certainly Japanese identity 50 years hence will be thoroughly Japanese. But if present trends are any indication, Japanese television, traffic, recreation, homes, and dress 50 years hence will be pretty indistinguishable from those of Western societies.

The mass media and modern transportation are a third factor promoting homogeneity. Mankind is in contact with common stimuli over a larger area, more rapidly than ever before.

Still other factors are reinforcing the trend toward a growing similarity of culture content among ethnic groups. One is the rather unexamined self-confidence of the adherents of the dominant culture that their way is best and that all enlightened people will adopt it if aided and advised. Philanthropically motivated aid and education programs are established to teach the "underdeveloped" how to enjoy the blessings of Western civilization. Another factor for homogenization is the practice of integrated universal education, together with civil-rights laws which help open the road for minority group members to jobs and facilities in the dominant society.

For all these reasons the pluricultural society of the Southwest 50 years hence will show far fewer differences between the ways of life of the Anglos, Indians, and Mexican-Americans than it does today.

But let us not overstate the case. The extension of the same industrial culture to ever larger numbers of ethnic groups and ever larger areas of the world does not necessarily imply a dull uniformity. One of the features of industrial society is the vast "cafeteria" it offers. Some may like wine and some yogurt; some may dance and some play chess. They are all available. Diversity may actually increase. But that is not the same thing as having separate coherent subcultures with their traditional ways. All the evidence seems to me to suggest that such distinct ways of life will inevitably weaken in face of the attractions of the great cafeteria. But, I repeat, that does not mean that the identities of those who adhere to these subcultures will weaken.

The Benefits of Pluralism

So much for prediction. Now let us become normative. What do we think of this prospect? A basic premise of most of us present at this conference is that pluriculturalism is a good thing. I concur: it is good for the members of the minorities, and it is good for the dominant society too. It is good because it eases the pains of social change for those whose culture is in transition. It is also good because it enriches and strengthens the life of the society.

Let us consider the pains of social change. As I have already indicated, there is no way in the modern industrial world to preserve traditional cultures from change. All cultures change. The dominant culture changes too. In the modern world all cultures change fast; non-dominant cultures in particular are buffeted by the powerful impact of the dominant culture. But fast as these changes go, their full completion is only generational. As Galarza wisely said in his paper, satisfactory acculturation occurs normally only once in a person's lifetime. To have to change after childhood is a painful experience. Tolerance of cultural diversity can help protect adults from such demands. Tolerance can thus make meaningful and satisfactory the lifetime experience of whole generations already inducted into their set ways. Even if in the long run many of these ways may and will change, the short run is the lifetime of human beings. A policy of cultural pluralism gives deference to the values of human beings already on this earth.

The other reason for favoring cultural pluralism is its enrichment and strengthening of the life of the entire society and, in particular, of the dominant system. In our discussions, the view was sometimes expressed that while the dominant culture imposes itself on the others, there is little influence the other way. I cannot agree. The dominant culture, being a cafeteria culture, continually adopts new items, even when it does not change its basic structural forms or values. A catalogue of Indian and

Mexican influences on Anglo life in the Southwest would not be a short one, even though most of the items listed would not be considered fundamental.

Further, there is a significant way in which cultural pluralism strengthens rather than weakens the great society. In a large and complex nation it is important for there to be patriotic identification by the mass of the people with the symbols of central power. But the central power is bound to seem somewhat remote and abstract to most people. They have no personal contact with the men in power and do not share their way of life. Farmers, craftsmen, factory workers, and students may have respect for the president, for example, but they have little commonality of experience with him. Strong identification and meaningful loyalties develop more easily towards more intimate groups that share common customs, history, and life circumstances. If these intermediary groups are in turn loyal to the nation, more solid cohesion results from having individuals tied-in through intermediary groups that are close and meaningful to them than by asking sole loyalty to a remote and impersonal national unit.

The fact that solid cohesion results from intermediary groups has been well understood in the Anglo-Saxon tradition of nation formation and was recognized by such observers as Tocqueville. Strong local government and federalism among the diverse units did not appear to them as antithetical to strong nationalism. In the Continental tradition of nationalism, however, the opposite view prevailed. Because Continental nationalism sprang from the revolt against the special castes and privileges of feudalism, national unity seemed to require the destruction of all intermediary groupings. Guilds, castes, local government, and ethnic regionalism all seemed to be threats to the nation. Rousseau, in the doctrine of general will, formulated the Continental view. Freedom under government, he argued, depended on the elimination of all intermediate groupings, so that each person could cast his vote unencumbered by segmental influences.

The difference between the Anglo-Saxon and Continental view of intermediary groups is visible in the American and French guarantees of human rights. The U.S. Constitution guarantees freedom of association as a natural adjunct of freedom of speech. The French Declaration of the Rights of Man, on the other hand, says: "Sovereignty resides in the Nation. No individuals nor body can exercise authority not derived expressly from it." Repression of association was perceived as the way to assure individual freedom. The republics of Latin America in their revolt from Spain followed in the tradition of Rousseau and the French Revolution. As León-Portilla noted in his paper, Mexico had a strong tradition of assimilation and unitary identification with the central government and did not accept the notion of Indian reservations as did the United States.

Culturally diverse groups can, of course, be schismatic. Historical circumstances determine whether they are or not. They need not be. Where people of different cultural legacies exist side by side, they can be knitted into a common national loyalty if their cultural traditions are treated with respect, so that loyalty to each ethnic group becomes a basis for loyalty to the larger society. That is one of the strongest arguments for a policy that favors cultural pluralism.

Unity with Diversity

It would, however, be unsophisticated in the extreme to label either pluriculturalism or the trend toward homogeneity of culture content over ever wider areas as simply good or bad. Human problems are not that simple. The desirable and the undesirable intertwine inseparably like the woof and the warp of a piece of cloth. A pluricultural society, if it is to be one society at all, must impose some values and practices on the communities that compose it. Let us consider a list of some of the impositions that American society has placed upon the ethnic minorities of the Southwest. They include monogamy (a major issue with the Mormons), compulsory education, respect for property rights, repression of violence, the draft, conservation practices (a major issue with the Navajos), rights-of-way for roads, respect for civil rights, and electoral self-government.

At other times and places dominated cultures have been forced to conform to the beliefs and practices of dominant cultures in such matters as adherence to the "true faith" and decency in dress. We each reveal our own values and prejudices when we declare which of these impositions we feel to be justified, and which we feel to be tyrannical. Many of us in the modern, post-Freudian liberal world see no necessity at all for control of subcultures in matters of dress, or faith, or marriage, but in that same value scheme we regard with indignation the Mormon denial of priestly sacraments to Blacks and would be all in favor of compelling Mormon acceptance of civil-rights principles. Clearly, a pluricultural society is not an anarchy in which, as in the law of nations, each sovereign unit decides all matters for itself. It is a society with a common system of law, values, and beliefs, as well as with some diversity. The common system is bound to have an impact upon the cultures within it.

But the acceptance of a common legal framework and a common value system is not, and has never been, inconsistent with the recognition of the value of diversity. That was the great insight of liberalism and of the framers of constitutions with bills of rights. Consensus and diversity are not in opposition to each other. On the contrary, a certain amount of consensus is a condition for diversity.

This point was well made by Adolph Löwe (1937) in a small pamphlet called *The Price of Liberty*. Löwe had gone as a refugee from his native Germany to Great Britain. Struck by the disappearance of freedom in Germany and its persistence in Great Britain, he asked why. The answer he gave was that the degree of consensus on a great many issues in Britain made it possible to tolerate freely the differences that remained, since those differences would not tear the society apart, whereas in Germany the aspects of the society at issue were too fundamental for tolerance of dissidence to flourish.

The same point can be seen clearly in the practice of freedom of religion in the United States. There is something remarkably similar in all our churches and synagogues. They all have weekend services with a sermon, prayers, and hymns; they advocate quite similar moral values and they worship an abstract God. American society would offer far less freedom for some of the very different kinds of religious revelations that human history has produced, for example, mortification of the flesh, or human sacrifice. It is well recognized in American law that freedom of religion does not justify acts against the law. Mormon polygamy was a case in point.

What is the relevance of this for the Southwest? We may well expect the gradual acculturation of the plural societies of the Southwest to certain basic American values, but that need not extinguish the sense of identity of those groups nor cause them to abandon the symbols of their cultures.

For example, under the impact of poverty programs, industrialization, and strong aspirations by each group for more wealth, Mexicans and Indians 30 years hence are likely to share much more nearly the dominant American standard of living and many of the styles of life and types of work that go with it. The contents of their market baskets and those of the Anglos may become more alike, and the furnishings of their homes more similar, but they need not become identical, any more than the many American churches are. Each group will also do with these material items different symbolically significant things, even if these seem only marginally different compared with how different they were in their origins.

In broad sweep, what we have offered above are some predictive and normative conclusions about the future of cultural pluralism in the Southwest. These conclusions as to the viability of a pluricultural society—the respects in which it will persist and the extent to which it will change—and as to the contributions it will make, are based on the general experience of the modern world with culture contact.

However, culture contact comes in many forms: migration, conquest, trade, uncontrolled private action, and planned public programs of development and education. What we propose to do now is to look at the public policy alternatives that arise when there are planned public programs for pluricultural development.

Planning for Integration

The prospective culture contact in the Southwest falls in that class of situations where a dominant group deliberately plans a policy for integrating one or more minority groups, not with the purpose of suppression, but for what it regards as the minority's own welfare. I should like to note some specific patterns that occur when a dominant society tries thus to influence (in its opinion, benignly) a less modern society, for the purpose of securing the cooperation and participation of the latter in national goals. Let me give four examples: Model Cities programs in the United States, community development programs in such places as India, the pacification program in Vietnam, and the Indian program of the U.S. government. All of these have much in common. All of them would be called "neocolonialist" by nihilists on the extreme left, on the valid grounds that they are attempts by a dominant society impelled by its own needs to influence another society. At the same time, with equal validity or invalidity, all of them would be called "altruistic" by those who optimistically seek the welfare and preservation of the less modern society through reform, and seek to help it achieve many things that the people in it also want. A social scientist has no interest in attaching any such simplistic labels; he seeks rather to describe objectively what is going on, regardless of the labels anyone may choose to attach to the facts.

Let me list a series of elements that are needed if one is to create an effective political structure for a subsociety so that it can both survive and be integrated into the larger national community. In the presence of these elements government programs are likely to succeed, and in their absence to fail. Ideally, I should like to construct the list in two dimensions: an enumerative one and a temporal one. For each element I should like to plot its developmental sequence, for each starts in one form and gradually changes into another as the process of education or influence advances. Unfortunately language does not lend itself to a two-dimensional presentation. Clarity of statement bars such complexity in formulation. Let me, therefore, state my list with the elements appearing in their initial form as they are found at the starting point when a highly modernized society approaches another society which to the former seems to be underdeveloped, disorganized, and in trouble. Along with some of the items on the list I shall also add some comments on how they may change with time:

1. *In creating the political structure the dominant authorities should seek to identify and rely upon the minority's accepted community leadership.*

In both the Navajo and Hopi cases, discussed in the papers by Young and Sekaquaptewa, and in the Yaqui and Papago cases mentioned in discussion, this was clearly a requirement for effective development of tribal political organization. All of these groups started out with only village or religious organization. The U.S. and Mexican governments desired to treat with a responsible tribal political leadership and therefore sought to set up tribal authorities. However, Yaqui municipal officials, set up without regard to traditional patterns, turned out to be mere fronts for the old religious leadership of elders. Navajo and Hopi history, too, shows that a tribal council was accepted only as it came to represent the prior leadership. In the case of the Papagos, the mistake of bypassing traditional tribal organization was avoided; the result was the slow but stable evolution of a complex three-level tribal organization based upon village leadership.

In similar programs in other parts of the world there are parallel histories. In Vietnam the French set up elective village councils which turned out to be nothing more than stooges for the long-established, prestigious village cult committees, whose members would not lower themselves to run for office.

With time, the new political forms, if based on previous leadership patterns, may and often do acquire a life and legitimacy of their own, and sometimes even become the base of a modern leadership that rivals the old. In Vietnam, Diem made the village councils, which by that time had acquired the legitimacy of time and experience, appointive instead of elective. The restoration of election of the village councils in 1967 was one of the most popular acts of the present government. Among the Navajo, by now, elections for chairman of the tribal council are hotly contested in modern campaigns, with use of all the mass media. The ascriptive traditional leadership with which the national government originally had to deal was in both instances eventually augmented or even replaced by a modern elective one.

2. *The community political structure should have control of a budget or other material resources which are significant to its clientele.*

The Navajo Tribal Council became important when it gained control of the millions of dollars that resulted from the discovery of oil. Model Cities administrators get their clout by having federal funds to spend. The elective village councils in Vietnam became important when each was given about $10,000 for locally chosen community projects. Community development projects in India and elsewhere get their leverage by having fertilizer, seeds, or medicine to distribute.

3. *The community political structure should be in possession of a security function wherever possible.*

There are Navajo and Hopi tribal police and courts. In some urban ghettos volunteer security patrols with arm bands have helped keep the local people safe. In Vietnam the local security forces are, of course, the all-important function of local government. The significance of such activity relative to others is a function of the character of the prevailing security problem.

4. *The community political structure and the national political structure should be mutually dependent.*

Political elites often fear effective community structures as sources of rebellion and resistance, and they have reasons for their fears. Indian tribal councils, for example, in response to the feelings of their constituents have sometimes served to block or modify programs of the Bureau of Indian Affairs. Given the natural and built-in tension between the community political structure as the voice of the community and the government as the voice of the dominant culture, they tend to work against each other, unless they find that they need each other. To keep them working together they must be mutually dependent.

The community structures are likely to be dependent on the government in many ways. They may get money from above or get other resources such as hospital care, schools, roads, guns, fertilizer, or seed. Indian tribes may be dependent for all of these things, and also for favorable adjudication of their rights in regard to land and natural resources.

The dominant society is, by definition, less dependent on the community power structure than vice versa, but in a healthy situation it too is dependent in some ways. In Vietnam and in Black or Mexican ghettos the nominal authorities may in fact be dependent on community organization to maintain security. Cooperation of the local community may be essential for effective control of terrorists and criminals. The government may also be dependent on community cooperation for resource conservation, disease prevention or population control. It took much effort to persuade the Navajos to change their grazing practices.

Community development programs may encourage peasants to use latrines or to practice contraception out of concern to protect the society as a whole from disease and poverty. The U.S. Government desires Indian cooperation in oil field development and bargains with the Indians to get it. Without substantial mutual dependence the growth of community political organization is indeed likely to be either a sham or, as the higher authorities fear, a prelude to revolution and secession.

5. *The cooperation of middle-level officials should be secured.*

Frequently the central government and the minority community may be in reasonable accord on policies for the development of community political structure, but middle- and lower-level officials may feel threatened by the growth of community political power and may sabotage it. In Model Cities programs mayors have been leading opponents of "maximum feasible participation" and of the autonomy of Model Cities administrations, for they felt threatened by the linkage over their heads between Model Cities officials and the federal government. In Vietnam, district chiefs have obstructed the transferring of control of Popular Force soldiers to the village chiefs as ordered by the national government. In India, local authorities have violated national laws against caste discrimination. In California, lower-level bureaucrats have helped the large farmers prevent the growth of autonomous community organizations which higher federal authorities would have welcomed—at least, under some administrations.

6. *Specialized intercultural staffs should be created.*

Among the citizens of the dominant society there will be some individuals who are more genuinely attached than most to the survival and welfare of the minorities. The dominant authorities, though perhaps engaged in exploitation at the same time, will put some of these dedicated individuals to work in a career of helping the minorities.

Léon-Portilla, in his paper, described how the Spanish missionaries preserved some of the Indian tribes by concentrating them around the missions, away from the haciendas and mines, and taught them new crafts. In India a major effort has been put into the training of thousands of community development workers at special training schools all over the country. In Vietnam about 3000 Americans are working in the districts and provinces as pacification workers. The Indian Service has had many able men devoted to the tribes with which they work. The Office of Economic Opportunity, VISTA, and Model Cities programs have developed a cadre of poverty specialists in the last few years. Applied anthropologists have long been particularly well-trained examples of development cadres.

When a wide gap of development separates the dominant society from the minorities, the development specialists will have objectives and interests of their own which are not identical with those of either the authorities or the minority members with whom they work: for example, proselytizing for their faith, or building personal careers. With the passage of time, as they become older and more numerous, early altruistic motives among community workers are likely to be buried in the self-interest of a routinized bureaucracy. For that reason, and also because of the rising expectations and capabilities of the developing minority, it becomes increasingly important to displace outside specialists in an ever-growing range of functions by members of the minority itself. Some educated members of the minority will be coopted into highly paid jobs in the specialized cadre. The Jesuits, the Indian Service, the Office of Economic Opportunity, and Model Cities administrations all sought to recruit staff from among the minorities with whom they worked, in the process of which they helped train a modern leadership for the minority, created a modernized bourgeois stratum among them, and drew off some of the natural leadership from the minority into compromised bureaucratic jobs.

Because of the last of these effects of cooption, a successful process of modernization requires that, at a later stage, some minority leaders refuse jobs in the regular bureaucracy and operate instead through autonomous organizations of the minority itself. Missionaries, social workers, and public officials, however altruistic and progressive their role may have been at an earlier stage, come to be the butts of anticolonialist feelings, and the minority members who leavened their cadres in the transition come to be seen as "Uncle Toms." That is, of course, both true and unjust, as would be any judgment pegged to any one stage of this evolving process of maturation. The specialized staffs may at different stages be both essential for the very survival of the minority and later on an impediment to its further development.

7. *There must be strong programs to educate, proselytize, and propagandize.*

The principles listed so far all relate to effective administration of public programs for community development. But community development cannot be achieved by bureaucratic means alone. The support and conviction of the people of the community must also be won. Thus, propaganda, persuasion, and education play a vital role in any development program. The Jesuits and Franciscans preached and established schools. The government of India uses posters and radio to teach farm and health practices and is planning to go into a national village television program via satellite transmission. Public schools have been the great instrument of Americanization in the United States; the Indian Service has gone even further in replacing familial influence by establishing boarding schools.

8. *Good works and welfare should be effectively promoted.*

Words by reformers from the dominant society will not alone win the credence of those representing minority cultures. The door has to be opened by evidence of good will and proofs of the benefits that will accrue from reform. For that reason virtually all programs that try to introduce social change start with health care or charity. Community developers come in with fertilizer or maternity clinics. Missionaries intent on saving souls often start by healing bodies. Some of the more naive doctrines of civic action seem to propose that if one builds schools, bridges, clinics, or housing this will be enough to win the hearts and minds of the poor or underprivileged. Cultures, values, or attitudes are not changed so casually. Good works play an essential role in any program of social change, but only as a point of entry. If good works are not coupled with all the other elements of a full program that we are here listing, they will achieve nothing beyond their own inherent good.

9. *Economic development should be promoted.*

Economic development may be the goal of a program of social change, or, if it is not the goal, it is in any case an essential condition for stable change. If the goal is peace and order then young men—whether villagers or in an urban ghetto—must see opportunities for advancement, excitement, and a good life in the jobs available to them in the economy. If the goal is to develop values of responsibility and achievement orientation, the discipline of industrial employment and the prospect of economic advancement may be the most effective means. Trade schools, small business assistance, agricultural loan banks, settlement of nomads, handicraft cooperatives, and industrialization may all serve to make the process of social change stable and self-generating rather than a mere political imposition.

10. *Links to the urbanized, assimilated elements of the minority should be established.*

A tribe on the reservation or an isolated village tends to lose its best young elements to the richer and more exciting life of the city. Sometimes these emigrants cut their ties, leaving the village as a sink of residual backwardness. Sometimes, however, the urban members of the ethnic community retain their ties to the ancestral hearth and become an important source of modernization. They send remittances home; the more successful ones establish schools, scholarships, and charities in their names. Merchants of village or tribal origin become a channel to market for crops and handicrafts, and invest in village enterprises. A well-thought-out development program will utilize links between the ethnic community in its traditional home and those members who have left.

This last point suggests a further strategy which has sometimes been tried as a means for producing social change and development, but which more often boomerangs than succeeds. That is the movement of the tribal or village people to a concentrated location convenient for the dominant authorities. Léon-Portilla tells us that the early missionaries saved the Indian tribes from destruction by concentrating them around the missions. The tribes of the Southwest have insisted on preserving the reservations which were imposed upon them, rather than breaking them into private holdings as the Anglo advocates of Americanization wished. However, more often than not reservations or strategic hamlets have been artificial constructions imposed on the living fabric of traditional communities and have resulted in resistance and chaos.

More generally effective in producing development than moving a people has been bringing roads and communications to them. There is a large literature on the transformation of villages when roads reached them (for example, Lerner 1958, Redfield 1950). Location, roads, migration from the community, and what ties the migrants maintain after they leave all affect the working of a development program.

Summary

Assimilation and diversity can coexist. Pluricultural societies will be more cohesive if differences within them are recognized and respected than if attempts are made to impose artificial uniformity upon them. But it is also true that there are severe limits to the elements of diversity that a modern highly organized society can tolerate. Consensus on some values and on some principles of mutual interaction between communities is a condition of diversity. Cultures living side by side are in a constant process of mutual influence and accommodation, as they exist and change. Programs for planned social change may reflect a desire shared by both the dominant culture and ethnic minorities for a chosen direction of modernization and development. Such programs for planned social change involving societies with different levels of power and different cultural values are likely to break down in mutual recriminations unless skillfully and sensitively conducted. We have tried to list certain common features that such programs must have if they are to achieve the shared objectives and the desired goals of both dominant and minority groups.

Contributors

ITHIEL de SOLA POOL is Chairman of the Department of Political Science and Director of the Center for International Studies at Massachusetts Institute of Technology. He has also taught at Hobart College and at Hoover Institute, Stanford University, and has been a Fellow of the Center for Advanced Study in the Behavioral Sciences. He is the author of *Symbols of Democracy*, *Symbols of Internationalism* and *Satellite Generals* and the editor of *Contemporary Political Science: Toward Empirical Theory* and *Trends in Content Analysis*.

ERNESTO GALARZA, scholar, poet, and lecturer, is an articulate and imaginative interpreter of Mexican-American life. Born in Mexico and a naturalized citizen of the United States, he holds a Ph.D. degree from Columbia University. He has worked for the Pan-American Union and has been organizer for the National Agricultural Workers Union, AFL-CIO. He has also served as a consultant for the government of Bolivia. the U.S. Civil Rights Commission, and the Department of Health, Education, and Welfare, and has been Visiting Professor at Notre Dame University and San Jose State College. Among his recent publications are *Merchants of Labor: the Mexican Bracero Story* and *Mexican-Americans in the Southwest*, written with Herman Gallegos and Julian Samora.

MIGUEL LEON-PORTILLA is Professor at the Faculty of Philosophy and Letters and Director of the Institute of Historical Investigations of the Universidad Nacional Autónoma de México. A student of both prehispanic and modern American Indian cultures, he has had a long association with the Instituto Indigenista Interamericano serving as its director from 1960 to 1966. He has written several books, three of which have been translated into English: *La filosofía Náhuatl* as *Aztec Mind and Culture*,

Visión de los vencidos as *Broken Spears: the Aztec Account of the Conquest of Mexico*, and *Literaturas precolombinas de México* as *Precolumbian Literatures of Mexico*.

THOMAS F. O'DEA is Professor of Sociology and Director of the Institute of Religious Studies at the University of California, Santa Barbara. Previously he taught at the University of Utah and Fordham University and was a Fellow at the Center for Advanced Studies in the Behavioral Sciences. He is the author of *The Mormons*; *American Catholic Dilemma: an Inquiry into the Intellectual Life*; *Alienation, Atheism, and the Religious Crisis*; and *Sociology and the Study of Religion: Theory, Research, Interpretation*, among other books and articles.

JOHN H. PARRY is Gardiner Professor of Oceanic History and Affairs at Harvard University. Previously he was Lecturer and then Professor of Modern History at the University College of the West Indies in Jamaica, and later served as Principal of the University College at Ibadan, Nigeria, and of the University College at Swansea, Wales. His works on European expansion include: *Europe and a Wider World, 1415-1715*, *The Spanish Seaborne Empire*, *The Age of Reconnaissance*, and *The Audiencia of Nueva Galicia in the Sixteenth Century; a Study in Spanish Colonial Government*.

EMORY SEKAQUAPTEWA is Assistant Coordinator of Indian Programs at the University of Arizona. Born at Hotevilla on the Hopi Indian Reservation, he is a graduate of the University of Arizona, from which he received the J.D. degree. Before he accepted his present position he worked in the production and marketing of silver jewelry and was associated with the Hopi tribal government in legislative, administrative, and judicial capacities.

EDWARD H. SPICER is professor of Anthropology at the University of Arizona. Since the 1930's, he has conducted field research in the Southwest, most extensively among the Yaqui Indians. During World War II he headed the community analysis section of the War Relocation Authority for Japanese-Americans. His writings on the Southwest include *Pascua, a Yaqui Village in*

Arizona; *Potam, a Yaqui Village in Sonora*; and *Cycles of Conquest: the Impact of Spain and the United States on the Indians of the Southwest, 1533-1960*. He has also edited and contributed to *Human Problems in Technological Change* and *Perspectives in American Indian Culture Change*.

ROBERT W. YOUNG, until his recent retirement, was the Albuquerque Area Tribal Operations Officer for the Bureau of Indian Affairs. Trained in anthropology and linguistics, he began his research on the Navajo language in the 1930's and later took the position of Specialist in Indian languages with the Bureau of Indian Affairs. In 1950 he was made assistant to the director of the Navajo Area Office of the Bureau, where he was concerned with the development of Navajo tribal government. He has written widely on Navajo language and culture, including *The Navajo Language* and *A Vocabulary of Colloquial Navajo*, and has also prepared a number of bilingual publications for Navajo schools.

References

References

Aberle, David F.
  1961 Navaho. In *Matrilineal kinship*, edited by David M. Schneider and Kathleen Gouth, pp. 96-201. Berkeley: University of California Press.

  1966 The peyote religion among the Navaho. *Viking Fund Publications in Anthropology*, No. 42. New York: Wenner-Gren Foundation for Anthropological Research.

  1969 A plan for Navajo economic development. In *Toward economic development for Native American communities*, Vol. 1, Pt. 1, pp. 223-276. Joint Economic Committee of Congress. Washington: U.S. Government Printing Office.

Aberle, S. D.
  1948 The Pueblo Indians of New Mexico: their land, economy, and civil organization. *American Anthropological Association, Memoir* 70.

Aiton, Arthur S.
  1927 *Antonio de Mendoza, first viceroy of New Spain*. Durham: Duke University Press.

Akzin, Benjamin
  1966 *States and nations*. Garden City: Doubleday.

Alegre, Francisco Xavier
  1956-60 *Historia de la provincia de la Compañia de Jesús de Nueva España*, 4 vols. Rome: Institutum Historicum Societatis Jesu.

Alessio Robles, Vito
  1931 *Francisco de Urdiñola y el norte de la Nueva España*. Mexico: Imprenta Mundial.

Anderson, Nels
  1942 *Desert Saints: the Mormon frontier in Utah*. Chicago: University of Chicago Press.

Anonymous
  1928 *Sonora, Sinaloa y Nayarit; estudio estadístico y socio-económico*. Mexico: Departamento de la Estadística Nacional (Imprenta Mundial).

Arlegui, José
  1851 *Crónica de la provincia de n.s.p.s. Francisco de Zacatecas*. Mexico.

Arrington, Leonard J.
  1958 *Great Basin kingdom: an economic history of the Latter-day Saints, 1830-1900*. Cambridge: Harvard University Press.

REFERENCES

Austin, Mary
1924 *The land of journey's ending*. New York: The Century Co.

Bailey, Paul D.
1948 *Jacob Hamblin, buckskin apostle*. Los Angeles: Westernlore Press.

Bailey, Wilfrid C.
1950 A typology of Arizona communities. *Economic Geography*, Vol. 26, No. 1, pp. 94-104.

Bannon, John F. (editor)
1964 *Bolton and the Spanish Borderlands*. Norman: University of Oklahoma Press.

Barth, Fredrik
1969 *Ethnic groups and boundaries*. Boston: Little, Brown.

Beals, Ralph L.
1932 The comparative ethnology of northern Mexico before 1750. *Ibero-Americana*, No. 2. Berkeley: University of California Press.

1943 Northern Mexico and the Southwest. In *El norte de México y el sur de los Estados Unidos*, pp. 191-199. Mexico: Sociedad Mexicana de Antropología.

Benedict, Ruth
1934 *Patterns of culture*. Boston: Houghton Mifflin.

Billington, Ray Allen
1938 *The Protestant crusade, 1800-1860: a study of the origins of American nativism*. New York: Rinehart.

1949 *Westward expansion: a history of the American frontier*. New York: Macmillan.

Bolton, Herbert E.
1917 The mission as a frontier institution in the Spanish-American colonies. *American Historical Review*, Vol. 23, No. 1, pp. 42-61.

1936 *Rim of Christendom: a biography of Eusebio Francisco Kino, Pacific Coast pioneer*. New York: Macmillan.

1947 The West Coast corridor. *Proceedings of the American Philosophical Society*, Vol. 91, No. 5, pp. 426-429.

1948 *Coronado, knight of pueblos and plains*. New York: Whittlesey House.

1964 The Northwest movement in New Spain. In *Bolton and the Spanish Borderlands*, edited by John F. Bannon, pp. 67-85. Norman: University of Oklahoma Press.

Borah, Woodrow, and Sherburne F. Cook
1966 Marriage and legitimacy in Mexican culture: Mexico and California. *California Law Review*, Vol. 54, No. 2, pp. 946-1008.

Brandt, Charles
1954 *Hopi ethics*. Chicago: University of Chicago Press.

Brewer, David L.
    1966 *Utah elites and Utah racial norms*. Doctoral dissertation, University of Utah. Ann Arbor: University Microfilms.

    1968 The Mormons. In *The Religious Situation: 1968*, edited by Donald R. Cutler, pp. 518-547. Boston: Beacon Press.

Brodie, Fawn M.
    1945 *No man knows my history: the life of Joseph Smith, the Mormon prophet*. New York: Alfred A. Knopf.

Brooks, Juanita
    1950 *The Mountain Meadows massacre*. Stanford: Stanford University Press.

Brown, Thomas N.
    1966 *Irish-American nationalism, 1870-1890*. Philadelphia: Lippincott.

Brown, Willie L., Jr., Jorge Lara-Braud, Vine Deloria, Jr., Theodore Freedman and Mildred Dickeman
    1970 *Thoughts on community and diversity in the Southwest*. Austin: Southwest Intergroup Relations Council.

Cabinet Committee Hearings on Mexican American Affairs, El Paso, Texas, 1967
    1968 *The Mexican American: a new focus on opportunity*. Washington: Inter-Agency Committee on Mexican American Affairs.

Chevalier, François
    1956 La formación de los grandes latifundios en México: Tierras y sociedad en los siglos XVI y XVII. *Problemas Agrícolas e Industriales de México*, Vol. 8, pp. 122-130.

Chin, Ai-Li
    1969 "Yellow" identity—"yellow" power? Cambridge: Center for International Studies, Massachusetts Institute of Technology.

    1970 Young adults want change. *PLUS Bulletin*, Spring. Cambridge: Massachusetts Institute of Technology.

Cohen, Felix S.
    1942 *Handbook of federal Indian law*. Washington: U.S. Government Printing Office.

Connelley, William E.
    1907 *Doniphan's expedition*. Kansas City (Mo.): Bryan and Douglas Book Co.

Day, John Marshall
    1963 A study of protest to adaptation. M.A. essay, Department of Sociology, University of Utah.

Decorme, Gerard
    1941 *La obra de los jesuítas mexicanos durante la época colonial, 1572-1767*. Mexico: Antigua Librería Robredo de J. Porrúa de Hijos.

REFERENCES

Dobyns, Henry F.
1964 *The Fiesta of St. Francis at Magdalena, Sonora, Mexico*. Doctoral dissertation, Cornell University. Ann Arbor: University Microfilms.

Dozier, Edward P.
1954 The Hopi-Tewa of Arizona. *University of California Publications in American Archaeology and Ethnology*, Vol. 44, No. 3. Berkeley: University of California Press.

1970 *The Pueblo Indians of North America*. New York: Holt, Rinehart and Winston.

Dunne, Peter M.
1940 *Pioneer Black Robes on the West Coast*. Berkeley: University of California Press.

1944 *Pioneer Jesuits in northern Mexico*. Berkeley: University of California Press.

1948 *Early Jesuit missions in Tarahumara*. Berkeley: University of California Press.

1952 *Black Robes in Lower California*. Berkeley: University of California Press.

Dwyer, Robert J.
1941 *The Gentile comes to Utah: a study in religious and social conflict (1862-1890)*. Washington: Catholic University of America Press.

Ericksen, Ephraim E.
1922 *The psychological and ethical aspects of Mormon group life*. Chicago: University of Chicago Press.

Fergusson, Erna
1940 *Our Southwest*. New York: Alfred A. Knopf.

Flanders, Robert Bruce
1965 *Nauvoo: kingdom on the Mississippi*. Urbana: University of Illinois Press.

Forbes, Jack D.
1960 *Apache, Navaho, and Spaniard*. Norman: University of Oklahoma Press.

Fried, Jacob
1969 The Tarahumara. *Handbook of Middle American Indians*, Vol. 8, pp. 846-870. Austin: University of Texas Press.

Galarza, Ernesto
1964 *Merchants of labor: the Mexican bracero story, an account of the managed migration of Mexican farm workers in California, 1942-1960*. Santa Barbara: McNally and Loftin.

Galarza, Ernesto, Herman Gallegos and Julian Samora
1969 *Mexican-Americans in the Southwest*. Santa Barbara: McNally and Loftin.

Gallegos, José Ignacio
1960 *Durango colonial, 1563-1821*. Mexico: Editorial Jus.

Gamio, Manuel, and others (editors)
1958 Legislación indigenista de México. *Ediciones Especiales*, No. 38. Mexico: Instituto Indigenista Interamericano.

Glanz, Rudolf
1963 *Jew and Mormon: historic group relations and religious outlook*. New York: Waldon Press.

Glazer, Nathan, and Daniel P. Moynihan
1963 *Beyond the melting pot: the Negroes, Puerto Ricans, Jews, Italians, and Irish of New York City*. Cambridge: M.I.T. Press.

González, Nancie L.
1967 The Spanish Americans of New Mexico: a distinctive heritage. *Mexican-American Study Project, Advance Report*, No. 9. Los Angeles: Graduate School of Business Administration, University of California.

Goodwin, Grenville
1969 *Social organization of the Western Apache*. Tucson: University of Arizona Press.

Gordon, Milton M.
1964 *Assimilation in American life: the role of race, religion, and national origins*. New York: Oxford University Press.

Grimes, Joseph E., and Thomas B. Hinton
1969 The Huichol and the Cora. *Handbook of Middle American Indians*, Vol. 8, pp. 792-813. Austin: University of Texas Press.

Hackenberg, Robert
1955 *Economic and political change among the Gila River Pima Indians*. Tucson: Bureau of Ethnic Research, University of Arizona.

Harris, T. George
1967 *Romney's way: a man and an idea*. Englewood Cliffs (N.J.): Prentice-Hall.

Hatch, Nelle Spilsbury
1954 *Colonia Juárez: an intimate account of a Mormon village*. Salt Lake City: Deseret Book Company.

Heizer, Robert F., and Alan J. Almquist
1971 *The other Californians: prejudice and discrimination under Spain, Mexico, and the United States to 1920*. Berkeley: University of California press.

Herberg, Will
1955 *Protestant, Catholic, Jew: an essay in American religious sociology*. Garden City: Doubleday.

REFERENCES

Hill, W. W.
1936 Navaho warfare. *Yale University Publications in Anthropology*, No. 5. New Haven: Yale University Press.

1938 The agricultural and hunting methods of the Navaho Indians. *Yale University Publications in Anthropology*, No. 18. New Haven: Yale University Press.

1940a Some aspects of Navajo political structure. *Plateau*, Vol. 13, No. 2, pp. 23-28.

1940b Some Navaho culture changes during two centuries. *Smithsonian Institution, Miscellaneous Collections*, Vol. 100, pp. 395-415. Washington.

Hinton, Thomas B.
1959 A survey of Indian assimilation in eastern Sonora. *Anthropological Papers of the University of Arizona*, No. 4. Tucson: University of Arizona Press.

1969 Remnant tribes of Sonora: Opata, Pima, Papago, and Seri. *Handbook of Middle American Indians*, Vol. 8, pp. 879-888. Austin: University of Texas Press.

Hughes, Everett C.
1943 *French Canada in transition*. Chicago: University of Chicago Press.

Hunter, Milton R.
1934 *Brigham Young, the colonizer*. Salt Lake City: Deseret News Press.

Inkeles, Alex
1969 Making men modern: on the causes and consequences of individual change in six developing countries. *American Journal of Sociology*, Vol. 75, No. 2, pp. 208-225.

Jiménez Moreno, Wigberto
1943 Tribus e idiomas del norte de México. In *El norte de México y el sur de los Estados Unidos*, pp. 121-133. Mexico: Sociedad Mexicana de Antropologia.

1958 *Estudios de historia colonial*. Mexico: Instituto Nacional de Antropología e Historia.

Joseph, Alice, Rosamond B. Spicer and Jane Chesky
1949 *The desert people: a study of the Papago Indians*. Chicago: University of Chicago Press.

Kelly, Lawrence C.
1968 *The Navajo Indians and federal Indian policy, 1900-1935*. Tucson: University of Arizona Press.

Kimball, Solon T., and John H. Provinse
1942 Navajo social organization in land use planning. *Applied Anthropology*, Vol. 1, No. 4, pp. 18-25.

Kluckhohn, Clyde, and Dorothea Leighton
1946 *The Navaho*. Cambridge: Harvard University Press.

Ladd, John
1957 *The structure of a moral code: a philosophical analysis of ethical discourse applied to the ethics of the Navaho Indians*. Cambridge: Harvard University Press.

Landes, Ruth
1965 *Latin Americans of the Southwest*. St. Louis: Webster Division, McGraw-Hill.

Left-handed Mexican Clansman
1952 The trouble at Round Rock. *Navajo Historical Series*, No. 2. Washington: U.S. Indian Service.

Lerner, Daniel
1958 *The passing of traditional society*. Glencoe: The Free Press.

Letherman, Jonathan
1856 Sketch of the Navajo tribe of Indians, Territory of New Mexico. *Tenth Annual Report of the Smithsonian Institution*. pp. 281-297. Washington: Smithsonian Institution.

Loomis, Charles P., Zona K. Loomis and Jeanne E. Gullahorn
1966 Linkages of Mexico and the United States. *Agricultural Experiment Station, Research Bulletin* 14. East Lansing: Michigan State University.

López-Portillo y Weber, José
1935 *La conquista de la Nueva Galicia*. Mexico: Talleres Gráficos de la Nación.

1939 *La rebelión de Nueva Galicia*. Mexico: Antigua Imprenta de E. Murguía.

Löwe, Adolph
1937 *The price of liberty*. London: Hogarth Press.

Malinowski, Bronislaw
1944 *A scientific theory of culture, and other essays*. Chapel Hill: University of North Carolina Press.

Mange, Juan Mateo
1926 *Luz de tierra incógnita en la América septentrional y diario de las exploraciones en Sonora*. Mexico: Talleres Gráficos de la Nación.

McCaskill, Joseph C.
1940 The cessation of monopolistic control of Indians by the Indian Office. In *Indians of the United States* [Vol. 2], pp. 69-76. Washington: U.S. Office of Indian Affairs.

McClintock, James H.
1921 *Mormon settlement in Arizona: a record of peaceful conquest of the desert*. Phoenix: Manufacturing Stationers.

REFERENCES

McWilliams, Carey
1949 *North from Mexico: the Spanish-speaking people of the United States*. Philadelphia: J.B. Lippincott.

Mecham, John Lloyd
1927 *Francisco de Ibarra and Nueva Vizcaya*. Durham: Duke University Press.

Mendizábal, Miguel Othón De
1930 *La evolución del noroeste de México*. Mexico: Departamento de Estadística Nacional (Imprenta Mundial).

Meriam, Lewis, and others
1928 *The problem of Indian administration*. Baltimore: Johns Hopkins Press.

Meritt, Edgar B.
1926 The American Indian and government Indian administration. *Bulletin* 12. Washington: U.S. Bureau of Indian Affairs.

Monroy Rivera, Oscar
1966 *El mexicano enano: un mal de nuestro tiempo*. Mexico: B. Costa-Amic.

Muck, Lee
1948 Survey of the range resources and livestock economy of the Navajo Indian Reservation. Report to the Secretary of the Interior.

Navarro García, Luis
1964 *Don José de Gálvez y la comandancia general de las Provincias Internas del norte de Nueva España*. Seville: Escuela de Estudios Hispano-Americanos de Sevilla.

Nelson, Lowry
1952 *The Mormon village: a pattern and technique of land settlement*. Salt Lake City: University of Utah Press.

[Nentuig, Juan]
1951 *Rudo Ensayo, by an unknown Jesuit padre, 1763*. Tucson: Arizona Silhouettes.

Nequatewa, Edmund
1936 Truth of a Hopi and other clan stories. *Bulletin*, No. 8. Flagstaff: Museum of Northern Arizona.

Ocaranza, Fernando
1934 *Capítulos de la historia franciscana, segunda serie*. Mexico.

1937-39 *Crónicas y relaciones del occidente de México*, 2 vols. Mexico: Antigua Librería Robredo de J. Porrúa e Hijos.

O'Dea, Thomas F.
1957 *The Mormons*. Chicago: University of Chicago Press.

1970 *Sociology and the study of religion: theory, research, interpretation*. New York: Basic Books.

O'Gorman, Edmundo
1966 *Historia de las divisiones territoriales de México*, 3rd. ed. Mexico: Editorial Porrúa.

Owen, Roger C.
1969 Contemporary ethnography of Baja California. *Handbook of Middle American Indians*, Vol. 8, pp. 871-878. Austin: University of Texas Press.

Park, Robert E., and Ernest W. Burgess
1921 *Introduction to the science of sociology*. Chicago: University of Chicago Press.

Pérez De Ribas, Andrés
1944 *Historia de los triunfos de nuestra santa fé entre las gentes más bárbaras y fieras del nuevo orbe,...*, 3 vols. Mexico: Editorial Layac.

Plancarte, Francisco M.
1954 El problema indígena Tarahumara. *Memorias del Instituto Nacional Indigenista*, Vol. 5. Mexico: Instituto Nacional Indigenista.

Pool, Ithiel de Sola (editor)
1967 *Contemporary political science: toward empirical theory*. New York: McGraw Hill.

Powell, Philip W.
1952 *Soldiers, Indians and silver: the northward advance of New Spain, 1550-1600*. Berkeley: University of California Press.

Redfield, Robert
1950 *A village that chose progress: Chan Kom revisited*. Chicago: University of Chicago Press.

Reeve, Frank D.
1943 The government and the Navajo, 1883-88. *New Mexican Historial Review*, Vol. 18, No. 1, pp. 17-51.

Reichard, Gladys
1924 Social life of the Navajo Indians, with some attention to minor ceremonies. *Columbia University Contributions to Anthropology*, Vol. 7. New York: Columbia University Press.

Riley, Carroll L.
1969 The Southern Tepehuan and Tepecano. *Handbook of Middle American Indians*, Vol. 8, pp. 814-821. Austin: University of Texas Press.

Rippy, J. Fred
1931 *The United States and Mexico*. New York: F. S. Crofts.

Romano, Octavio Ignacio (editor)
1969 *El espejo: selected Mexican American literature*. Berkeley: Quinto Sol Publications.

Rubio Mañé, Jorge Ignacio
1959-61 *Introducción al estudio de los virreyes de Nueva España, 1535-1746: Expansión y defensa*, vols. 2, 3. Mexico: Instituto de Historia, Universidad Nacional Autónoma de México.

Russell, Frank
1908 The Pima Indians. *26th Annual Report, Bureau of American Ethnology*, pp. 3-390. Washington: Smithsonian Institution.

Samora, Julian
1971 *Los mojados: the wetback story*. Notre Dame: University of Notre Dame Press.

Saravia, Atanasio G.
1940-56 *Apuntes para la historia de la Nueva Vizcaya*. 3 vols. Mexico: Instituto Panamericano de Geografía e Historia.

Service, Elman R.
1969 The Northern Tepehuan. *Handbook of Middle American Indians*, Vol. 8, pp. 822-829. Austin: University of Texas Press.

Shepardson, Mary
1963 Navajo ways in government: a study in political process. *American Anthropological Association, Memoir* 96.

Shepardson, Mary, and Blodwen Hammond
1970 *The Navajo Mountain community: social organization and kinship terminology*. Berkeley: University of California Press.

Spicer, Edward H.
1940 *Pascua, a Yaqui village in Arizona*. Chicago: University of Chicago Press.

1953 People of Pascua: a study of participation in Yaqui culture. MS, Arizona State Museum Library, University of Arizona.

1954 Potam, a Yaqui village in Sonora. *American Anthropological Association, Memoir* 77.

1962 *Cycles of conquest: the impact of Spain, Mexico, and the United States on the Indians of the Southwest, 1533-1960*. Tucson: University of Arizona Press.

1969a *A short history of the Indians of the United States*. New York: Van Nostrand Reinhold.

1969b The Yaqui and Mayo. *Handbook of Middle American Indians*, Vol. 8, pp. 830-845. Austin: University of Texas Press.

Spicer, Edward H., Asael Hansen, Katherine Luomala and Marvin Opler
1969 *Impounded people: Japanese-Americans in the relocation centers*. Tucson: University of Arizona Press.

Spier, Leslie
1933 *Yuman tribes of the Gila River*. Chicago: University of Chicago Press.

1936 Cultural relations of the Gila River and Lower Colorado tribes. *Yale University Publications in Anthropology*, No. 3. New Haven: Yale University Press.

Stone, Robert C., Frank A. Petroni and Thomas McCleneghan
1963 Ambos Nogales: bi-cultural urbanism in a developing region. *Arizona Review of Business and Public Administration*, Vol. 12, No. 1, pp. 1-29.

Tanner, Clara Lee
1957 *Southwest Indian painting*. Tucson: University of Arizona Press and Arizona Silhouettes.

1968 *Southwest Indian craft arts*. Tucson: University of Arizona Press.

Thompson, Laura
1950 *Culture in crisis: a study of the Hopi Indians*. New York: Harper and Row.

Turner, Wallace
1966 *The Mormon establishment*. Boston: Houghton Mifflin.

Tyler, S. Lyman
1964 *Indian affairs: a study of the changes in policy of the United States toward Indians*. Provo: Brigham Young University Press.

Van Valkenburgh, Richard
1945 The government of the Navajos. *Arizona Quarterly*, Vol. 1, No. 4, pp. 63-73.

Vogt, Evon Z.
1955a *Modern Homesteaders: the life of a twentieth-century frontier community*. Cambridge: Harvard University Press.

1955b A study of the Southwestern fiesta system as exemplified by the Laguna fiesta. *American Anthropologist*, Vol. 57, No. 4, pp. 820-839.

Vogt, Evon Z., and Ethel M. Albert (editors)
1966 *People of Rimrock: a study of values in five cultures*. Cambridge: Harvard University Press.

Vivó, Jorge A.
1958 *Geografía de México*, 4th ed. Mexico: Fondo de Cultura Económica.

Ward, John
1968 Letter to S.F. Tappan. Washington: National Archives. (Microfilm copy in Coronado Library, University of New Mexico.)

Weber, Max
1963 *The sociology of religion*. Boston: Beacon Press.

Weld, Isaac
1968 *Travels through the states of North America*, 2 vols. New York: Johnson Reprint Corporation.

REFERENCES

Werner, Morris R.
1925 *Brigham Young*. New York: Harcourt, Brace.

West, Robert C.
1949 The mining community in northern New Spain; the Parral mining district. *Ibero-Americana*, No. 30. Berkeley: University of California Press.

Williams, Aubrey W., Jr.
1970 Navajo political process. *Smithsonian Contributions to Anthropology*, Vol. 9. Washington: Smithsonian Institution Press.

Woodward, Arthur (editor)
1966 *The Republic of Lower California, 1853-1854, in the words of its state papers, eyewitnesses and contemporary reporters*. Los Angeles: Dawson's Book Shop.

Wyman, Leland C.
1970 *Blessingway; with three versions of the myth recorded and translated from the Navajo by Father Berard Haile, O.F.M.* Tucson: University of Arizona Press.

Young, Kimball
1954 *Isn't one wife enough?* New York: Henry Holt.

Zavala, Silvio
1968 *Los Esclavos indios en Nueva España*. Mexico: Colegio Nacional.

Index

Index

Aberle, David F.: "A plan for Navajo economic development," 234ff.

Acculturation: frequency of, 263; among Norteños, 109ff.; pressure for, 116; remedial, 286; and self identity, 278-9, 330; and self image, 265, and traditional institutions, 274.

African Nations: parallel to Navajo, 234.

Agrarian proletariat, 283, 292.

Agriculture: braceros and wetbacks, 283-5; Chicano, 318; decline in the North, 102; effect of, 96; Hopi traditions, 243; Indian, 91, 300; in Mexico, 88; Mexican peon, 272-3; modern technology, 108, 307; Mormon, 124-5, 136-8; Navajo, 169, 173, 192; Norteño, 85; Pueblo, 302; in the revolution, 104-5.

Akzin, Benjamin: *States and Nations*, 45ff.

Alviso, California: culture and annexation, 280ff.

Anglos (see also: Dominant societies): ethnic policies, 44ff.; intercultural exchange, 73-4; production of goods and services, 317.

Annexation of Texas, 80.

Anthropological approach: attitude, 293-4; in New Guinea, 311; Verbal arts in Mexican Southwest, 68-9.

Apaches: ethnic policies, 49; literature, 68; Mormon attitude to, 158; Norteño fear of, 103; as raiders, 303; schools on reservations, 62; as semi-nomads, 300-1.

Arizona Boundary Bill: passage of, 196.

Arlegui, José: *Crònica*, 93-5.

Arts and crafts: fusion with European, 67; graphic and plaster, 67ff.; interchange at Gallup, 72-3; pottery, 85, 91; revival of, 318.

Assimilation: of Blacks, Jews, Chinese, 323-4; coexistence with diversity, 338; disappearance of distinct groups, 13; domestication of Indians, 176; governmental attempts, 3; identity loss, 53; Indian attitude to, 310; individual, 75; inevitability of, 4, 7; limits to, 116ff.; Mexican resistance to, 277; Mormon Hopi, 41; Opatas, 44; at Oraibi, 251; pressure on Hopi, 259; prospects for, 310; reasons for, 310; tribal links to assimilated minority, 337.

Baja California: Missionaries in, 78, 99; part of Mexican Northwest, 82, 87; proposals for U.S. acquisition, 81.

Ballet Folklórico: deer dancer, 76.

Bear clan: role in Hopi tradition, 240.

Benedict, Ruth: *Patterns of Culture*, 269.

Beyond the Melting Pot : persistence of sense of identity, 323.

Bilingualism: end of, 273; Indians, Chicanos, 69-70; shifting Spanish and Anglo balance, 275-6.

Blacks: in Anglo experience, 35, 58; identity system, 41; and Indians, 45; intermarriage, 156; and Mormon priesthood, 142, 144-6, 165; separatism of, 295; as slaves, 95.

Book of Abraham: controversy over, 146-9.

Book of Mormon, 120ff.

Border Belt and Mexican migration, 267ff.

Boundaries: Arizona, 196; awareness of, 56ff.; as border region, 300; features of Southwest b. system, 57; fluidity of, 56ff.; Hopi-Navajo, 246; language as, 56ff.; New Mexico, 199; problems in understanding of, 56; reinforcing ethnic, 73; reservation as, 56ff.; Treaty

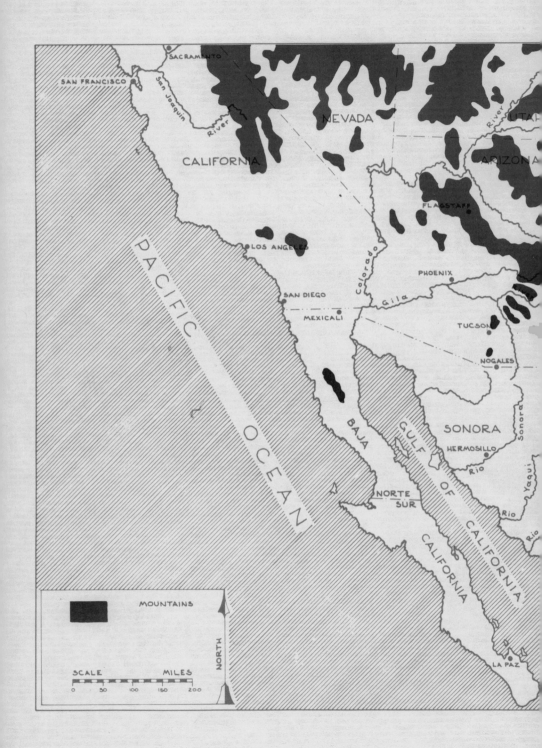